Magic's Reason

Magic's Reason

An Anthropology of Analogy

GRAHAM M. JONES

The University of Chicago Press
Chicago and London

The University of Chicago Press, Chicago 60637
The University of Chicago Press, Ltd., London
© 2017 by The University of Chicago
Published 2017
Printed in the United States of America

26 25 24 23 22 21 20 19 18 17   1 2 3 4 5

ISBN-13: 978-0-226-51854-1 (cloth)
ISBN-13: 978-0-226-51868-8 (paper)
ISBN-13: 978-0-226-51871-8 (e-book)
DOI: 10.7208/chicago/9780226518718.001.0001

Library of Congress Cataloging-in-Publication Data
Names: Jones, Graham M., author.
Title: Magic's reason : an anthropology of analogy / Graham M. Jones.
Description: Chicago ; London : The University of Chicago Press, 2017. |
    Includes bibliographical references and index.
Identifiers: LCCN 2017015013 | ISBN 9780226518541 (cloth : alk. paper) |
    ISBN 9780226518688 (pbk. : alk. paper) | ISBN 9780226518718 (e-book)
Subjects: LCSH: Magic—Social aspects.
Classification: LCC BF1621 .J66 2017 | DDC 306.4—dc23
    LC record available at https://lccn.loc.gov/2017015013

♾ This paper meets the requirements of ANSI/NISO Z39.48-1992
(Permanence of Paper).

For
Val, Augie, and Momo
with love

This is the essence of magic, which does not create but summons.

FRANZ KAFKA, 1921

CONTENTS

FIGURES

Dangerous Doubles

I first met the seventy-year-old cabaret magician Jack Alban on a blustery December afternoon in a sleepy 18th arrondissement Parisian café. Jack occupied a unique position in the world of French entertainment magicians—or *magicos*, as they refer to each other within the profession—and I was eager to hear about his career. He had started out with a hypnosis act as a teenager in the 1940s, and then worked the bohemian left-bank cabarets in the 1950s after his military service, specializing in what he called "electric" magic—especially producing and manipulating glowing lightbulbs (figure 1).

In 1982 he became president of France's National Illusionists' Union (Syndicat National des Illusionnistes), which helps magicos file suit against employers who cheat them out of benefits. It sounded like frustrating work. Jack told me that his fellow magicians often didn't know anything about France's byzantine employment regulations, and came to him years after the fact when they realized that they weren't receiving retirement benefits they assumed they had coming. As part of my anthropological fieldwork on the subculture of magicos, I was hoping he could help me understand how the professional prospects for French magicians had evolved over the six tumultuous decades leading up to our meeting in 2004.

Given his serious position, I was surprised to find Jack homey, jovial, boisterous, and irreverent. He also happened to be bald, a feature I probably wouldn't have thought significant if he hadn't called it to my attention. "You might not recognize me next time we meet, because I usually have a wig," he chortled. "When it's windy, I don't bother anymore. If it blows away, I'm too old to chase it!" It sounded like he was delivering a punch line, and we both laughed, but I later found out it was true.

Jack always jokingly referred to me as "le Chinois," because when I cold-called him to introduce myself as an anthropologist studying magic—to

Figure 1. Illusionist Jack Alban, 1950s. Collection of Didier Morax.

avoid confusion, I used the French word "prestidigitation," which specifically denotes entertaining sleight of hand—he thought I sounded Chinese. One of Jack's friends, Alain, a lanky, bespectacled Afro-Antillean computer engineer, joined us at the café. He and Jack met at least once a month to swap the latest issues of magic magazines and dissect the secrets they contained. Alain kept an engineer's meticulous ledger of each exchange in a computational note-book. When Jack found out I was of African American descent, he said he was tickled to be the milk with two coffees, even if one of them was Chinese.

At one point Jack reached into his satchel and presented me with a hand-written sheet of paper. "A magician friend of mine knows something about anthropology, so I asked him to write down some things you could use for your research."

It was a bibliography (figure 2).

At the top of the page, the bibliographer had drawn a large bullet point, and had written next to it in large letters, "Marcel MAUSS anthropologist." This was clearly a reference to the coauthor of the classic *Outline of a General Theory of Magic*, in which Henri Hubert and Mauss (1902–1903) boldly proposed that supernatural magical rites like casting spells or using charms could be explained strictly in terms of social relationships. Scanning the rest of the page, I recognized other similarly influential names. Under the heading "Magic in Traditional Societies," the bibliographer had listed James Frazer's *Golden Bough* (1900), an encyclopedic Victorian work of comparative mythology that locates the origins of religion and even science in ancient magical beliefs. Under the same heading, the bibliographer included

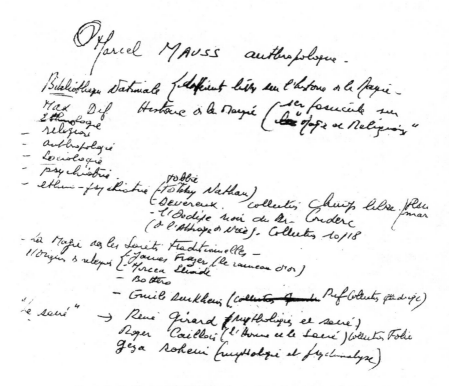

Figure 2. An illusionist's bibliography on the anthropology of magic.

Mauss's uncle, Émile Durkheim, whose *Elementary Forms of the Religious Life* (1912) famously distinguishes religion, which constitutes a lasting community in the form of church, from magic, which has no institutions that transcend fleeting encounters between magicians and their clients.

Whoever had written this bibliography indeed knew more than just "something" about anthropology! He appeared to be widely conversant in the field. But perhaps there had been some misunderstanding, for he had included only references concerning occult magic and its relationship with ritual and religion—works peopled with sorcerers, shamans, witches, wizards, alchemists, and astrologers. These texts constituted the cornerstone of what I will henceforth refer to as *anthropological magic theory*, a speculative and empirical tradition devoted to explaining the prevalence and persistence of occult beliefs and practices—a tradition that is, along with the study of topics like kinship and ritual, an intellectual centerpiece of anthropology as a discipline.

I knew all too well that, with a few isolated exceptions, the scholars working in this tradition mostly treated the ludic, rabbit-in-a-hat, lady-in-a-box kind of magic that interested me as superfluous if not altogether irrelevant to their core concerns, scarcely referring to it at all. As Tanya Luhrmann (1997: 299), neatly summing up the logic of this exclusion, writes, "the deliberate attempt to fool an audience that knows that it is being fooled" just "does not involve the same kind of intellectual problems as the study of magic as instrumental action." The bibliography included only one item manifestly pertinent to illusionism, magician and magic historian Max Dif's (1986) standard French reference work *Histoire illustrée de la prestidigitation*. Even here, the bibliographer specified that I should look at the first section on "Magic and Religion," which covers materials similar to those addressed by Mauss, Frazer, and Durkheim: magical rites and shamanistic practices in prehistoric and ancient societies. Surely I wasn't studying *that* kind of magic!

With its potential to simultaneously denote both supernatural ritual and secular entertainment, the word "magic" (*magie*, in French) often seems to introduce categorical confusion, and the English word "conjuring" never seemed to me any less equivocal. Definitions of magic have been shifting and uncertain since the Greeks in the fifth century BCE began nervously speculating about the esoteric powers of the *magi*—Zoroastrian priests from Persia—who represented fearful foreign Others (Cheak 2004; Kieckhefer 2000: 10). In everyday parlance, "magic" can still easily refer to illusionism, sorcery, or superstition—not to mention its extension into other domains as a metaphor for the virtuosic skill of anybody from politicians (Jones 2015b) to artists (Kris and Kurz 1979).

The concept remains so ambiguous, and its definition so changeable, that no one ever really can be sure what they are talking about when they talk about magic. Given the centrality of the term in the field, one contention of this book is that to successfully disambiguate it would be practically tantamount to solving anthropology.

In my fieldwork and later writing, I have generally stuck with terms like "illusionism" (*illusionnisme*) and "prestidigitation" (*prestidigitation*), and their associated agent nouns "illusionist" (*illusionniste*) and "prestidigitator" (*prestidigitateur*)—terms that highlight the skillful production of enjoyable deceptions central to magic as a form of entertainment. Still, occult, supernatural associations have always seemed to seep into my ethnographic conversations, not because magicos haphazardly bandied about the ambiguous term *magie*, but because they systematically emphasized, exploited, and called analytic attention to its polysemy.

I would have chalked the bibliographer's seemingly incongruous references to anthropological magic theory up to a simple misunderstanding if it didn't fit such a pronounced pattern. The few magicos who knew a bit about anthropology inevitably referred me to authors like Mauss or Claude Lévi-Strauss, whose extraordinary essay "The Sorcerer and His Magic" (1963) describes how a Kwakwaka'wakw shaman named Quesalid comes to believe that tricks he once dismissed as charlatanism are curatively effective. Magicos were keenly interested in the way that sorcerers like this approached legerdemain, magic as they practiced it themselves. A far greater number of magicos, though unfamiliar with anthropology and its esoteric canons, made arguments with a decidedly anthropological cast, suggesting connections between the kinds of entertainment they performed and the ritual practices and religious beliefs of what they called "traditional" or "primitive" peoples.

For me, the problem wasn't necessarily that these parallels were far-fetched, but rather how they came to be embedded in a historical narrative of cultural progress that opposed tradition, occult magic, and irrationality, on the one hand, with modernity, entertainment magic, and rationality, on the other. Often the people making these arguments would assert an equivalence between medieval or premodern France—a time *when* Europeans still believed in magic—and contemporary cultures in the global south, particularly Africa—places *where* people still believe in magic.

Anthropologists generally refer to models that map contemporary cultural differences onto a historical scale of unidirectional progress as *social evolutionism* (or simply *evolutionism*). Blending a potent cocktail of Darwinian theory and colonial chauvinism, social evolutionists in the nineteenth century argued that human societies developed along a unilinear, teleological path, passing through predictable phases of savagery and barbarism before reaching the apogee of civilization exemplified by European metropoles. According to this model, contemporary societies that lacked the complex technological achievements of industrial capitalism were essentially historical curiosities: living vestiges of a primitive past that Western Europe had long surpassed. Although it long stood as a dominant paradigm for explaining cultural difference, by the dawn of the twentieth century, social evolutionism had been largely repudiated as an unscientific, ethnocentric byproduct of European colonialism (Fabian 2002; Wolf 1995).

Viewed in light of the evolutionist perspectives that I had already encountered in the field, the bibliography seemed to threaten—or so I thought—some of my deepest intellectual convictions. I politely folded it away, and Jack returned to a story about his six-month stint performing with a trained duck in an Egyptian cabaret. (The Egyptians, it seemed, considered ducks dirty and unrespectable, but Jack thought it would be a funny gag to use one in lieu of a rabbit. The first time he pulled it out of a box, everyone laughed. He looked down to find that it had shat all over his sequined suit. When he put a diaper on the duck the following night, its resultantly pressurized feces splattered his face. The duck went on to become the star of his act.)

All in all, I thought it best to stay focused on issues that seemed ethnographically most pertinent to Parisian magicos' day-to-day activities, be they off-color cabaret anecdotes, or any of the other topics that registered much more prominently in my notes from the conversation with Jack and Alain: illusionists' career strategies and creative processes; relationships between amateurs and professionals; exchanges of technical secrets as a form of collegiality; the experience of life on the road. I certainly did not want to get sucked into what could never amount to more than armchair speculations about the way entertainment magicians may or may not be comparable to occult, instrumental magicians.

I filed the bibliography along with other magic ephemera. But sometimes my thoughts would drift back to it and the impression that receiving this ponderous reading list from such a rollicksome intermediary had made on me, and I wrestled with a vague sense of unease. After all, why should comparisons between occult and entertainment magic that seemed so compelling from the perspective of contemporary Western illusionists be so disconcerting from the perspective of contemporary Western anthropology? Why were illusionists so eager to invoke anthropological magic theory while anthropologists seemed to have studiously ignored the form of magic arguably most prevalent in their own societies: illusionism? What might it be like to write the anthropology of illusionistic magic based on a bibliography like the one that Jack had given me?

This book is an attempt to answer these questions, though in a somewhat perverse way, reading "athwart" (Helmreich 2011) anthropologists' and illusionists' theories of magic to uncover some unexpected patterns of convergence. Excavating beneath surface dissimilarities, I show how anthropologists and illusionists have, in fact, engaged in complementary and at times collaborative projects of defining magic in ways that shaped the culture of Western modernity, while also furthering their own parochial interests as professionals and experts.

Taking Jack's bibliography as a historiographical warrant leads me back in time to formative moments in the history of both stage magic and anthropology as Euro-American cultural traditions, particularly the second half of the nineteenth century. This period coincides with the beginning of what magicians call the "Golden Age of Magic," when illusionists were at the height of their creative prowess and cultural influence, and with the consolidation of anthropology as a new academic discipline. As a source of vitality in both domains, I discern something of a representational feedback loop linking the entertainment industry and anthropological scholarship in parallel efforts to define magic. I am not arguing that stage magicians and anthropologists closely collaborated, aside from a few fleeting encounters. Rather, I am arguing that they were operating in convergent milieux, each promulgating images and ideas that the other could productively incorporate into their own projects of cultural production, albeit at somewhat of a distance via mediated channels.

My argument is largely organized around tracing the legacies of two figures, the French illusionist Jean-Eugène Robert-Houdin (1805–1871) and the English anthropologist Sir Edward Burnett Tylor (1832–1917). Both were towering, internationally renowned professionals who established positions of unprecedented institutional influence and wrote foundational texts that shaped the future of their respective fields. Both were deeply engaged in Enlightenment projects of what Bruno Latour calls "purifying" (1993b: 35) theories of magic, seeking to overturn "the obscurity of the olden days, which illegitimately blended together social needs and natural reality, meanings and mechanisms, signs and things," to pave the way for a "luminous dawn that cleanly separated material causality from human fantasy." Robert-Houdin exemplified an approach to defining his brand of magic as an unambiguously modern combination of skill and expertise, hostile toward any obscurantism and akin to science. In anthropology, Tylor staked his scientific reputation on a rational account of occult magic as an unambiguously primitive set of delusions.

Entertainment magicians and cultural anthropologists such as these came to assert claims of expertise by distinguishing themselves from primitive magicians, but the comparisons they drew in terms of difference also carried the potential to highlight something more destabilizing: similarity. Latour argues that a proliferation of unavowed "hybrids" always accompanies any process of purification, and elsewhere (Latour 1993a) he suggests theories of magic as an example of this paradoxical process of simultaneous purification and hybridization—an idea that other scholars have confirmed and extended (Styers 2004; Wiener 2003, 2013). The modern construct of primitive magic exemplifies hybridity, yoked as it is to the service of guaranteeing the purity of other constructs: modern magic (for illusionists) and modern science (for anthropologists). The surface-level projects of purification pursued by illusionists and anthropologists converged in this undercurrent of hybridization. In the rest of this introduction, I will begin to describe how, in making (their) magic modern, illusionists incorporated anthropological imagery of primitive magic and, in making (their) magic primitive, anthropologists incorporated illusionistic imagery of modern magic.

As I will show, Robert-Houdin and Tylor both contributed actively to the ideological apparatus of Western imperialism, helping articulate a rationale for colonialism in terms of the cognitive supremacy of rational, modern Euro-Americans whom they compared to irrational, non-modern Others. In aspiring to account for something as broad and nebulous as Western modernity, my story emphasizes the transnational circulation of signs. Most of the anthropological work I single out for discussion has been influential across French, British, and American anthropological traditions, and reflects areas of shared concern. The topic of magic engendered a fertile academic trading zone, with scholars maintaining an active exchange across national borders. Likewise, illusionists were cosmopolitans in an industry that incentivized touring abroad and rewarded it with international fame. In both anthropology and entertainment, comparisons between rational and irrational stances toward magic came to circulate widely in nineteenth-century Euro-American cultural spheres, via scholarly publications and illusionistic performances that crisscrossed national frontiers.

Making Magic Modern

In some ways, it took considerable resolve not to bring anthropological theories of magic into my earlier ethnographic research. As one of the discipline's cardinal concepts and a topic of some of its most canonical texts, occult magic carried with it the allure of weighty intertextual associations. What's more, my informants themselves were convinced that this work (or at least what it represented) should be closely pertinent to anything I might have to say, as an anthropologist, about their craft, and they actively encouraged these associations. Among magicos, it was nearly a truism that entertainment magic derived from occult magic, or at least that there was a relationship, if not of ancestry, then of family resemblance that bound the figures of the occult, instrumental magician and the secular, entertainment magician conceptually together. Quite fairly, they reasoned that I would be well positioned, as someone ostensibly versed in anthropological magic theory, to confirm and clarify this relationship.

There are a variety of deep historical reasons why magicos would associate illusionistic and instrumental magic. Medieval taxonomies blurred boundaries between magic as entertainment, proto-science, and demonic perversion of religion (Kieckhefer 2000; Zetterberg 1980). Medieval books of secrets, for instance, often jumbled information about practical techniques for the home (remedies, dyeing procedures, etc.) together with instructions for sleight-of-hand tricks and practical jokes, spellcasting, making magical charms, and controlling demons through necromancy (Eamon 1994). A process of categorical clarification beginning in the thirteenth century (Kieckhefer 1994, 1998) gained currency among learned elites during the Enlightenment, giving entertainment magic a valence distinctive from science and the supernatural (Butterworth 2005: 180–81).

Illusionists played a crucial role in redrawing these cultural categories, taking an active lead in the process that Max Weber (1958: 139) famously termed the "disenchantment" of the world. When "increasing intellectualization and rationalization" convince people that "there are no mysterious incalculable forces," Weber writes, "one need no longer have recourse to magical means in order to master or implore the spirits, as did the savage, for whom such mysterious powers existed. Technical means and calculations perform the service." As I detail in this section, highlighting technical skill, cultivating associations with science, and discrediting mysterious (i.e., supernatural) powers constituted a set of cultural strategies that Euro-American illusionists used to style themselves as modern professionals. Disenchantment, however, was not a static condition that they attained once and for all, but rather an ongoing process of working through the fundamental ambiguities of a performative practice that appears to engage rational and irrational impulses simultaneously. Entertainment magic retained strong associations with enchantment that performers actively managed through discourses of disenchantment.

From the publication of the earliest manuals devoted to the art of legerdemain in the sixteenth century, illusionists rhetorically positioned themselves as crusaders for the cause of disenchantment, exposing the trickery of home-grown charlatans, and seeking to dispel a credulous public's superstitious beliefs by revealing ingenious technical means of illusion-making (During 2002; Mangan 2007). Consider, for instance, the Frenchman Jean Prévost's *Subtiles et Plaisantes Inventions* (Subtle and Pleasing Inventions), published in January 1584. At a time when charlatans plied European fairgrounds and marketplaces, performing impressive tricks and making fantastical claims about the magical virtues of the talismans and elixirs they hawked (Eamon 1994: 234 ff), Prévost professed to write with the goal of educating the misguided public. In the preface, he states that "having seen . . . simpleminded and crass people charmed and enchanted by a horde of imposters who . . . chase money under the pretext of doing things they cannot do," he hopes to show that "all the charms, feats, and illusions that we attribute to these deceivers are nothing but physical agility or manual dexterity through which they trick the eyes" (Prévost 1584: 4–5).

The kind of self-reflexive stance required for audiences to regard magical deceptions as a source of amusement ultimately made it a popular parlor recreation during the European Enlightenment and, subsequently, a vector for the democratization of Enlightenment values and ideas (Stafford 1994). Commenting on this development, historian of religion Leigh Eric Schmidt (1998: 275) writes that the "Enlightenment did not so much assault magic as absorb and secularize it," transforming it into "a widely distributed commodity of edifying amusement," and a medium for conveying "the skeptical professions of the *philosophes* in a performative and entertaining mode" (277).

This proliferation of edifying trickery may have accelerated the process of disenchantment by encouraging enthusiasts to think in naturalistic, rather than supernatural, terms about paranormal phenomena. For instance, in an entry on "Tricks with Cards and the Hands," in Diderot's *Encyclopédie*, Jaucourt (1765: 463) writes that learning about illusionism can "teach men to search for the causes behind sundry things that may strike them as very surprising." According to Weber (1958: 139), disenchantment does not imply that people actively possess a scientific account of how the world works; "it means something else, namely, the knowledge or belief that if one but wished one *could* learn it at any time." Magic as a mode of entertainment thus disenchants by promoting the view that seemingly supernatural phenomena must have a naturalistic explanation, even if performers titillate by intentionally obscuring that explanation.

By the turn of the nineteenth century, illusionism had become the prototypical form of what Simon During (2002) calls a *modern enchantment*—in other words, an expressive form "that enchants and disenchants simultaneously: one that delights but does not delude" (Saler 2006: 702). By convention, modern magical showmen were expected to present tricks *as tricks* to audiences eager to be deceived, but not so credulous as to mistake illusions for reality. These performers agentively carved out associations with science, exposing the public to new technological advances in fields such as optics and electricity, even adopting the performative conventions of scientific lectures, experiments, and demonstrations (Lachapelle 2015; Nadis 2005).

Just as a long tradition of East Indian performance magic enacts the cosmological principal of *maya*, the world-as-illusion (Siegel 1991), Western illusionism converged with modern materialist cosmology and empiricist epistemology. Cook (2001: 169) argues that, by the beginning of the nineteenth century, the illusionist had emerged as "a powerful symbol of progress" in the West, as a scientific popularizer and a debunker of superstitions, but also as a catalyst of critical controversy in the expanding public sphere, claiming "disenchantment as [a] *raison d'être* in the post-Enlightenment world" (179). As a popular representative of European cultural modernity, the Western-style magician also became an icon of progress outside the West—in early twentieth-century China (Pang 2004) or contemporary India (Srinivas 2015). The close association of entertainment magic with Enlightenment values of rationality, skepticism, and materialism made it a powerful resource for signifying secular modernity and defining its thresholds.

During (2002: 81) argues that entertainment magicians defined themselves as modern by provoking comparisons with "dangerous doubles"—charlatans, con men, cardsharpers, psychics, and mediums—whose dishonest, disreputable use of trickery risked tainting stage magic by association. By aggressively attacking these doubles, modern magicians consistently allied themselves with the cause of progress and, in the process, policed the boundaries between normative and non-normative forms of magic (Lachapelle 2015; Lamont 2013). Through public (and publicized) attacks, magical entertainers carefully managed and productively channeled troubling resemblances with figures of simultaneous attraction and repulsion. In denouncing these doubles, modern magicians also promulgated perspectives that worked their way, more or less circuitously, into anthropological texts.

The era of colonialism invigorated Enlightenment discourses of progress by dramatizing the dominion of Western European powers over less technologically advanced peoples of the global south. It also provided magicians with a new foil: "primitive"—or, in Weber's parlance, "savage"—magicians reputed to hold sway among colonial populations. More than Europe's fairground quacks or village soothsayers, ritual experts in non-Western traditions came to figure in the literature and lore of entertainment magic as conceptual embodiments of premodern, non-modern, or antimodern approaches to magic. Magic authors drew on a variety of ethnographic representations and erudite commentaries in constructing these discourses, equating the benighted outlook of present-day colonial subjects with the superstitious beliefs of Europe's historical past. Often, the ritual performances reported in these ethnographic annals involved awe-inspiring artifice or displays of superhuman prowess, and inspired oral traditions attesting to ritual experts' paranormal feats. These kinds of practices were particularly susceptible to illusionists' increasingly well-honed tactics of disenchantment.

One author contributed more than any other to establishing the primitive magician as a figure of dangerous doubleness in the lore of European illusionists, and he is central to the story I tell in this book: Jean-Eugène Robert-Houdin. Known around the world as the "Father of Modern Magic," Robert-Houdin set performative and presentational standards that still serve as a touchstone for magicians today. Although born three years after Robert-Houdin's death, a young American named Ehrich Weiss was so impressed by the Frenchman's imposing legacy that he took the stage name "Houdini" as an homage to his idol.[1]

If Robert-Houdin "fathered" something called "modern" magic, it was by positioning himself, onstage and in print, as a standard-bearer for progress. This involved calling attention to his own originality, ingenuity, and tastefulness while actively repudiating a tradition of uncouth predecessors whom he described as dressing up in absurd wizard costumes, comporting themselves like buffoons onstage, and possessing little by way of real technical skill. The poster for an 1849 performance in London (figure 3) shows Robert-Houdin precisely how he wanted to be seen: in the middle of an elegant salon, dressed in stylish eveningwear, demonstrating sophisticated automata that he himself designed and built—a genial mondain with an aura of erudition.

Crucially, Robert-Houdin also burnished his image as a paragon of progress by contributing to France's civilizing mission in colonial Algeria. In 1856, at the behest of the French Army, he traveled to the relatively new colony to stage a series of didactic performances designed to challenge the influence of popular religious figures known as *marabouts*. According to army intelligence, these marabouts were using magic tricks to convince people that they were anointed with supernatural powers, and then leading their awestruck followers in messianic, anticolonial campaigns. Robert-Houdin's mission was to one-up the marabouts with technologically advanced trickery, and to ultimately discredit them as charlatans among Algerian Muslims.

Figure 3. Poster from British tour of Robert-Houdin's Soirées Fantastiques, St. James's Theatre in London, circa 1849. Harry Ransom Center, The University of Texas at Austin.

In writing about this episode in his mythopoeic memoir *A Conjuror's Confessions*, Robert-Houdin (1859) created what may well be the most widely circulated anecdote in all of modern magic. Reprised in virtually every history of the genre and familiar to most magicians, the story still even crops up in the news: the American illusionist Teller (1999) recounted it in the *New York Times Magazine*; a recent story in the *Boston Globe* called it "the only documented instance, at least since antiquity, in which a conjurer changed the course of world affairs" (Bennett 2008). More importantly for my purposes, this narrative played a vital role in ushering an anthropological style of argumentation into the discourses of modern magic. As I will show, Robert-Houdin's *Confessions* mobilized ethnographic representations and evolutionist models of cultural difference in a way that left an indelible ideological imprint on the history of illusionism. The confrontation with the marabouts was both literal and allegorical, providing yet another way for Robert-Houdin to define what it meant for magic to be modern by delineating a contrast with colonial ritual experts whom he classified as "magicians" and characterized as "primitive."

The central objects of Robert-Houdin's ethnographic gaze were the 'Isawa,[2] members of a mystical North African Sufi order (the 'Isawiyya), whose ecstatic rituals involve displays of seemingly miraculous invulnerability to otherwise harmful self-mortifications: eating glass and cactus spines, stabbing themselves, walking on coals and sabers, handling snakes and scorpions, touching red-hot metal implements, dislodging their eyeballs, and so forth. Accused of using tricks to feign supernatural powers, the 'Isawa had already come to figure in colonial rhetoric as embodiments of Muslim difference (Spadola 2008; Trumbull 2007). In Chapter One, I describe how Robert-Houdin drew on representations in French colonial ethnography to narratively fashion the 'Isawa as archetypically "primitive" African charlatans. In Chapter Two, I argue that those representations anticipated Robert-Houdin's appropriation by incorporating images of more-or-less "modern" magicians as comparative foils.

Manipulating doubleness was key to the way illusionists made their kind of magic modern, and the 'Isawa occupied pride of place in Robert-Houdin's extensive writing about modern magic's Others. Central to my argument is an account of how these particular dangerous doubles came to feature so prominently in his memoir and, consequently, in magicians' lore. Representations of the 'Isawa were astonishingly common in French popular culture more broadly, resulting in a dense archive of texts and images that makes this a particularly rich historiographical focus. In writing about these representations, I am anxious not to reanimate the racism and

Islamophobia that infuse them, but instead to show how ideas about magic operated to create invidious contrasts in the context of colonial culture, informing troublesome stereotypes.

My approach is essentially an ethnohistorical one, not because my objective is to rediscover Algerian ritual meanings obscured in earlier, biased ethnographic accounts. Although I do hazard some conjectures in that direction by drawing on more sophisticated recent research among contemporary 'Isawa, it is primarily to cast earlier ethnographic perspectives into analytic relief. My ethnohistory, as an anthropologist of France, is primarily of *French*, not Algerian, understandings of the cultural parameters of magic, precisely as reflected in what I take to be manifest ethnocentric biases in the history of ethnographic representations.

Popular and highly publicized performances first in North Africa, then in Europe, reinforced the 'Isawa's iconic status. As I describe in Chapter Three, the 'Isawa achieved some degree of show-business celebrity by exhibiting their devotional feats of self-mortification alongside Western illusionists in Paris and London in the late nineteenth century (figure 4). These performances stoked public controversy about artifice and authenticity at a time when intellectuals were already fiercely divided about another set of religious figures: Euro-American occult mediums widely performing feats of spiritism, hypnotism, and mesmerism. In Chapter Four, I describe how French esotericists and their allies hailed the 'Isawa as purveyors of profoundly significant otherworldly knowledge, which they eagerly incorporated in their heterodox cosmology, directly challenging the demystifying assertions of Robert-Houdin and other illusionists.

That the 'Isawa became contested objects of intellectual controversy serves as an important reminder that, then as now, Europeans' ideas about magic were far from uniform. Historian Karl Bell (2012) rightly cautions that accounts stressing connections between modern magic and disenchantment run the risk of simplifying a much more complicated reality: modern magicians not only traded on the allure of occult associations, but also seemed to revel in distinctly counter-Enlightenment antics when it suited their interests. Public reception is always something of a mystery, but for his part, Bell proposes that nineteenth-century "magic shows were as likely to enchant or re-enchant as much as disenchant" (95), and that we should seriously consider their potential for "sustaining genuine magical beliefs" (99) by translating and transforming them. Along with Bell's insistence that enchantment is not only a premodern condition, I would also want to stress the anthropological corollary: that disenchantment is not only a modern condition (Lewis 2002).

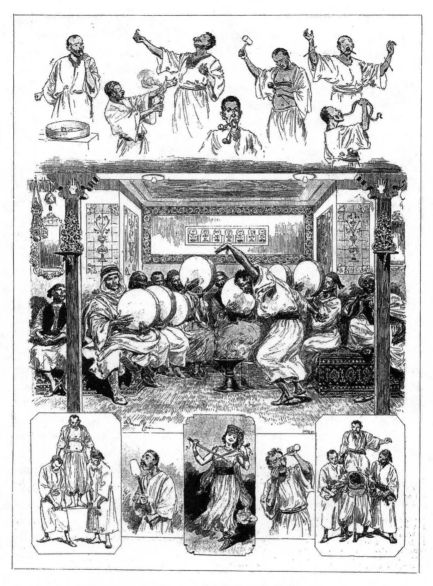

Figure 4. French representation of 'Isawa. *Le Monde illustrée*, October 12, 1889. Courtesy Firestone Library, Princeton University.

Even if the motif of disenchantment in modern magic comingled with contradictory, countervailing tendencies, it resonated unequivocally with certain sectors of the Euro-American intelligentsia, such as the ethnographers and anthropologists who drew it into their analyses of primitive magic. The theories they propounded were so influential that, generations later, a historian like Bell, writing in an entirely different discipline, can offhandedly refer to occult magic writ large as "ethnographic magic" (2012: 79, 90), magic in the anthropologists' sense. Ultimately, I will suggest that, just as emphasizing disenchantment was a strategy for modern magicians to manage associations with enchantment, anthropologists' evolving engagements with instrumental magic offered a way of working through the discipline's enduringly equivocal status as both colonial and anticolonial, scientific and hermeneutic.

Making Magic Primitive

Around the time Western illusionists were formulating ideas about the relationship between primitive and modern magic, the fledgling field of anthropology was itself beginning to stake out convergent claims of authoritative expertise in all matters relating to occult magic—claims it maintains to this day. Instrumental magic came to captivate Western anthropologists curious to understand participants' *belief* in the influence of symbolic actions on natural events or supernatural forces. Assured of their own imperviousness to superstition, nineteenth-century anthropologists asked what could lead other rational human beings to hold seemingly irrational beliefs, even in the face of disconfirming evidence. Emphasizing this epistemological theme of belief, they contrasted occult magic with other explanatory systems, classifying it as a primitive cultural formation in respect to religious faith and, especially, the kind of modern scientific knowledge that anthropologists themselves claimed to espouse.

To the present day, anthropologists have continued to debate how best to understand the nature of belief in instrumental magic, particularly as—in seeming contradiction with the master narrative of disenchantment—occult phenomena have not only persisted but proliferated under the postmodern, postcolonial, postsocialist conditions of global capitalism (e.g., Ashforth 2005; Buyandelgar 2013; Comaroff and Comaroff 1999; Geschiere 2013, 2016; James 2010; Lemon 2013; Meyer and Pels 2003; Romberg 2009). Moreover, ideas about the backwardness of magic spread with Western ideals of modernity, progress, and development, creating new modern syncretisms within magical traditions (Pigg 1996). Magic remains germane for another reason that will figure more centrally into my discussion. At the same time that anthropological modernity has hinged on the ability to rationally ana-lyze apparently irrational beliefs, it is also connected with the anthropolo-gist's ability to enchant Western publics with exoticized imagery of native Others and romanticized narratives of contact. The topic of instrumental magic represents a point, within anthropology, where motifs of enchant-ment and disenchantment converge.

In contrast to instrumental magic, entertainment magic seems to rely on an attitude of *disbelief* that allows people to enjoy mystifying deceptions as play or amusement. At least as a manifestation of Euro-American popular culture, it largely fell outside the purview of the agenda nineteenth-century anthropologists set for themselves. With a few fleeting exceptions, Western illusionism seemed mostly to escape the attention of anthropologists until I began my study of the French magic scene. But my struggle to reconcile an-thropological magic theory, attuned as it was to supernatural beliefs, with the seemingly incompatible magical practices of the self-avowedly disenchanted illusionists in my ethnography left me with some unanswered questions.

Along with Peter Pels (2014: 234–35), it continued to strike me as odd that, for all the ink spilled in debates over instrumental magic, Western an-thropologists had, paradoxically, written so little about the practice most commonly referred to as "magic" in their own societies. This silence seems stranger still when considering that the discipline of anthropology matured during what my informants wistfully refer to as the "Golden Age of Magic," the period from the late nineteenth to early twentieth centuries when illu-sionists ranked among the entertainment industry's top-billed celebrities, crisscrossing the globe with sensational, blockbuster stage illusions (see Steinmeyer 2003).

There are a few reasons, I think, for this silence. On one level, any schol-arly neglect is part of a legacy of anthropological disdain for cosmopolitan entertainment industries more generally. P. T. Barnum may have coined the term "show business" around the time anthropology adopted "culture" as its central concern (Boon 2000: 431), but as opposed to the density of sub-stance that anthropologists imputed to exotic cultures (Silverstein 2013), they found it easy to dismiss Western popular culture as thinned and tainted by market forces. Edward Sapir, to cite one famous example, lamented that, while genuine culture "reaches its greatest heights in comparatively small, autonomous groups" (1924: 425), the "admirable machinery" of modern civilization produces blandly homogenized and passively consumed "canned culture" (429). By this standard, it would be difficult to recognize any mass entertainment as an instance of culture sufficiently "authentic" to merit sustained consideration, even if, as I will argue, they repeatedly insinuated themselves into anthropologists' thinking.

A second reason has to do with a historical tendency among social scientists to overlook phenomena that conform so closely to researchers' own expectations about what is normal that they may even supply normative interpretative frames. Many topics that seemed to lack sufficient alterity to constitute legitimate objects of anthropological interest—topics like science (Latour 1993b), Christianity (Bialecki, Haynes, and Robbins 2008), or whiteness (Frankenberg 1993; Mullings 2005)—long escaped anthropologists' attention. In a similar fashion, entertainment magic so fully embodied the "correct" way of engaging in magical practices that, even when it did enter into explicit focus, it never received the same kind of sustained treatment that "deviant" occult magic elicited. It simply didn't pose an analytic problem.

In a definitive intellectual history of anthropological magic theory, Randall Styers (2004: 8) shows that anthropologists viewed occult magic as so deviant that they came to treat it as the "archetypically nonmodern phenomenon" and the ultimate analytic challenge. Primitive and occult magic thus "offered scholars and social theorists a foil for modern notions of religion and science and, more broadly, a foil for modernity itself." In the words of Peter Pels, "anthropology, more than any other scholarly discourse on magic, was responsible for the interpretation of magic as an antithesis of modernity" (2003a: 5). Secular stage magic, which helped fashion the cultural scaffolding for this interpretation, had become so utterly suffused with the attributes of modernity that it elicited little analysis from scholars seeking to position themselves as experts on magic as a quintessentially non-modern phenomenon.

I do not purport to offer the kind of overarching critical history of the development of anthropological magic theory that scholars like Styers, Pels, and others (e.g., Brown 1997; Greenwood 2009; Tambiah 1990; Wiener 2013, 2015) have already so expertly provided. By approaching the process of "theoretical development" (Snow, Morrill, and Anderson 2003) in terms of a topic that most of these other histories almost entirely exclude—entertainment magic—what I do offer is a new way of seeing underlying continuities between the intellectual history of anthropology and the cultural history of Euro-American showbiz.

Simon During's alluring notion of "dangerous doubleness" suggested itself as the title for this introductory essay (and as an overarching leitmotif for this book) not only because I focus on the way that illusionists defined normative modern magic through oppositions with deviant primitive alternatives.

Anthropologists also positioned the primitive magician as the ultimate cultural Other against which to test their explanatory prowess as modern social scientists capable of systematically accounting for even the most aberrant (by Enlightenment standards) beliefs and practices in terms of universal laws and generalizable theories. The joint attention they trained on the figure of the primitive magician linked illusionists and anthropologists themselves in another curious relationship of doubleness: illusionists articulated an anthropology of magic while anthropologists quietly absorbed the imagery of illusionism into their ethnographic and theoretical accounts of magic. When anthropologists wrote about primitive magicians, I argue, modern magicians were often also implicitly present in their texts as points of conceptual comparison to be leveraged, if not explicitly by juxtaposition, then figuratively, through tropes of metaphor and simile. Sometimes they even sought to enlist the help of illusionists as scientific allies.

From at least the seventeenth century, denigratory allusions to European illusionary performance were not uncommon in ethnographic accounts that missionaries, colonial officials, travelers—and eventually also prestidigitators such as Robert-Houdin—wrote about magico-religious practices among indigenous colonial peoples. In colonial ethnographers' descriptions of indigenous ritual experts as "jugglers" (not to mention "conjurers," "mountebanks," and "prestidigitators," etc.), one can discern a hidden history implicating theatrical magic more deeply in the formation of primitive magic as an anthropological category.

Tropes of trickery were not uncommon in the *Jesuit Relations* or other traditions of ethnographic writing (Flaherty 1992; Taussig 1999, 2003), but it was not until the nineteenth century that anthropologists began to compile and collate the scattered accounts of magico-religious practices of which they formed but a part. From a patchwork of disparate and more-or-less reliable evidence, these scholars stitched together something like a coherent theory of primitive magic—one that incorporated accusations of charlatanic trickery and implicit contrasts with the disenchanted trickery of entertainment magic at its very core. In Chapter Five, I consider how this process unfolded in the work of one exemplary anthropological theorist, Edward Burnett Tylor.

The first chair of anthropology at Oxford, Tylor is widely credited with systematizing earlier ethnographic writing, creating unified categories of anthropological analysis and, in so doing, building an intellectual framework for the discipline (Stocking 1987, 1995). Like Robert-Houdin, he is often, if controversially, touted as the father of modern anthropology, a reputation that also largely rests on a major text. Tylor's 1871 magnum opus *Primitive*

Culture[3] articulated the paradigmatic modern perspective on primitive magic and helped cement it as one of anthropology's paramount concerns.

The archetypal social evolutionist, Tylor viewed magic as the simplest and most wrongheaded way people might go about making sense of the world, contrasting it with more advanced forms of what he called "intellectual culture" (1873: 112): religion and, ultimately, science. The belief in magic, he declared, was "one of the most pernicious delusions that ever vexed mankind," belonging to the "lowest known stages of civilization, and the lower races." He formed his view of primitive magic by bringing together an impressively learned omnigatherum of superstitious practices, paranormal beliefs, and magical rites culled from ancient literature, European peasant folklore, and travelers' accounts of far-flung exotic peoples. Regardless of whether it came from European history or contemporary non-Western cultures, in the machinery of Tylor's evolutionism, any example of irrational belief became an interchangeable token of the same type of thing: primitive magical thinking.

Tylor wrote about magic alongside a vast number of other topics: language, mathematics, kinship, religion, weaponry, tools, jurisprudence, and games, to name but a few. But magic wasn't just a topic like any other for Tylor—it was crucial to his conception of what anthropology was and what it could do. It occupied a pivotal place in his system-building enterprise for three reasons. First, the challenge of giving a rational account of something as ostensibly irrational as magic made for a methodologically alluring demonstration of scientific prowess. Tylor (1873: 19) argued that invoking "notions of arbitrary impulses, causeless freaks, chance and nonsense and indefinite unaccountability" to explain "absurd superstitions" simply wouldn't do. It was itself the anthropological equivalent of magical thinking. "The great task of rational ethnography" demanded the scientific "investigation of the causes which have produced the phenomena of culture, and the laws to which they are subordinate" (20), even when dealing with practices as intellectually muddled as magic. He proposed that this approach would reveal the magico-religious beliefs and practices of savage people to be "far from . . . a rubbish-heap of miscellaneous folly . . . consistent and logical in so high a degree as to begin, as soon as even roughly classified, to display the principles of their formation and development," principles that are "essentially rational, though working in a mental condition of intense and inveterate ignorance."

In addition to providing a propitious proving ground for his new science, magic was, in the second place, important to Tylor because its indisputable prevalence in the midst of technologically advanced Victorian

Britain threatened to fundamentally contradict his model of progress and its rigid stratigraphy of primitive and modern thought. In Tylor's day, Spiritualist mediums were everywhere. Offering not only the promise of speaking with the dead, but also producing a variety of spectacular phenomena to substantiate their extraordinary claims, these mediums attracted throngs of followers and drew enormous crowds on both sides of the Atlantic (Lamont 2006; McGarry 2008; Owen 2004). Their strange noises, ectoplasmic excretions, and other mysterious manifestations were easy for stage magicians to write off as the trickery of dangerous doubles, but that didn't stop them from replicating the same phenomena themselves—helping stir up a controversy that embroiled the British, American, and French intelligentsia for decades (Lachapelle 2015; Lamont 2004, 2013; Natale 2011).

Tylor positioned himself in the middle of the scrum, even conducting fieldwork among Spiritualists and their clients in 1872 (Collins 2015; Pels 2003a, 2003b; Stocking 1971). His evolutionist theory predicted that if magic persisted in the modern era, it should be in the "liminoid" (Turner 1982) form of play, fantasy, theater, or entertainment. "The serious business of ancient society may be seen to sink into the sport of later generations, and its serious belief to linger on in nursery folk-lore," he wrote (Tylor 1873: 16). Thus, Tylor allowed that the hollow shell of occult magic could unproblematically persist in the form of disenchanted diversions: "From the earliest times . . . tricks of sleight-of-hand etc., have been passed off by magicians as miracles to deceive their dupes; our language still testifies to this in the use of the word conjuror, the wonder-worker still carrying on the old juggling, although no longer evoking demons to give him mysterious power" (Tylor 1883: 206). Here, Tylor's account of the resignification of legerdemain is indistinguishable from the narrative of progressive disenchantment to which entertainment magicians themselves, like the magicos I worked with in contemporary France, subscribe.

The problem for Tylor was that, as he put it, "sometimes old thoughts and practices will burst out afresh to the amazement of a world that thought them long since dead or dying; here survival passes into revival, as has lately happened in so remarkable a way in the history of modern spiritualism" (1873: 16–17). The concept of "survivals" (or "revivals") was Tylor's way of reconciling the Spiritualist craze with his theory of progress, ensuring that whenever anything resembling his definition of primitive magic cropped up in a context he defined as modern, it could be safely categorized as a vestigial holdover, dismissed as mere anachronism, or swept aside as "matter out of place" (Douglas 2002: 44). Key to Chapter Five is an examination of how Tylor interpreted Euro-American Spiritualism by invoking parallels with Amerindian shamanism—a comparison mediated by the trope of trickery. At the heart of Tylor's theory of primitive magic sits the notion of the trick, an electrically charged point of contact between disenchanted entertainment and enchanted ritual.

The third reason Tylor had so much at stake in the topic of magic has to do with the way he framed it—dangerously—as a double for his own scientific activities. Tylor placed magic on the opposite end of a continuum with science, along a pathway of intellectual progress leading from the most primitive to the most modern mode of thought (Marett 1936: 76–78). But as a precursor to science, magic inevitably had to share something in common with the enterprise of anthropology that Tylor was endeavoring to fashion as scientific. That commonality was the use of *analogy*, which Tylor (1873: 115) called "the very foundation of human reason, but . . . of unreason also." Elsewhere, he explained,

> In the earlier days of knowledge men relied far more than we moderns do on reasoning by analogy or mere association of ideas. In getting on from what is known already to something new, analogy or reasoning by resemblance always was, as it still is, the mind's natural guide in the quest of truth. Only its results must be put under the control of experience. [In] matters beyond his limited knowledge, [the rude man] contents himself with working on resemblances or analogies of thought, which thus become the foundation of magic. (Tylor 1881: 338–39)

For Tylor, magical thinking involved treating analogies as facts about the world, mistaking "ideal" connections existing only in the mind for "real" ones (1873: 116). Scientific thinking, by contrast, treated analogies heuristically, identifying resemblances that could be subjected to further tests. Contrasting the deviant, magical use of analogies with the normative, scientific use of analogies, Tylor formulated a comparison that continues to stir debate: in practice, just how scientific are magicians, and how magical are scientists?

Analogy is where magical thinking and the anthropological imagination meet, for if occult magicians rely on analogical resemblances, then so too do anthropologists. In seeking to substantiate the scientific nature of anthropology, Tylor doubly deploys the notion of analogy, arguing that anthropology is analogous to natural science in terms of its concern with laws, and that anthropologists should use analogies the way that biologists do when comparing plants and animals in different regions. "Just as distant regions so often produce vegetables and animals which are analogous, so it is with the details of the civilization of their inhabitants," he writes (Tylor 1873: 8). "How good a working analogy there really is between the diffusion of plants and animals and the diffusion of civilization, comes well into view when we notice how far the same causes have produced both at once." This analogy is particularly striking given the importance of Darwinian theory as a source for Tylorian evolutionism.

To substantiate the concept of magic, Tylor, for instance, analogizes a variety of magical practices themselves appearing to involve the use of analogy to interpret and influence the world—and here, I quote only in part:

> The North American Indian, eager to kill a bear to-morrow, will hang up a rude grass image of one and shoot it, reckoning that this symbolic act will make the real one happen. The Australians at a burial, to know in what direction they may find the wicked sorcerer who has killed their friend, will take as their omen the direction of the flames of the grave-fire. The Zulu who wants to buy cattle may be seen chewing a bit of wood, in order to soften the hard heart of the seller he is dealing with. (Tylor 1881: 340)

Here, Tylor compares three examples, from three different cultures, of people who seem to believe that there are cause-and-effect connections between symbolic activities and external processes that are—so he says—analogous in appearance but unrelated in fact. However, the analogy that Tylor draws between North American, Australian, and African cases itself rests upon a set of assumptions about comparison and classification that a future generation of anthropologists—with Franz Boas (1896) leading the charge—would dismiss as unscientific in its tendency to confuse appearance and reality.

In the wake of this critique, anthropologists became more cautious in framing comparisons. However, following a number of influential theorists—notably Roy Wagner (1981) and Marilyn Strathern (2007a, 2007b, 2008, 2011)—I will argue that cross-cultural analogy remains, in some form or another, the cornerstone of the way that anthropologists produce knowledge. Anthropological fieldworkers continue to explore analogies between the cultures they come from and the cultures they are trying to understand; as authors of ethnographic studies, they try to generalize from their own localized cases by plotting out analogies with studies conducted both in the immediate vicinity and elsewhere in the world; as educators, they challenge students to confront experiences analogous to their own but in unfamiliar circumstances, or unfamiliar experiences in closely analogous circumstances. The continuing, but contested, importance of analogy to the way anthropologists work makes the disciplinary history of this intellectual device particularly rich and relevant.

Anthropologists' analogies, comparisons in terms of similarity, are always also *disanalogies* (Shelley 2002b), comparisons in terms of difference. Comparisons between things that are too similar or too different are meaningless; as Poole (1986: 417) puts it, paraphrasing Jonathan Smith: "difference makes a comparative analysis interesting; similarity makes it possible." For an anthropological comparison to have some value, analogy and disanalogy must be dynamically co-present—though as a kind of shorthand, I often refer to both under the umbrella term "analogy" (cf. Gentner and Markman 1997). Throughout this book, I carefully attend to the complex interplay of analogy and disanalogy in the comparisons magicians, ethnographers, and anthropologists draw between modern and primitive magic. I argue that, in order to make contrasts between enchanted and disenchanted perspectives particularly stark, these comparisons often emphasize analogies in terms of the way that tricks are performed and disanalogies in terms of the way that tricks are intended and interpreted.

In Chapter Six, I explore how an originary analogy-cum-disanalogy between primitive and modern magic shaped the formation of the anthropological magic concept and determined the course of its future development. At the same time, I use magic as an example of how analogy shapes *any* concept in anthropology—kinship and ritual would be other notable examples. I examine how anthropologists since Tylor have thought about the place of analogy in cross-cultural comparison, and use this as the basis for a more general model of how anthropological concepts such as magic change through time, within a dominant disciplinary framework.[4]

Here again, we are confronted with the issue of doubleness: for scholars whose primary means of knowledge production is cross-cultural comparison, the promises and perils of doubling are especially pronounced. Appearances of doubleness can guide but also often mislead, making any operation of positing doubleness inherently dangerous. Tylor (1873: 14) himself was well aware of this problem, confessing that "it has more than once happened to myself to find my collections of traditions and beliefs thus set up to prove their own objective truth." How are we to know if our analogies are valid, and the concepts that facilitate them sound? Generally, the response is through "reflexivity" (e.g., Davies 2008; Herzfeld 2001), critical self-reflection incorporated iteratively into the process of ethnographic research and writing. Reflexivity is a prescription for applying careful scrutiny to analogies that seem too obvious, dampening the epistemological danger of doubleness.

Marilyn Strathern (1992b: 47) writes that "culture consists in the way people draw analogies between different domains of their worlds," be they anthropologists or people whom anthropologists study. Concentrating on two particularly active arenas of analogy-making, what I ultimately want to show is how deeply comparisons between modern and primitive magicians, enacted by illusionists like Robert-Houdin and theorized by anthropologists like Tylor, can take us in thinking about the cultural construction of European modernity, with its cognitive hallmarks of rationality, skepticism, and disenchantment. In the final chapter of the book, I use a technique I call "ethnohistorical reflexivity" to explore the ideology of cognitive singularity central to European modernity by enfolding the intellectual history of European anthropological magic theory back into my ethnography of contemporary European entertainment magic. The result is a view of modernity itself as an artifact of active analogy-making, as seen from the close comparative vantage of two professions claiming the expert ability to mediate some of its operative binaries—especially the disanalogy between magical and rational thought.

ONE

The War on Miracles

On September 16, 1856, gentleman illusionist Jean-Eugène Robert-Houdin boarded a steamship in Marseille bound for the embattled French colony of Algeria. Thirty-six hours later, a detachment of French soldiers met him in the port of Algiers. Recently retired as an entertainer to pursue research in optics and the emerging field of applied electricity, Robert-Houdin was about to return to the stage in a series of magic performances that a French general later called the single most important campaign in the pacification of indigenous Algeria (Chavigny 1970: 134).

Although France had captured Algiers over twenty years earlier, in 1830, Algeria remained a tinderbox of anticolonial resistance. The political director of the Bureau of Arab Affairs, army colonel François-Edouard de Neveu, was particularly concerned about the subversive influence of charismatic Muslim religious figures whom he identified as *marabouts*. According to his intelligence, some of these marabouts feigned supernatural powers with conjuring tricks, gaining religious veneration as living saints and using their influence to oppose the French. Faced with what appeared to be a dangerous form of charlatanism, de Neveu, with possible encouragement from Emperor Napoléon III himself (Fechner 2002: 39–40), solicited the help of France's most famous magician, Robert-Houdin. It took de Neveu nearly two years and three requests to sway him, but Robert-Houdin eventually agreed to undertake an improbable mission. His task was to counteract the sway of wonder-working holy men by performing modern, European magic for Algeria's Arab elites.

Two years later, Robert-Houdin wrote extensively about this experience in his memoirs, *Confidences d'un prestidigitateur* (A Conjuror's Confessions). Cunningly devised to solidify its author's reputation as the greatest magician of all time, this magical bildungsroman also functions to magnify the status of entertainment magic by aligning it with values of science, progress, and modernity.[1] A vivid cast of transgressive Others populate the *Confessions*, violating Robert-Houdin's elevated standards of propriety and proficiency, and serving as rhetorical foils for his own brand of enlightened illusionism. The marabouts embody the narrative's most extreme form of alterity, inverting the progressive principles Robert-Houdin posits as the quintessence of modern magic. As he describes it, these

> intriguers claiming inspiration from the Prophet, and whom the Arabs regard as God's messengers on Earth, incited most of the revolts that have had to be suppressed in Algeria . . . Now, these false prophets, these holy marabouts, are no more sorcerers than I am (indeed, even less so), but nevertheless succeed in igniting the fanaticism of their coreligionists with the help of conjuring tricks as primitive as the audiences for whom they are performed . . . It was hoped, with reason, that my performances would lead the Arabs to understand that the marabouts' trickery is naught but simple child's play and could not, given its crudeness, be the work of real heavenly emissaries. Naturally, this entailed demonstrating our superiority in everything and showing that, as far as sorcerers are concerned, there is no match for the French. (Robert-Houdin 1859, vol. 2: 249–50)

This description suggests a tension between activities of *disenchanting* local modes of religious authority and *enchanting* European dominion that ultimately remains unresolved in Robert-Houdin's narrative.

Beginning with an account of the overall significance of Robert-Houdin's *Confessions* as perhaps the ultimate statement of what and how modern entertainment magic signifies, this chapter goes on to analyze the place of his Algerian mission within the narrative. In the next chapter, I examine the cultural logic behind the French Army's curious choice of magic as a mode of "imperial spectacle" (Apter 2002), arguing that it hinged on the way colonial ethnographers had already used entertainment magic as an analogy for describing Algerian religious practices. I ultimately want to suggest that one of the reasons modern magic could creep into ethnographic texts as a tropological resource for contrastive interpretations was because contemporaneous cultural producers like Robert-Houdin were working so hard to elaborate the secular meaning of their marvelous performances, to provide audiences with normative interpretive frames, and to burnish their overall image as heralds of modernity.

The Ur-Text of Modern Magic

The most influential illusionist in nineteenth-century Europe, and the most famous French illusionist of all time, Robert-Houdin is a pivotal figure in the historiography of magic (Cook 2001; During 2002; Mangan 2007; Metzner 1998; Steinmeyer 2003). In the recent estimation of one historian, "with his fascination with all that was scientific and technological, his promotion of strict and detailed rules of conduct for a successful magic show, and his interest in the supernatural drama" of the Spiritualist controversy, "Robert-Houdin personified this era in which conjurers presented their magic as entertaining and spectacular but also instructive and respectable" (Lachapelle 2015: 136).

It is difficult to distinguish Robert-Houdin's impact as a performer on the history of magic from the indelible mark he left as a writer on the historiography of magic. His literary output includes a tantalizing exposé of card-sharpers' techniques (Robert-Houdin 1861) and a book many consider the first comprehensive primer on the art of conjuring, *Les secrets de la prestidigitation et de la magie* (1868). In that latter work, he famously proclaimed that "the illusionist is not a juggler, but an actor playing the role of a magician" (54). This clever dictum reflects the aesthetic predilections of a figure who strove to transform illusionism from a disreputable popular amusement into legitimate theatrical entertainment. It also encapsulates a worldview in which the appropriate experience of anything magical lies within a circumscribed arena of suspended disbelief,[2] safely sequestered from real pre-, non-, or antimodern belief.

It is Robert-Houdin's extraordinary autobiography, the *Confessions*, that remains the definitive objectification and crowning achievement of a career. In that book, Robert-Houdin presents himself as reforming magic into a respectable form of bourgeois entertainment by purging it of its problematic associations with low culture, the criminal demimonde, and backwards superstition. That the *Confessions* inspired a young American reader to take the stage name "Houdini" only begins to suggest the impact of the book on the cultural history of magic.

Written after his retirement from the professional stage, the *Confessions* are a meditation on the meaning of a career, animated by Robert-Houdin's desire to establish the magician as a respectable figure and magic as a respectable profession in distinctively modern terms. Surveying gushing contemporary reviews of the English-language translation, James Cook affirms that "what these opinions documented most of all was Robert-Houdin's

virtuosity as a maker of powerful new literary images" (2001: 194). Referring to the "long shadow" Robert-Houdin cast over subsequent generations,
magic historian Jim Steinmeyer calls him "the model magician . . . because,
more than anything else, magicians had been captivated by his astounding
memoirs, an inspiring piece of literature that painted the portrait of a magician
as an artist. It might be the most influential book in the world of magic"
(2003: 141).

A contemporary reading like Steinmeyer's, emphasizing the romantic
model of the creative *artist* as the ultimate measure of cultural distinction,
appears somewhat anachronistic; Robert-Houdin emerges from the *Confessions* as an author much more concerned with securing his status as an
inventor and man of science.[3] Participation in industrial and scientific activity
was central to nineteenth-century French notions of bourgeois masculinity.
During this period, "science, as both a discursive field and a realm of social practice, was capable of making bourgeois manhood appear a solid,
homogenous unity set in opposition to the more frivolous occupations of
women and noblemen" (Harrison 1999: 64). To harness the legitimizing
prestige of science, Robert-Houdin, both in print and onstage, drew attention to his technological savvy as an inventor and craftsman, figuring himself as a reformer who could refashion the relatively anonymous folk tradition of magic, mired as it was in out-of-date techniques, into a modern
profession propelled forward by striving individual talent—not unlike the
revolution Tylor purported to effect in anthropology. In so doing, Robert-
Houdin induced magicians and their audiences to think in new ways about
progress as central to the cultural significance of magic as a form of cultural
production.[4]

Robert-Houdin depicts his predecessors as "mystifiers" who compensate
for their lack of technical skill with crass hijinks and crude stagecraft, and
similarly decries the intellectual shortcomings of spectators who succumb to
mystification. In the relationships of correspondence he plots between modes
of apprehending magic and spectators' social stations, the male monarch,
Louis-Philippe, typifies an appropriate attitude of playful, self-reflexive detachment, and members of the working class, women, and African colonial
subjects embody naïve, uncritical perspectives. The Algerian episode serves
not only to burnish the author's reputation as a national hero, but also to
buttress his distinction between modern magic—a harmless mode of entertainment amenable to bourgeois sensibilities—and retrograde charlatanism
linked with superstitious fanaticism. For Robert-Houdin, narrating the confrontation with the marabouts was therefore part of a broader strategy of
staking out professional status and establishing illusionism as a legitimate

form of expertise, compatible with a scientific worldview and opposed to unscientific forms of knowledge.

Robert-Houdin's memoirs make explicit a normative assumption that the performance of a trick should always elicit from spectators a line of etiological reasoning leading back to the magician's skill and intelligence. Magicians invite audiences to speculate about their methods even as they systematically thwart possible hypotheses (Jones 2011: 57). As Robert-Houdin himself puts it elsewhere, "Nothing should be neglected which can help mislead the minds of the spectators: therefore, when you perform any trick, try to induce spectators to attribute the effect produced to any cause other than the real one" (1868: 45).

Modern conjurors, while often dabbling in occult iconography (Robert-Houdin's calling card, for instance, depicted a devil signing his name), generally do not intend audiences to perceive in their performances the action of supernatural forces or agents. Far from it—they want individual credit for their technical prowess (Metzner 1998). Thus, in Robert-Houdin's narrative, misconstruing tricks as evidence of anything other than the conjuror's manual dexterity or mechanical ingenuity becomes a potential mark of unreason or even insanity. By contrast, the ability to marvel self-reflexively at an illusionist's displays of sophisticated skill reflects both intellectual and cultural sophistication, and indeed comes to serve as a metonym for modernity writ large.

The *Confessions* themselves function like precisely this kind of magic act, demanding playful self-reflexivity from its readers: key to Robert-Houdin's literary self-fashioning (and to the text's cultural impact) is a parallelism between the theatrical performance of magic and the writerly performance of biography. In the preface, Robert-Houdin alerts the reader to the use of literary artifice, describing the memoirs as a "continuation of the performances of yesteryear in a new form" with "the reader as an audience, the volume as a stage" (Robert-Houdin 1859, vol. 1: vii). The autobiography-as-magic-act conceit justifies the fanciful confections that constitute some of the text's most memorable episodes, but poses serious challenges for using it as anything like factually accurate historical record. For instance, the valiant efforts of generations of magic historians have failed to surface even the slightest trace of the dashing aristocratic figure who purportedly mentored Robert-Houdin—save for the hundred-odd pages devoted to him in the *Confessions*. Most have reluctantly concluded that he is a fictional character (Jones 2008: 42).

There are ample sources corroborating that Robert-Houdin indeed went to Algeria at the army's behest, but besides the *Confessions*, few of them provide much detail about the precise nature of his activities there. I have chosen to set aside some of the more questionable (if most colorful) episodes in Robert-Houdin's narrative, focusing on details that strike me as reasonably plausible given other established facts. Still, his narration of even plausible events is colored by his objectives as an unabashedly self-aggrandizing raconteur. Although I use the *Confessions* as the primary source for describing Robert-Houdin's exploits in Algeria, I want it to be clear that my ultimate object of analysis is not the events themselves (which want for corroborating testimonials), but rather the cultural logic of Robert-Houdin's textual representations thereof, and the web of intertextual, interdiscursive (Silverstein 2005) relationships that he establishes as a writer. For, although Robert-Houdin is not a reliable narrator when it comes to reporting facts, he is steadfastly consistent in articulating a self-servingly idealized vision of himself and of modern magic.

The French Marabout

Robert-Houdin reports that his magic shows in Algeria were scheduled to coincide with an annual festival honoring Arab chiefs, on evenings of the second and third days of extravagant equestrian games. By the time the magician and his wife reached Algeria, however, armed rebellion had broken out in Kabylia, to the west of Algiers; military operations would postpone his performances for five weeks, until October 28. The evening of the first show found Robert-Houdin restless with anticipation. He recalls anxiously peering out from the wings of the cavernous Theater of Algiers at the Arab chiefs, with their large entourages and flowing burnouses, squirming uncomfortably in the unaccustomed seats (Robert-Houdin 1859, vol. 2: 261). When the show finally began, the magician confesses, "I felt a bit like laughing . . . presenting myself as I was, with a magic wand and all the gravitas of a veritable sorcerer. I didn't give in. This wasn't a matter of entertaining a curious and receptive audience, but of striking a powerful impression on crude imaginations and backwards minds. I was playing the role of a French marabout" (262).

Unsure how this untested audience would respond, Robert-Houdin says that he proceeded cautiously, opening with his most trusted material from the genteel magic act that had made him the toast of European polite society. The spectators were impassive at first, but when he produced cannonballs from an ordinary hat, he says, they began to thaw, expressing, as the conjuror puts it, "their joyous admiration through the strangest and most energetic gestures" (263). Encouraged, he moved on to *La corne d'abondance*

("The Horn of Plenty"), a trick depicted in the upper left cameo of the poster in figure 3. He held an ornate lacquered metal cornucopia up for all to see. It was clearly empty. The audience was amazed when he then pulled dozens of small presents from within the mysterious object and distributed them throughout the theater. More cheers. A seasoned professional, Robert-Houdin knew exactly how to choose tricks that would win over a diffident—and, in this case, potentially hostile—audience, even in an unfamiliar cultural setting. In Europe, one of his trademark routines, called "The Inexhaustible Bottle," consisted in serving seemingly limitless amounts of any liquor the audience requested from an improbably small receptacle. Respecting Muslim prohibitions on alcohol, he instead magically filled an empty tureen with piping hot coffee. At first reluctant to ingest a seemingly diabolical beverage, Robert-Houdin says that the spectators were soon "unwittingly seduced by the perfume of their favorite liquor" (265) and the temptation of accompanying sweets, also magically procured.

But these were all trifles compared to the "irrefutable proofs" of supernatural power Robert-Houdin intended to provide. For this, he had prepared three blockbuster tricks. First, he invited a muscular young Arab to join him onstage, boldly announcing that he could take away all the man's strength and restore it at will. He placed a small wooden box at the man's feet and bade him pick it up. Easily obliging, the volunteer set it back down, scoffing, "is that all?" (267). Then, with a portentous wave of his hands, Robert-Houdin proclaimed, "Presto! You are now weaker than a woman!" When the man tried to lift the little box a second time, it would not budge. Behind the scenes, stagehands had thrown a switch activating a powerful electromagnet hidden beneath the stage. The strongman struggled in vain. Panting and furious, he began to skulk back to his seat defeated, but shouts from the audience persuaded him to venture a second attempt. This time, however, Robert-Houdin signaled his assistants to pass an electric current through the handle of the box, toppling the stunned volunteer to the floor in a convulsive heap. Regaining his wits, the Algerian dashed from the stage. A ponderous silence fell upon the audience. Robert-Houdin reports hearing murmurs of "*Shaytan*" and "*Junun*" (which he glosses as "Satan" and "genii") passing among the spectators he calls "credulous" (269).

In Europe, Robert-Houdin had performed the same "Light and Heavy Chest" trick, describing it as a magical security device for protecting valuables, but here in Algeria he used it to simulate the ensorcellment of a volunteer. This resignification points to the difference between two aspects of a trick that magicians call *effect*—the illusion an audience sees—and *presentation*—the performed framing of that effect as somehow significant (Lamont and Wiseman 1999: 104–5).[5] Here, a secular effect is presented in a way suggestive of supernatural forces at work.

For his next effect, the magician staged a classic of nineteenth-century magic, simply called the "Gun Trick," hoping to match an alleged indigenous conjuring feat.[6] It had been reported that marabouts, as proof of invincibility, would sometimes ask followers to shoot firearms at them. After the holy men uttered a few cabalistic phrases, the guns would not discharge. Robert-Houdin reasoned that the marabouts secretly tampered with the firing mechanisms in advance, rendering the weapons useless. French military officers were particularly eager to discredit this kind of false miracle, which they feared could embolden Algerians to defy the occupying forces.

According to Robert-Houdin, when he announced to the audience that he would perform this stunt, a wild-eyed man shot up from his seat and bounded onto the stage. "I want to kill you," the volunteer announced impertinently (270). An interpreter nervously whispered to Robert-Houdin that this eager volunteer was, in fact, a marabout. Steadfast, Robert-Houdin handed the man a pistol to inspect. "The pistol is fine," he responded, "and I will kill you" (271). The magician then instructed him to make a distinguishing mark on a lead bullet and load it into the pistol with a double charge of powder for good measure. "Now you're sure that the gun is loaded and that the bullet will fire?" Robert-Houdin asked. The marabout could not but assent. "Just tell me one thing: do you feel any remorse, any scruple about killing me in cold blood, even if I authorize it?" By this point, the marabout's response was comically predictable: "No, because I want to kill you" (272). The audience laughed nervously. Robert-Houdin shrugged. Stepping a few yards away, he held up an apple in front of his chest, and asked the volunteer to fire right at his heart. Almost immediately, the crack of the pistol rang out. Spectators' eyes darted from the gun's smoking barrel to the place where Robert-Houdin stood grinning across the stage. The bullet previously marked by the volunteer himself was lodged in the apple. Taking it for a powerful talisman—the magician reports—the marabout would not give the bullet back.

In his final trick, Robert-Houdin invited a handsome "Moorish" gallant—in fact, a secret accomplice—up from the audience. He stood the elegantly dressed volunteer on top of a table and covered him with a cloth canopy. Just moments later, he tipped the canopy over. The lad had vanished without a trace, having passed through a hidden trapdoor. According to Robert-Houdin, "the Arabs were so impressed that, besought by an indescribable terror, they instantaneously leapt from their seats in a frantic devil-take-the-hindmost scramble for the exit" (273). When the panic-stricken mob reached the door, it was amazed to find the resurrected boy waiting contentedly outside.

After repeating these same feats in a second performance the following day, Robert-Houdin instructed his interpreters to spread the word that his "seeming miracles were only the result of skill, inspired and guided by an art known as *prestidigitation*, and having nothing whatsoever to do with sorcery" (275). He claims an Arab who witnessed his performance was later heard to say, "Now our marabouts will have to work much more powerful miracles to impress us" (282). Several days later, on November 5, the colony's official French-language newspaper, *Le Moniteur algérien*, reported enthusiastically on the performances:

> the Marshal considered that showing the Arabs a Christian superior in the genre [of sleight of hand] to their phony shereefs, who have tricked them so often, would encourage them to uncover and frustrate future impostures, and to resist—through knowledge of the cause—their own shameful excitation. May these performances, of which all of Algeria long will speak, have their desired effect! (reproduced in Seldow 1971: 13)

The following year, a story about Robert-Houdin's mission in the metropolitan newspaper *Le Moniteur universel* concluded triumphantly: "today the marabouts are totally discredited among the natives, who, by contrast, hold the famous prestidigitator as an object of veneration" (reproduced in Seldow 1971: 17). Contemporaries mythologized Robert-Houdin as a modern-day Moses triumphing over Pharaonic magicians (Vapereau 1859: 335). Years later, another Algerian newspaper recalled Robert-Houdin as the "extraordinary man who spared France much bloodshed and moved colonization forward twenty years" (quoted in Fechner 2002: 59).

A Most Precious Souvenir

Apart from such self-congratulating discourses, the actual reception and impact of these performances is difficult to assess, and I have located only a single archival trace. In his monthly report submitted on October 31, 1856 (a few days after the shows at the Theater of Algiers), the head of the Bureau of Arab Affairs in nearby Blida noted that the performances were the subject of much discussion in his district: "The skillful prestidigitator's marvelous tricks made a profound impression on the [indigenous] imagination; within days, word of them flew from mouth to mouth and they are now everywhere the topic of conversation, between townsfolk in the Moorish cafés and *fellahs* in their tents or huts."[7] But what exactly those simmering conversations may have been about remains an object of speculation.

The closest thing I have found to evidence of how the Algerian spectators may have viewed Robert-Houdin's performances comes in the form of testimonial penned by Algerian hands, but which was clearly constructed to serve as a prop in a theatricalized form of diplomacy—a "text act," as Chau (2005) puts it. The conjuror himself reports that, three days after his second performance, he was summoned to the governor's palace, where thirty Arab leaders formally presented him with a stunning gold and turquoise illuminated certificate (figure 5). Handsomely calligraphed in parallel columns of Arabic and French, the bilingual certificate heralds Robert-Houdin as "the marvel of the moment and of the century." After the calligrapher declaimed the Arabic text, sixteen of the most important chiefs solemnly impressed their seals on the document. A seventeenth seal, from Colonel de Neveu himself, confirms the portent of this ceremonial transaction. Calling it the "most precious souvenir" of his career, Robert-Houdin (1859, vol. 2: 279) introduces the text of the certificate in his memoir as corroborating the success of his Algerian mission. Until only recently, it hung in a museum in his native Blois, seeming confirmation of France's triumph over the marabouts and modern magic's triumph over primitive magic (it has recently been stored for preservation). Examined more closely, however, the certificate proves deeply equivocal.

The Arabic text is a highly conventionalized rhyming panegyric. The parallel French translation offers an accurate, idiomatic rendering, without replicating difficult effects of rhyme and meter (for instance, all end-words in the first paragraph of Arabic verse rhyme with "Robert-Houdin"). As the author makes extensive use of rhetorical formulae associated with formal eloquence, the terms of praise are relatively generic: "Our age has seen no one who can compare to Robert-Houdin. The radiance of his talent surpasses history's most brilliant achievements. Because it can boast him, his century is the most illustrious of all." In a formulaic expression of indebtedness, the signatories promise to "keep [Robert-Houdin's] memory alive, attempting to elevate [their] praise to the level of his merit," and apologize to the magician directly for insufficient ability: "Nature gifted you with rich eloquence and before you, we admit our weakness. Excuse us, if we offer you so little. Is it fitting to offer nacre to one who owns the pearl?" The terms of encomium, while lavishly poetic, do not sound significantly different from compliments Robert-Houdin might have received from contemporary European spectators: "He has stirred our hearts and dumbfounded our minds . . . Such

Figure 5. Certificate presented to Robert-Houdin by Algerian Arab chiefs, 1856.
"Generous and knowledgeable men went to admire the marvels of his science." Ville de Blois.

feats had never before fascinated our eyes . . . Thus, friendship for him has taken root in our hearts, and our bosoms preciously enfold it." Nothing about this language suggests that the performances evoked supernatural associations, and the author neither acknowledges the French project of demystification nor mentions the marabouts.

Quoting the French text of the certificate in his memoirs, Robert-Houdin writes, "I am going to give the translation . . . as it was done by the Arab calligrapher himself." Technically, the text he presents is in the calligrapher's words, but Robert-Houdin has made significant expurgations, removing phrases and entire sentences, present in both languages, that were potentially discordant with his construal of the situation.[8] It is unfortunate that subsequent biographers and magic historians overlooked these omissions, as much of the French column of text (but surprisingly not the Arabic) has now faded into illegibility. Comparing the parallel texts using archival photographs, I have been able to make out all but a few omitted words. A number of Robert-Houdin's omissions link his magic with intellectual achievement. For instance, he leaves out sentences comparing him to three archetypically learned figures—a Greek philosopher, a Hellenistic magus, and a legendary Persian king: "He seems like a Greek sage. He has the profound genius of Aristotle, the science of sage Hermes [Trismegistus], and the wisdom of Chosroes [i.e., Khusraw Anushiravan]." One can only speculate why Robert-Houdin chose to elide these lines, but the effect is to suppress a clear indication that his Arab interlocutors were not just primitive outliers on the fringes of modernity, but heirs to one of the world's great literary traditions.[9] Likewise, in omitting a later sentence describing his "accomplishments" as "the obvious mark of his elevated intelligence, his knowledge, and his wisdom," Robert-Houdin removed a further indication that the Algerian audience unproblematically construed his performances in terms of technical savvy rather than potentially supernatural agency.

Another omitted line gives a concrete sense of how the local Arab elite categorized Robert-Houdin's performances. The French text states, "Generous and knowledgeable men went to admire the marvels (*prestiges*) of his science." Striking this sentence, Robert-Houdin suppressed a fundamentally accurate description of his performances as entertainments offered in the honor of Arab notables, instead promoting a more exoticizing narrative. In fact, French officials presented these spectacles as diplomatic prestations intended to mediate the tensions of empire; insofar as the primary spectators saw them as such, the certificate itself can be seen as a diplomatic counter-gift. A gloss of the Arabic counterpart of this same omitted line reveals more nuanced meaning still: "He brought the marvels of his crafts an illustrious group to entertain." The word translated as "marvels" is 'aja'ib, a complex term associated with both natural wonders and man-made works inspiring astonishment (see Hees 2005); here, it refers specifically to astonishing crafts-manship. The phrase translated as "entertain," tusli al-khawatir, could be more literally rendered as "divert the thoughts" or "distract from cares." The overall connotation is that Robert-Houdin's act was seen as a prodigiously amusing curiosity of skilled performance—not terrifying sorcery, as the magician's nar-ration implies.

Despite its limitations as a record of reception, the glimpse this certificate offers into indigenous perspectives suggests that Robert-Houdin was per-haps less dramatically successful in demystifying Algerian systems of belief than the French might have liked to think. This underlines questions about the fungibility of Western stage magic and local forms of ritual performance within popular religious traditions that Muslim elites would have them-selves rejected as illegitimate. In the following section, I begin to examine how the French came to equate some Algerian religious practices with secu-lar entertainment magic, focusing in particular on colonial encounters with the 'Isawiyya, a Sufi order famous for spectacular performances of improb-able marvels.

A Lesson on Miracles

Robert-Houdin's mission is an extraordinary example of the use of spec-tacle in European imperialist projects to astound, frighten, and/or beguile indigenous spectators and dramatize knowledge differentials, enacting and reinforcing assumptions about the superiority of European civilization (Fa-bian 2000; Taussig 1991, 1993). Europeans' production of such imperialist performances went hand-in-hand with the consumption of Orientalist im-ages of North African Muslims as irrational, childish fanatics (Said 1979). In Algeria, Robert-Houdin was not only a performer, but also a spectator eager for such Orientalist imagery. Like many other tourists, he witnessed a ceremony of the 'Isawa (singular, 'Isawi), members of a mystical Sufi order famous for ecstatic rituals that involved displays of seemingly miraculous invulnerability to otherwise painful and potentially lethal self-mutilations. The 'Isawa emerge from Robert-Houdin's narrative as the magician's prin-cipal adversaries, epitomizing the primitive trickery that he supposed kept Algerian Muslims in a state of religious thralldom.

After his performances in Algiers, Robert-Houdin remained in Algeria almost three more weeks.[10] During this time, he says he hoped to attend "a conjuring performance by the marabouts or by some other native jugglers"

(1859, vol. 2: 283), and expressed particular curiosity about the "the 'Isawa and their marvels," which "few French travelers, even after a short stay in Algeria, haven't heard about." Asserting an illusionist's expert claim of "professional vision" (Goodwin 1994), he writes, "I was sure that all their miracles were nothing but more-or-less clever tricks (*trucs*) that I would be able to see right through." Colonel de Neveu, whose position gave him supervisory authority over the Algeria's Sufi brotherhoods, easily arranged a performance. Along with their wives, the colonel and the magician visited an Arab house for a *hadra*, the 'Isawa's trance ceremony infamous for its feats of self-mortification.

Robert-Houdin describes what he saw, and how he saw it, in the following terms. After the male guests were seated in a large inner court and the women in an overlooking gallery, the devotees filed in and arranged themselves in a closed circle. They began chanting slow prayers and devotions, eventually taking up cymbals and tambourines. The intensity gradually mounted. After approximately two hours, some of the chanters stood and began to yell "Allah!" at the top of their lungs. The mood quickly became paroxysmal. Sweat-drenched devotees shed much of their clothing. Some suddenly dropped to all fours, imitating wild animals. Only when the ceremony had reached this frenzied peak did the much-anticipated wonder-working begin.

Hidden behind a column to better detect any imposture, so he says, Robert-Houdin observed a number of the feats for which the brotherhood was so reputed. With the *muqaddam*, or spiritual leader, officiating, some of the 'Isawa devotees devoured dangerous and inedible substances—glass, rocks, and cactus spines. Some placed scorpions and poisonous snakes in their mouths. When one 'Isawi struck his left arm with his right hand, a profusion of blood began to flow—yet when he removed his hand, the flesh was completely intact. Others handled a red-hot iron bar, touching it with their tongues, and walked upon a white-hot iron plate. Others still struck themselves with knives and swords, proving themselves impervious to razor-sharp blades.

In the *Confessions*, Robert-Houdin devotes a long epilogue to debunking the apparently miraculous feats of the 'Isawa, both those he directly observed and others only reported to him. The title he gives this section, "*Un cours de miracles*," is an untranslatable play on words. While it literally means "a course on miracles," it also evokes the French expression "*une cour des miracles*," or "a court of miracles." Historically a lawless urban alleyway populated by lowlifes, brigands, and women of ill repute, the court of miracles was reportedly so called because crippled beggars returning there after a day's mendicancy were suddenly healed of their presumably feigned afflictions.

As a showman, Robert-Houdin was struck by the highly rehearsed nature of the 'Isawiyya order's rite, as evident in both the specialization of individual ritualists and the carefully orchestrated collusion between them. "Not a soul among [the 'Isawa] has any illusion about the true nature of their phony miracles," he writes (327). "Indeed, they all help each other produce these feats." Comparing them unfavorably to second-rate mountebanks, Robert-Houdin systematically demystifies each of their apparent miracles, showcasing his knowledge of illusionary principles: the 'Isawi who appeared to stick a knife into his cheek was merely stretching his skin with a blunt instrument; the adept who ate the prickly pear spines must have prepared them in advance—"otherwise, he would not have failed to [let us examine them] . . . thereby doubling his prestige" (330); to create the illusion of a bleeding wound, one need only secretly palm a sponge soaked with red liquid; before laying bare-bellied on a sharpened saber, the devotee turned his back, providing an ample occasion to cover the likely dull blade with a protective cloth; finally, the apparently poisonous snakes the 'Isawa handled were either defanged or altogether harmless varieties, he says.

To Robert-Houdin's eyes, some other feats performed by the 'Isawa clearly relied on scientific principles. While the 'Isawa who swallowed rocks and broken bottles distributed by the muqaddam probably discreetly deposited them, while prostrating, back into the leader's robes, others had unquestionably chewed and swallowed shards of glass. Unimpressed, Robert-Houdin fed an "enormous meatball full of pounded glass" to one of his housecats (333). After the cat survived, he frequently repeated the procedure as a party stunt for friends, eventually consuming (much more carefully pulverized) glass himself. The fire-handlers fared no better against his withering positivism. Robert-Houdin cites research suggesting that a preparation of powdered alum could be used to protect the tongue from extremely high temperatures, and he claims to have experience confirming that a thin layer of moisture provides sufficient buffer against red-hot—even molten—metal. Finally, Robert-Houdin reasons that the frequently barefoot Arabs developed feet calloused "like horses' hooves," enabling them to walk on the white-hot iron plate without discomfort (340).

Robert-Houdin's memoirs, the most significant text in the history of modern magic, end on this note of disenchantment, as if the case against primitive magic had been definitively laid to rest. He substantiates his characterization of the 'Isawa as charlatanic impostors by exposing and explaining the alleged trickery behind the hadra ceremony. In the process, he makes the 'Isawiyya Sufi order—a centuries-old, entirely apolitical, religious confraternity with codified ceremonies and long-standing centers of worship throughout the Muslim world (see Andézian 1996, 2001)—seem equivalent to the opportunistic, prophetic "intriguers" that he was sent to discredit. Yet this elision seemed to satisfy contemporaries. Favorably reviewing Robert-Houdin's memoirs, one literary critic wrote: "Hoping to see for himself the marvels of the indigenous prophets, the magician was lucky enough to procure a performance. He includes a chapter . . . explaining the most alarming tricks of jugglery used to impress the Arabs' imagination" (Vapereau 1859: 336).

Conclusion

In the following chapter, I will begin to account for how Robert-Houdin and others came to identify the 'Isawa as embodiments of Muslim fanaticism and to construct a cultural image of them as the antithesis of secular, modern Western magicians. What is important for me to establish here is that, in the context of the *Confessions*, the 'Isawa—and their local Muslim audiences—represent the heroic modern magician's ultimate adversaries: primitive superstition, unsophisticated artifice, and naïve credulity. Rhetorically, Robert-Houdin's point was not so much to give an ethnographic account of Algerian ritual practice, as to use the image of the 'Isawa allegorically, in staging an argument about modern magic.

The kind of self-reflexive subjectivity Robert-Houdin presents as essential to the appreciation of modern entertainment magic is a cognitive skill that Algerian Arabs were widely depicted as lacking in colonial literature. Bishara (2013: 51), for instance, describes the ongoing legacy of what she calls the trope of "epistemic otherness" applied to Arabs "presumed to have a different and lesser relationship to knowledge than Euro-Americans." She writes that "Arabs are presumed by many who align or identify themselves with Western civilization to have radically different and lesser ways of knowing and representing the world."

It is not entirely clear whether, in deploying a magician, the French colonial power intended to dispel the ignorance they attributed to indigenous people, or to exploit it (Robert-Houdin himself suggests both motives). Either way, the subsequent representation of his performances as a successful instance of the modern disenchantment of primitive superstition reaffirmed French convictions of cognitive superiority—as did the ethnographic representation and performative presentation of the 'Isawa as insufficiently disenchanted magicians. By unfavorably comparing Algerians' supposed credulity toward the alleged trickery of indigenous ritual practices to their own attitude of incredulity toward conjuring as a form of disenchanted entertainment, the

French used magic as a powerful marker of cultural difference and social evolution.

Baudelaire wrote that "only an unbelieving society would send Robert-Houdin to turn the Arabs from miracles" (1887: 77). As the poet implies, employing a modern magician to wage symbolic war on saintly figures does not suggest a high view of religion, but it does suggest a high view of modern magic. Though often dismissed as culturally trivial (During 2002: 2) or overlooked because of anthropologists' historical aversion to showbiz (Boon 2000), Western illusionism emerges through the exceptional sequence of events I have examined in this chapter as a potent signifier of modernity, particularly in terms of the specific cognitive outlook and interpretative practices associated with it. Stage magic provided colonial observers a convenient interpretative framework for ethnographic descriptions of the 'Isawa and a sensational mode of imperial spectacle. Equating the hadra with illusionism gave the French compelling evidence of Algerians' primitive credulity, while diacritically confirming their own characteristically modern incredulity—a stance indissociable from Western magic as a form of entertainment.

TWO

Disanalogy

The army colonel who orchestrated Robert-Houdin's mission and served as his guide in Algeria, François-Edouard de Neveu, was at the time the most influential French expert on North African Islam. A gifted young officer trained in topography at France's prestigious Saint-Cyr military academy, de Neveu had been appointed as a surveyor to the 1839 scientific commission set up to explore Algeria (Faucon 1889: 417–18; Triaud 1995: 15–16). The commission's projects of detailing the territory's natural resources and describing its inhabitants would lay an empirical groundwork for the colonial administration (Burke 2014: 28–29; Lorcin 1995: 41–51).

While serving on the commission, de Neveu seems to have transformed into both an Arabophilic ethnographer and a devotee of Saint-Simonianism—the utopian movement whose members saw colonialism as an opportunity to conduct grand experiments in social reform that would promote progress by wedding the best in Algerian and French civilization (Abi-Mershed 2010: 73; Pilbeam 2014: 133–34). Often at odds with settler colonists, these ideologues "were sympathetic with many features of Algerian society, and adopted a paternalistic attitude toward the Muslim populations" (Burke 2014: 32). Like other Saint-Simonian military officers, de Neveu married an indigenous Muslim woman (Lorcin 1995: 55; Siari-Tengour 2009: 225; Triaud 1995: 16). His mastery of Arabic and his commitment to causes of indigenous reform led him to occupy a variety of administrative positions in the Arab Bureaux that administered local populations, as he gradually ascended the ranks to general (Levallois 2012: 763).

By the time Robert-Houdin visited in 1856, de Neveu was chief of the Political Bureau in Algiers—which is how he was identified in this contemporaneous photograph (figure 6). The photographer Félix Moulin also arrived in Algeria that year, under the auspices of a colonial administration

Figure 6. Colonel François-Edouard de Neveu, army ethnographer of Algerian Sufi orders, photographed by Félix Moulin, circa 1857. Bibliothèque Nationale de France.

Figure 7. Algerian 'Isawa photographed by Félix Moulin,
circa 1857. Bibliothèque Nationale de France.

eager to celebrate its military achievements and popularize the new colony. Although he spent a full eighteen months in Algeria, the sheer difficulty of producing daguerreotypes—Moulin traveled with almost 2,500 pounds of baggage—imposed technical constraints that required him to focus selectively on "what was crucial to reproduce: the most important sites and the most significant people" (Zarobell 2010: 116).

In addition to the portrait of the ascending young colonel, Moulin's nearly 300 photographs included two images of the 'Isawa: one focuses on the central figure of an 'Isawi eating a spiny cactus leaf while his confrère lifts a heated plate to his mouth; the other (figure 7), an 'Isawi in a state of cataleptic trance, stretched out in the arms of another adept in a kind of pietà. In contrast to the portrait of de Neveu standing erect and at attention, Moulin portrays the 'Isawa as fully absorbed in seated, supine, and even dissociative ritual activities. These 'Isawa images were quickly duplicated as a mass-produced engraving that incorporated the activities of both photographs into one tableau (see Hugonnet 1858: 232), thus amplifying their circulation.

Prochaska (1990b: 406) comments that "what is striking about early photographs of the Orient" produced by Moulin and the other French photographers flocking to Algeria during this period "is not how novel they are, but how much they recapitulate Orientalist imagery and pictorial strategies." It is intriguing to consider how these two images of martial sobriety and mystical intoxication work together iconographically given Moulin's complementary efforts "to comprehend and master indigenous society" and "especially to glorify military virility" (Clancy-Smith 2006: 27–28). As a matter of fact, de Neveu himself had already significantly contributed to making—and perhaps even promoting—the 'Isawa as iconic figures in French colonial culture. Crucially, he appears to have been the first European to describe them as theatrical magicians guilty of inadequately disenchanting their own trickery.

A decade earlier, in 1845, de Neveu published *Les Khouan: Ordres religieux chez les Musulmans d'Algérie*. This was a groundbreaking—if far from impartial—field manual on the Sufi orders (which he referred to as *khouans*, from the Arabic *ikhwan*, "brotherhood").[1] Long a feature of North African society, these orders have become widely documented by anthropologists in the intervening years.[2] Drawing principally on questionnaires administered near Constantine in the northeast of the country, de Neveu posited a link between a recent surge of messianic rebellion against colonial rule and the Sufi orders. At the same time, he also purported to give an authoritative account of seven of the orders themselves—including the 'Isawiyya.

As substantial subsequent scholarship has established, the North African Sufi orders (*turuq*, sing. *tariqa*) trace their origins to founding saints (*awliya'*) whose teachings inspire their practices. Considered to be friends of God, these founding saints and their most revered followers are widely believed to possess *baraka* (divine blessing), which they are able to transmit through contact and which enables them to perform miracles—especially of healing, protection, and divination. As the baraka of saints is believed to persist after their death, their graves attract believers in search of blessing and intercession, while leadership of the order passes from the charismatic founder to his descendants. The brotherhoods establish small buildings or larger complexes (*zawaya*, sing. *zawiya*) to provide for the devotional and material needs of their members. Zawaya are often connected to sanctified gravesites and are directed by a sectional leader (*muqaddam*). As de Neveu ascertained, these Sufi complexes were paramount social institutions throughout North Africa, serving, especially in rural settings, a wide array of religious and sociopolitical functions.[3]

In writing about the brotherhoods, de Neveu frequently used the term "marabout" to describe the Sufi saints. Derived from the Arabic *murabit*, "a religious disciple or military volunteer" (Maarouf 2012: 35) connected to a fortified outpost (*ribat*), the transliterated French term *marabout* can denote any kind of Islamic spiritual broker tied to God (Rhani and Hlaoua 2014: 24). The term's ambiguity did significant analytic work in French colonial ethnography, allowing observers to concatenate a variety of holy figures associated with gifts of baraka, including "political chiefs, founders and leaders of the Sufi brotherhoods, eponymous ancestors and tribal chiefs, pious men, hermits, healers" (Andézian 1996: 390)—a list that also could include messianic insurgents (Clancy-Smith 1990: 232). Thus, the very term that de Neveu and subsequent colonial ethnographers variously employed for both the general veneration of holy figures and the regulated religious life of Sufi orders—"maraboutism" (*maraboutisme*)—threatened to distort the complicated relationships between charismatic rebels and well-established mystical orders (Clancy-Smith 1994; Spadola 2014: 12), precisely the elision Robert-Houdin effects in the *Confessions*.[4]

In *Les Khouan*, de Neveu argued that, due to "maraboutic" influence, what had begun as nationalistic resistance to French occupation was evolving into a religious crusade against Christian invasion.[5] Pointing to their hierarchical organization, transnational and interethnic scope, well-established communication networks, customary secretiveness, and devoted veneration of charismatic leaders, de Neveu (1846: 194) considered the khouans a particularly pernicious threat. In the short term, he recommended "constant surveillance" through the infiltration of spies within the brotherhoods. Ultimately, he advocated supplanting radical leaders with members of the French-educated—and Francophilic—indigenous elite that Robert-Houdin's performances were supposed to help nurture.

The book had an enormous impact, and was quickly reissued in an expanded 1846 edition. As Lorcin (1995: 57–58) explains, it stood as the authoritative work on not just the Sufi brotherhoods, but all of Algerian Islam, for the next forty years. Similarly, Saaïda points to *Les Khouan* as that period's "ineluctable reference" (2013: 80); although de Neveu had no qualifications as a "specialist of Islam" and focused on political rather than religious themes, "his book became a 'colonial Bible' on the religious brotherhoods. Its scholarship . . . did not attract attention so much as its organizing theme: dangerousness."

Today, historians and anthropologists are in wide agreement about the ideological biases inherent in the ethnographic accounts produced by French colonial officers. Even if currents of Saint-Simonianism did provide a basis for heterodoxy (Siari-Tengour 2009) and the officers' close involvement with the everyday life of the peoples they administered afforded a measure of nuance (Burke 2014: 29), the French Army's ultimate rationale for producing any ethnographic knowledge at all was clearly to dominate and control. Trumbull (2009: 20) calls this kind of ethnography "participant-observation surveillance," and Clancy-Smith (1994: 9) likens the often painstaking literature produced by the Arab Bureaux to "police reports." For the French colonial officials, she explains, "the principal aim of the literature of surveillance was to ascertain the causes and motives underlying insurrection as well as to identify the prime movers." This had profound consequences when it came to interpreting religious phenomena: Saaïda (2013: 79) describes how army officers, "whose mastery of Arabic alone sufficed to make them experts on Islam," came to exert an "intellectual monopoly" in their view of "Islam as an ideological system rather than a religion, which they saw as an obstacle to pacification."[6]

After the publication of de Neveu's study, French preoccupation with Sufi orders quickly spiraled into "hysteria" (Clancy-Smith 1990: 225), shifting "the attitude of French officialdom toward Muslim religious and educational institutions . . . from calculated disregard to near obsession with their role in disseminating subversive doctrine and mobilizing anticolonial sedition" (Abi-Mershed 2010: 106). Colonial observers were profoundly uncomfortable about what they saw as an interdependence of religion and politics in Islamic civilization, but their particular aversion to Sufism was overdetermined by other factors. As Patricia Lorcin (1995: 60–61) argues, the potent anticlericalism that the 1789 Revolution had unleashed into French politics proved particularly influential in the military academies that trained the majority of colonial officers. Thus, many of the same anxieties French Republicans had long harbored about the subversive activities of Catholic religious orders and parish priests were easily transferable to these supposedly secret Sufi societies (cf. Abi-Mershed 2010: 103; Triaud 1995: 10–11; Trumbull 2007: 453–55).[7] In addition, prevailing racialist stereotypes led the French to view the Algerian Arabs as naïve, irrational fanatics, easily stirred to religious excess by rabble-rousers feigning divine inspiration (Lorcin 1995: 60; Silverstein 2004: 50).

Given these preconceptions, the 'Isawa, with their apparently false miracles and seemingly unhinged ecstatics, represented a particularly troubling fulfillment of France's Orientalist fears and fantasies. As George Trumbull (2007: 451) expertly shows, the 'Isawa's "vipers and iron, fire and poison, knives and hatchets brought with them first a sense of menace, [and] later of spectacle . . ." For the adepts themselves, "the mortification of the flesh" signified a "pursuit of communion with the divine," but "it exerted an entirely different pull on the French ethnographers, metropolitan tourists, and administrators who watched." For these colonial spectators, these "practices seemed exotic, threatening, the embodiment of liminality." Trumbull reasons that accusations of artifice may have come naturally to French observers "in the context of the secular ideology" of Republican France (475). In the next section, I examine how what he calls "the language of artifice, of dishonesty, or rejection" that cast the 'Isawa "not as spiritual men but as liars and fakes, or as grotesque charlatans" (476), originated in de Neveu's text—in particular through the analogy he draws between the 'Isawa's performances and French secular magic.

The Authority of Tricks

As de Neveu (1846: 67–68) explains in the chapter of *Les Khouan* devoted to the 'Isawiyya, the order emerged in early sixteenth-century Morocco around Sidi Muhammad Ibn 'Isa, a maraboutic saint reputed for piety, asceticism, and miraculous deeds. According to tradition, during a long desert sojourn, Ibn 'Isa saved his disciples from starvation by miraculously enabling them to eat noxious substances—scorpions, poisonous snakes, rocks, and prickly desert plants (92–93). Later, Ibn 'Isa's long-standing adversary the sultan of Meknes challenged his disciples to reproduce this miracle publicly by ingesting large quantities of dangerous and taboo substances, which they did (102–4). From Morocco, the movement spread eastward through North Africa and into the Middle East. Especially in Algeria and Tunisia, the 'Isawiyya were infamous for reenacting the miracles of invulnerability associated with Ibn 'Isa in their ecstatic hadra ceremony.[8]

For de Neveu, these reenactments of miracle stories were nothing but legerdemain, however deft. Describing a typical performance, he writes that "everything is done with sufficient art that one cannot guess the secret methods they use to protect themselves from harm. Among themselves, the 'Isawa must not be under any illusions about how their surprising feats are done, but the spectating public is easily duped" (90). This trickery would be harmless in itself, but de Neveu argues that it is rendered dangerous because of audiences' naïveté and penchant for fanaticism. In essence, de Neveu writes,

> these 'Isawa's ceremonies are more or less the same kinds of sideshow stunts and sleight-of-hand tricks that, in the fairgrounds of France, attract and fascinate peasants who are awe-struck but not convinced. For there is one

fundamental difference: in Algeria the Muslim religion imparts a powerful authority to these tricks, and the true believer thinks that God grants some of his power to the followers of Ibn 'Isa. By contrast, in France, everything unfolds with Mr. Mayor's permission, and the peasant walks away thinking to himself, "Wow, those guys sure are nimble!" (1846: 91)

Making a clear distinction between the performance of trickery under the auspices of laic, temporal power ("Mr. Mayor") and spiritual power ("the Muslim religion"), de Neveu claims that even the most stereotypically backward Frenchman—a peasant—would not mistake the virtuosic feats of skilled performers for divine miracles.

To get a sense of the kind of performer de Neveu probably had in mind when drawing this analogy, we might turn again to Robert-Houdin's *Confessions*. Reminiscences of illusionists and their performances pepper the narrative, providing a chronicle of the author's creative influences but also establishing a historical baseline—a veritable prehistory of modern magic—so that readers can better appreciate the revolution Robert-Houdin purports to effect.

The first sort of illusionist Robert-Houdin encounters in the course of the narrative (according to his chronology, it would have been in the early 1820s) is an itinerant mountebank named Dr. Carlosbach performing in the marketplace of his native Blois. Clearly marked as an ethnic outsider with "dark skin" and "kinky hair" (Robert-Houdin 1859, vol. 1: 19), Carlosbach has all the romantic allure of a fairytale gypsy. After attracting a crowd with humorous banter, Carlosbach performs a classic "Cups and Balls" routine, then goes on to peddle a false tract of conjuring secrets. While the figure of Carlosbach may be a literary construction, he typifies the open-air conjurors who plied European fairgrounds and marketplaces for centuries (figure 8). Like the morally suspect conjuror in Hieronymus Bosch's late fifteenth-century painting, such figures seem to have occupied a murky social station; for his part, Carlosbach uses an elaborate ruse to skip out on his bill at a local inn.

A carnival magician named Castelli later strikes Robert-Houdin as being "charlatanism incarnate" (92). Advertising on giant posters that he will "eat a man alive," Castelli packs his theater with rubes. As Robert-Houdin watches from the audience, Castelli begins the show by performing some crude conjuring feats, then asks for volunteers willing to be eaten onstage. Selecting a corpulent boy, Castelli uses a giant saltshaker to cover him with a fine white powder. He then takes the volunteer's hand and bites it with such force that the boy runs squealing from the stage. Unable to get another

Figure 8. Depiction of Parisian street illusionist performing Cups and Balls effect. *Le Journal pour rire*, November 11, 1853. Bibliothèque Nationale de France.

volunteer for his "dinner," Castelli admits the impossibility of fulfilling his promise. This comic scene unfolds in an atmosphere of great hilarity. "One must remember," Robert-Houdin writes, "that legerdemain, at the time, was not the object of serious performance . . . People attended magic shows with the purpose of laughing at the expense of the conjuror's victims, even if that meant exposing themselves to attack" (93). In the partisan framework of Robert-Houdin's narrative, Castelli's humiliation of volunteers for the sake of entertainment coupled with his unscrupulous advertising marks his style as retrograde and uncouth and, by extension, casts negative light on the type of spectators who would delight in such antics.

Robert-Houdin uses evocations of predecessors like Carlosbach and Castelli to contrastively accentuate his own virtues: while they are crass, tasteless, and inexpert, he emerges from the narrative as progressive, refined, and elite. Given the importance that cultural historians have attributed to sincerity and trustworthiness as constitutive values of bourgeois religious, economic, and social life in the context of European modernity (Keane 2007; Shapin and Schaffer 2011), it is not surprising that Robert-Houdin makes an especial effort to differentiate his brand of modern magic from the mystification his predecessors and rivals in the *Confessions* incarnate. His contemptuous depiction of the kinds of magicians who performed in French fairs and carnivals in the early nineteenth century (as well as the types of spectators who would have frequented them) can probably also serve as a fairly accurate indicator of the type of image de Neveu has in mind when drawing his comparison with the 'Isawa. For elites like Robert-Houdin and de Neveu, the fairground and its denizens were clearly, in the words of Stallybrass and White (1986: 191), "marked out as 'low'—as dirty, repulsive, noisy, contaminating."[9] Robert-Houdin regards fairground conjurors contemptuously, and de Neveu presumably mobilizes these figures with similar disdain.

Ultimately, de Neveu concludes that the use of trickery among contemporary 'Isawa constitutes probable evidence that the order's founding saint was not a miracle worker, but an exceptional trickster:

> it is difficult not to consider Sidi Ibn 'Isa himself a consummate juggler, a great prestidigitator, who managed to overwhelm the public with his skill, and who doubtless supplemented his talents as an actor with the exhibition of trained animals. The entire history of Sidi Ibn 'Isa depends on sideshow stunts and sleight-of-hand. (1846: 105–6)

While terms like "prestidigitator" (*prestidigitateur*) make de Neveu's analogy with modern magic unmistakable, his use of the term "juggler" (*jongleur*), in particular, merits some further comment. He applies it not only to the saint Ibn 'Isa, but to the 'Isawiyya in general (185), and dismisses their "marvels" as "jugglery" (*jongleries*) that only ignorant people take seriously (87).[10] These terms crop up repeatedly in nineteenth-century descriptions of the order. Robert-Houdin, for his part, quotes de Neveu's description of an 'Isawa performance verbatim in his *Confessions* and, hewing closely to his predecessor and guide's interpretation of what and how the hadra signifies, refers to the 'Isawa as "jugglers" (1859, vol. 2: 283) and to their rituals as "jugglery" (285).

According to the 1986 *Grand Robert* etymologicon, the word "jongleur" first appeared in French in the Middle Ages, when it referred to "itinerant minstrels who exhibited trained animals, performed magic tricks and acrobatic feats, and sold unguents and herbs."[11] By the sixteenth century, it came "to designate a person who performed tricks," gradually acquiring its modern meaning: "a person who adroitly throws things in the air." In the eighteenth century, a specialized use emerged in ethnographic writing about North America, with the identification of indigenous ritual experts as "jugglers." The *Grand Robert* suggests that the novel use of "jongleur" to designate "a sorcerer among the Amerindians" depended on an "analogy with the medieval meaning." It is clear from explorer and missionary narratives, however, that French observers regarded these "jugglers" not just as quacks, but also as venal tricksters—charlatans who deluded people with legerdemain and exploited primitive credulity to establish themselves in positions of influence (see Flaherty 1992). Thus, the word "juggler" used in reference to the 'Isawa can be taken as either simply synonymous with "prestidigitator" (as the above quotation from de Neveu implies) or as describing a cross-cultural category of primitive ritual experts with strong connotations of charlatanism.[12]

In some ways, de Neveu's account of the 'Isawa as jugglers could be read as construing the marvels of the hadra as the performed equivalent of fetishes. Nineteenth-century social theorists understood fetishism as the most primitive form of religion, based on the worship of a material thing with "no transcendent meaning beyond itself, no abstract, general, or universal essence with respect to which it might be construed as a symbol" (Masuzawa 2000: 248). Denying the possibility of a more complicated symbolism, de Neveu imagined that whatever awe indigenous Algerians attached to marvels like those of the 'Isawa could be easily transferred to the high-tech trickery of a Western magician, a disenchanting double.

Analogy and Disanalogy

In the following chapter, I follow the cultural half-lives of de Neveu's categorization of the 'Isawa as jugglers, mediated by the influence of *Les Khouan* on future authors. The trope of insufficiently disenchanted magic proved a stubbornly resilient feature in ethnographic representations of the 'Isawa, reinforced by a variety of exhibitionistic conventions. Yet alongside denigratory depictions ran an often equally Orientalist counternarrative celebrating the paranormal significance of the order's performative marvels. Challenging connections between the hadra ceremony and theatrical magic had a way of trapping even sympathetic writers in dichotomies of truth/falsity, reality/illusion, and authenticity/inauthenticity that, I argue in Chapter Four, threatened to fundamentally distort its nature as ritual performance.

Before exploring broader resonances of de Neveu's portrayal of the 'Isawa as charlatans, however, it is essential to examine how exactly he effected the textual parallel between divergent domains, and what it can, in turn, tell us about the dangerousness of doubling in ethnographic representation. The parallelism that de Neveu posited (and which Robert-Houdin in turn enacted) between entertainment magic and 'Isawi ritual practices was a form of cross-cultural analogy. Through this analogy, de Neveu likened a relatively well-known institution in his own culture with a relatively un-known foreign institution.

De Neveu's ethnographic account of the 'Isawa involves a transfer of ideas from the familiar domain of the magic show to the novel domain of an exotic ritual. What kind of knowledge does this analogy produce—or occlude? It hinges on surface resemblances between two genres of perfor-mance involving the spectacular display of seemingly superhuman, super-natural abilities. What interests de Neveu is the epistemological relationship that—in Gell's (1998) terms—the "patient" who spectates maintains with the "agent" who performs, as mediated by the "index" of the trick itself: the Frenchman is "fooled" but "not convinced," while the Algerians "believe" that the 'Isawa have divinely inspired powers.

De Neveu, in other words, makes it quite clear that the analogy *breaks down*: the magic show is like the hadra only superficially; the opposing laic and Islamic frameworks generate contrastive stances toward conjuring effects in France and Algeria, respectively. That analogical breakdown is what matters most for de Neveu, leading him to the inference that the 'Isawa are religious charlatans who present techniques that Europeans easily recognize as tricks, deviously, for devotional purposes. What is striking here is that de Neveu aligns two domains based on what he considered to be a common feature (namely, the performance of "tricks") in order to emphasize not a higher-order similarity, but rather a difference.

Philosopher of science Mary Hesse explains that "the relation of anal-ogy . . . generally implies differences as well as similarities," which she terms "negative" and "positive" analogies, respectively (1967: 355). In most com-monplace analogies between disparate domains, she argues, "there is always a negative analogy that is implicitly recognized and tacitly ignored" (356) in favor of exploiting generative similarities.[13] Shelley (2002b) notes that theo-ries of analogy that overemphasize the significance of positive analogy in promoting knowledge production risk underestimating the important role of what he calls "disanalogy" in scientific endeavors: emphasizing rather than deemphasizing negative aspects of analogy can also generate knowledge.[14] In this way, de Neveu treats a disanalogy as the crucial component of a contras-tive comparison: the tricks may be more or less the same, but the Algerians believe them and Frenchmen do not.

In treating this specific disanalogy as ethnohistorical evidence, my primary objective is not so much to reassess understandings of the domain it sought to illuminate (Algerian Sufism) as to see how de Neveu—and the other colo-nial ethnographers who would follow his example—conceptualized French magic as a foil and emphasized certain salient aspects of it for the purposes of contrastive comparison. What were the cultural conditions that made entertainment magic such a generative analogue? Beyond superficial resemblances, an association with modern cognitive repertoires, the availability of normative interpretive frames and, somewhat paradoxically, an aspect of triviality all contributed to making illusionism an attractive counterpart for invidious cross-cultural comparison.

In propounding a comparison that seeks to highlight a differential correspondence, what de Neveu achieves is not a failed analogy but rather a successful—at least in terms of his particular ideological agenda—disanalogy. For colonial ethnographers, Algerian credulity and French incredulity were contrastive epistemological differences in the disanalogy between the hadra and a magic show. Beyond simply framing the 'Isawa as charlatans and their hadra ceremony as fraudulent magic, on the wider scale of de Neveu's text, this disanalogy buttresses representations of Algerian Sufis—and Algerian Muslims more generally—as fanatics who view the world through a skein of irrational belief rather than normatively rational disbelief.

In drawing his analogy between illusionism and the 'Isawa's hadra, de Neveu articulated an ethnographic representation that was, if not empirically accurate, ideologically quite potent—as evidenced by its subsequent circulation. It had a successful career in ethnographic representations for many decades to come. In the next chapter, I add to recent research on the place of the 'Isawa in French colonial culture (Spadola 2008; Trumbull 2007), with a particular focus on the trajectory of this trope. The enfolding of entertainment magic as an analogue in this particular ethnographic tradition reflects recurring tendencies in colonial representations of other indigenous ritual systems that informed incipient theorizations of magic as an anthropological abstraction.

THREE

Conjuring Equivalences

Amid significant changes in both politics and scholarship, the characterization of the Algerian 'Isawa as insufficiently disenchanted magicians proved a resilient thematic in colonial ethnography from the mid-nineteenth well into the twentieth century. In this chapter, I show how it rippled from de Neveu's and Robert-Houdin's texts through the work of subsequent ethnographers and illusionists. Moreover, I explore the intermedial and transmedial relationships that textual accounts came to have with visual representations and touring performances by 'Isawa themselves. I conclude with some thoughts about how the sensationalistic fixation on this relatively small Sufi brotherhood fit into and perhaps helped shape persistent patterns in French attitudes toward Islam.

"The 1880's mark the advent of a second phase of colonial writing devoted to Islam in the Maghrib," writes Clancy-Smith (1990: 238), ushered in by the 1884 publication of Louis Rinn's *Marabouts et Khouan*. An army officer and the head of the Algerian Service of Indigenous Affairs, Rinn was "situated at the confluence of the military-amateur ethnographer tradition and that of the Orientalist-academic school marked by an increasing professionalism and specialization based upon textual analysis rather than knowledge gained in the field" (239). In this sense, Rinn certainly complicated the picture presented by de Neveu, introducing new sources, new categories of analysis, and an increased acknowledgment of competing perspectives within Algerian religion (cf. Clancy-Smith 1990: 241–43).[1]

Still, *Marabouts et Khouan* remained primarily a practical manual for colonial administration. In matters pertaining to the 'Isawa, Rinn did not deviate markedly from de Neveu's charges of mendacious charlatanism. But, by pointing to a variety of contradictory perspectives on the order internal to Algerian society, the book did introduce a leavening measure of ethnographic context. Of the 'Isawa, Rinn writes:

> For the ignorant and credulous majority of Muslims, they are saints inhabited by the spirit of God and possessing the power to perform miracles . . .
> For other Muslims, as for most outside observers, they are but jugglers and prestidigitators, lacking in religious substance, mere exploiters of human stupidity. The smartest observers point out that most of their extraordinary feats that aren't sleight-of-hand tricks are simply phenomena of neurosis, hysteria, magnetism and hypnotism—all easily explainable. (1884: 303)

Rinn is careful to differentiate between the naïve viewpoint of Algerian commoners and the disdainful skepticism of more orthodox Muslim intellectuals and urban elites, who share a common stance with critical French observers, and whom French authorities often supported. Moreover, he noted dissention within the 'Isawiyya order itself, reproducing a letter from an 'Isawi sheikh condemning mendicant performers demonstrating physical feats as impious "conjurors" (329–31).[2]

Rinn's approach reflected the nascent scholarly interest in the scriptural sources of Sufism, and an effort to distinguish between "orthodox" orders "closer to true Islam by virtue of doctrine and ritual" and "heterodox" orders "led by tricksters who pandered to popular tastes for the miraculous and superstitious," which "were a deviation from Islam" (Clancy-Smith 1990: 242). He situated the 'Isawa firmly in the latter category, describing them as "religious ecstatics who abandon themselves to practices that are essentially but bizarre outgrowths of a zealous, unhealthy mysticism" (Rinn 1884: 303). Still, for Rinn, there remained two separable parts to the 'Isawa's ritual practices: a pious core of musical and poetic ceremonies and the degenerate showmanship that overgrew it. He describes the poetic aspect of the 'Isawa's hadra in great detail, arguing that "without a doubt, the 'Isawa leaders and the truly devout stop there. But more is needed to dazzle the eyes of the masses and call forth their superstitious veneration" (329). In other words, the 'Isawa's conjuring emerged from the desire to make a sophisticated form of mysticism meaningful to the ignorant multitudes. Like de Neveu, Rinn's ultimate assessment was that it would be prudent to keep the 'Isawa under close military surveillance (332).

Talal Asad (1983, 2011) has identified a tendency to privilege doctrine and belief over ritual and practice as a common feature of Euro-American theories of religion. Not surprisingly, Rinn's emphasis on theology was appealing to subsequent generations of French Orientalist scholars, who were eager to find commonalities between vernacular Sufism and a learned, scriptural Islam that they found more congenial (Eickelman 1998: 277), and whose clerics themselves scorned Sufism (Gellner 1981). In a well-regarded monograph on the 'Isawiyya order in Morocco, René Brunel dismisses the spectacular forms of ritual performance as vulgar decadency traceable to rural Algeria. Brunel (1926: 98) draws a sharp contrast between allegedly degenerate Algerian and Tunisian 'Isawa who "in ecstatic furor stoop to the worst charlatanism" and their relatively austere Moroccan counterparts who, "eschewing all eccentricity, content themselves with a state of ecstasy" induced strictly through dance.

In a short monograph on an 'Isawiyya group in Tlemcen, Orientalist scholar Edmond Doutté essentially concurred with de Neveu that the hadra "reeks slightly of charlatanism" (1900: 11), that "its tricks reek a bit too much of the conjurer (*bateleur*)" (12), and that the 'Isawa "attract the curiosity of crowds through jugglery" (24). Doutté ends his essay with a recapitulation of Robert-Houdin's performances in Algeria and his demystifications of the 'Isawa's tricks, but questions the overall success of the conjuror's mission:

> Robert-Houdin was simply taken as an extraordinary sorcerer, and I doubt that his performances had any other effect. Those who planned the mission obviously did not consider sufficiently that childish peoples like indigenous Algerians are much less surprised than us by supernatural things. Or, more accurately, they do not distinguish, as we do, between the natural and the supernatural; the notion of the immutability of natural law is unfamiliar to them. Sorcery is, for them, a given; it is therefore easier for them to attribute a surprising phenomenon to occult powers than to offer a scientific explanation, which in most cases they would be incapable of understanding . . . Recalling what our own Middle Ages were like will make us more indulgent toward today's Africans. (29–30)

Doutté frames illusionism as supernatural. Algerians, he says, have no scientific conception of nature that is devoid of occult powers, so the supernatural, for them, is natural. As a consequence, a secular magic show could never surprise them—in the normative manner of European spectatorship—but would only serve to corroborate their already irrational worldview. According to Keller (2007: 112), Doutté essentially conceived of "maraboutism . . . as an Islamicized form of magical thought," claiming that marabouts "operated as transitional figures in the Islamicization of superstitious practices." Here, the ethnography of the 'Isawa's allegedly magical trickery begins to connect with the anthropological theorization of magical thinking—a convergence I explore more fully in Chapter Five.[3]

Evolving Iconography

These stereotypes of the 'Isawa—particularly in Algeria—as jugglers and charlatans were well established not only on the pages of colonial ethnography; they accrued widespread cultural support though emergent mass-media representations and exhibitionary practices. By the mid-nineteenth century, colonial publicity was a multimedia enterprise, harnessing a wide array of verbal and nonverbal representational modalities (Sessions 2011). Orientalist paintings circulated images of the 'Isawa beyond North Africa: Eugène Delacroix painted an image of an 'Isawi procession in Tangiers for the 1838 salon; and Paul Lazerges, an 'Isawi hadra for the 1861 salon.[4] Meanwhile, "many topics of discussion within sociological and anthropological circles were mainstreamed by scientifically vulgarized publications. These latter were then picked up by the major media outlets, and used to feed colonial discourse" (Lemaire, Blanchard, and Bancel 2014: 88). Throughout the second half of the nineteenth century, French illustrated newsweeklies ran frequent features on the 'Isawiyya with accompanying engravings; lurid accounts of the 'Isawa's rituals made congenial subject matter for artists.

I have collected nearly thirty engravings of this sort dating between 1850 and 1900, not to mention imagery contained in paintings, photographs, and postcards. This corpus even includes a diagram of an Isawi's autopsied stomach (Maire 1883). Here, I compare two representative engravings from *L'Illustration*, France's first mass-market illustrated newsweekly (Martin 2006: 24–29) and a publication that was deeply engaged in hawking mythical images of Algeria to metropolitan readers (Lemaire and Blanchard 2014: 90–91; Sessions 2011: 222–26). Considered longitudinally, these images, separated by three decades, indicate a significant evolution in style and stance.

The first engraving accompanies an eyewitness account of an 'Isawi ceremony published in the April 27, 1850, issue. The author, Vivant Beaucé (1850: 263), describes a disorienting, phantasmagorical nighttime scene: "to illuminate everything, there were only two candles on the ground, and all the people blocking the light . . . became black shadows, assuming an otherworldly quality." Accordingly, the artist's rendering (figure 9) obscures the hadra almost entirely: onlookers encircle the ritual space, largely blocking our view. On the left, the muqaddam prepares to heat an iron implement;

Figure 9. French representation of 'Isawa, *L'Illustration*, April 27, 1850.
Courtesy Firestone Library, Princeton University.

on the right, we glimpse seated musicians and seven or eight ecstatic dancers. The action in the center seems to correspond to a moment in the narrative when an ecstatic 'Isawi lunges toward the author:

> he rose nearly erect in front of me. His wild eyes, unseeing, bulging from their sockets, the drops of sweat covering his tensed face, the violent gnashing of his teeth, the opening and closing of his fists in nervous spasms, the topknot spread over his shaved head in disordered strands—all conspired to make his person a terrifying image of human unreason. I instinctively leapt up, on the defensive.

Torn between fascination and fear, desire and disgust, Beaucé struggles to make sense of the 'Isawa. What this drawing illustrates—and enacts—is the frustrated attempt to interpret intractable exoticness. By blocking clear sight lines, it invites viewers to imagine the disturbing ritual for themselves. A complementary engraving from this same period, which ran in a competing illustrated newsweekly, *Le Monde illustré*, gives a similar impression of visual overload (figure 10). Here, observers are relegated to the background, leaving various components of the ritual activity visible but in such densely pulsating simultaneity as to remain almost entirely illegible.

Figure 10. French representation of 'Isawa, *Le Monde illustré*, January 16, 1858.
Courtesy Firestone Library, Princeton University.

With time, a new representational strategy emerged, one that would iso-
late each performative feat as an easily digestible individual vignette. The
later engraving, from the August 13, 1881, edition of *L'Illustration* (figure 11),
exemplifies this strategy. The sole illustration for a pair of reports on Algeria's Sufi brotherhoods (Ney 1881a, 1881b), the engraving separately depicts the 'Isawa in several phases of a performance for a European audience
in Algiers (clockwise from top): ingurgitating cactus leaves; ingurgitating a
live scorpion; piercing the cheeks; walking on red-hot iron; dancing ecstati-
cally; and balancing on a sword. In the central frame, an 'Isawi presents the
scorpion to European spectators for inspection; the lower left-hand frame
depicts a regal individual identified as "the spectacle promoter." This image
does more than just dissect the hadra. The synecdochical representation of
the hadra in terms of its most strikingly dramatic moments overshadows its
overall religious significance, instead segmenting a devotional ritual into
graphic highlights and reframing it as sensational spectacle.

Compare this image to Robert-Houdin's 1849 poster (figure 3), in which
small, framed scenes depict the magician's marquee tricks—the sensa-
tions you wouldn't want to miss. This kind of showcasing was a common

Figure 11. French representation of 'Isawa, *L'Illustration*, August 13, 1881.
Courtesy Firestone Library, Princeton University.

graphic-design element in nineteenth-century magicians' advertisements, which touted a performer's signature talents. The convergent visual rhetoric of the 1881 image of the 'Isawa stylistically evokes the iconography of popular entertainment, consciously or unconsciously reinforcing parallels between the 'Isawa and stage magicians. The tricks, the image seems to say, are the whole point of the show. A short text explaining the image underscores this reading: "Is this the work of saints, whose sanctity changes the very conditions of life, or the work of charlatans? It doesn't matter. Whatever the case . . . their stunts are certainly surprising, and they don't disdain to perform . . . for *roumis* [Europeans], and for money. They make a deal with a Barnum who exhibits and engages them in their best financial interests" (*L'Illustration* 1881: 116).

It is crucial to recognize that, while these images accompany texts, they also produce meanings and associations of their own, both independently and through relationships with other images. Focusing on visual representations of the Franco-Prussian War, Michèle Martin (2006) explains the complex technical, artistic, editorial, and commercial processes involved in the production of engraved images for nineteenth-century illustrated newsweeklies. She shows that, despite the verisimilar artifice these publications employed to give imagery the semblance of unmediated reality, their illustrations were also ideologically charged constructions of the very objects they claimed to merely depict. Examining artists' renderings of 'Isawa in *L'Illustration* bears out this assessment. Taken together, the engravings from 1850 and 1881 exemplify an evolving visual idiom that, in tandem with other representational and presentational strategies, conspired to make the 'Isawi hadra increasingly legible as a genre of spectacle.[5]

Exhibitionary Recontextualizations

Given their notoriety, it is not surprising that the Parisian World's Fairs of 1867, 1889, and 1900 featured 'Isawa as ethnographic exhibits. Their ecstatic self-mortifications and reputation for charlatanism suited them perfectly for events where ethnographic exhibitions were carefully designed to arouse curiosity about the exotic Other while providing ocular vindication of France's colonial projects (Boëtsch 2014; Çelik 1992; Çelik and Kinney 2008; Hale 2008; Lemaire and Blanchard 2014; Mitchell 1989). The circulation of narrative and visual representations of the 'Isawa had whetted the curiosity of metropolitan spectators and, as audiences flocked to see the Algerians perform their repertoire of marvels firsthand, the exhibitions provided an impetus for the production of new texts and images.

At least in print, the 'Isawa received a somewhat ambivalent reception in 1867.[6] The Romantic poet and chronicler Théophile Gautier (1867), who had attended a hadra in Blida, Algeria, over two decades earlier, complained that the "vaguely oriental decor" lacked the mysterious charm of a real "Arab courtyard." Still, he wrote, "the spectacle, such as it is, maintains a high African flavor, and is well worth seeing." In another account, a medical doctor, who leapt at the opportunity to clinically assess the 'Isawa's performances up close, fulminated, "It's not in a country like ours, where nobody still believes in miracles, that African jugglers will succeed in convincing even the most credulous souls that, thanks to the prophet Mohammed, they are endowed with supernatural power" (Warnier 1867: 39). He felt "sorry that indigenous Algerians . . . didn't have any specialty more noble, human, and worthy of sympathy for Europeans to admire," but was "very happy to see France finally enlightened about the real state of indigenous civilization" in the colony. Charles Desprez gives a mischievous account of the 'Isawa's first Parisian appearance:

> A kind of hangar—hardly Levantine in appearance—was requisitioned for them on the Champs de Mars. Detailed posters, like those for a comic sketch at the [*Théâtre des*] *Funambules* or an operetta at the *Folies-Bergères* [music-hall], announced their sacrosanct exercises. At first, crowds flocked—we've heard so much about them! But Parisians and their foreign guests—Kalmyk, Chinese, or Kamchadal—quickly lost their taste for such savage exhibitions. Women closed their eyes and plugged their ears. Men yelled, "enough!" And taking those "enoughs" for "bravos," our jugglers ferociously redoubled their furor. All fled, and the hall was empty well before the end of the performance. (1880: 202–3)

However shocked Parisians may have been in 1867, the year 1889 found them as curious as ever about the 'Isawa. After initially performing in the Café Algérien on the Esplanade des Invalides, the 'Isawa soon moved to the more favorable Concert Marocain on the rue du Caire, achieving "widespread and consummate success" (Pougin 1890: 117–18). On August 3, *Le Figaro* reported that "because of the immense success that the 'Isawa now enjoy, the director of the Moroccan Concert . . . has decided to give one performance a night instead of three times a week" (Grison 1889). Lenôtre (1890: 276) called them "one of the most extraordinary spectacles that one can see at the Exposition . . . *extraordinary* if not *agreeable*."[7] Although it is often difficult to trace the identities of individual performers, at least three of these 'Isawa sat for a series of ethnological photographs depicting the staff of Café Algérien, and accompanied by a handful of biographical details (figures 12–14).[8]

Exhibitionary recontextualization of the hadra invited renewed accusations of charlatanism. Branding the 'Isawa "mountebanks" (*baladins*), the acerbic Pougin (1890: 117) wrote, "there's obviously nothing to it but jugglery, even if it depends on one or more secrets that we find impossible to penetrate." French magicians eagerly stoked suspicions that 'Isawi ritual was nothing more than an inadequately disenchanted magic show. After witnessing the hadra at the 1889 World's Fair, music-hall illusionist and wicked satirist Édouard Raynaly wrote: "In the famous [Algerian Concert], where there were many things, with the exception of music, I had the chance to see

Figure 12. Mahmoud, 30-year-old cobbler from Algiers, 'Isawi at 1889 Paris Exposition Universelle. Bibliothèque Nationale de France, Société de Géographie.

Figure 13. Kaddour, 28-year-old embroiderer from Algiers, 'Isawi at 1889 Paris Exposition Universelle. Bibliothèque Nationale de France, Société de Géographie.

the epileptic frivolities (*calembredaines*) of a bunch of humbugs (*fumistes*) working their little angle" (1894: 215–16). Imputing meretricious motives to the 'Isawa, Raynaly took great pleasure in divulging what he considered the "crude" secrets behind their "little tricks" (217). His explanations of many mortifications largely follow Robert-Houdin's text (which he dutifully cites). In accounting for the ingestion of inedible substances, he points to surreptitious substitutions of harmless doubles—for the cactus leaves (219), scorpion (228), and serpent (230)—made under the cover of misdirection. "Thus," he concludes,

> with these facetious Arabs, those who have strong hearts can observe a pe-
> culiar kind of prestidigitation. It's not their tricks that I reproach, but the
> exaggerated importance they seem to attach to those tricks and, more than

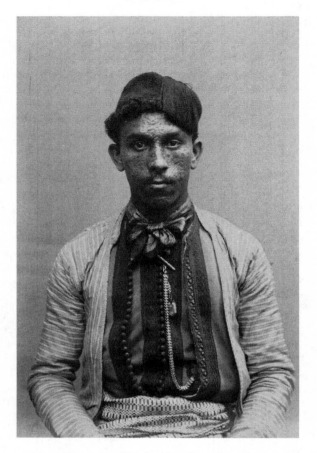

Figure 14. Bassar (?), 24-year-old embroiderer from Algiers, 'Isawi at 1889 Paris Exposition Universelle. Bibliothèque Nationale de France, Société de Géographie.

anything, the role they play in fanaticism. When real fanatics—they do exist, alas!—want to go about their mysteries, they do it at home, in a context appropriate to their religious convictions . . . They don't cross the sea and act like mountebanks (*saltimbanques*), ballyhooing to attract crowds. (231)

While bringing a professional magician's zeal to demystifying what he considered insidious humbuggery, in his ultimate assessment of the 'Isawi hadra, Raynaly seems to have been more disturbed by a fundamental incompatibility between religious ritual and show-business spectacle—two performative modalities that World's Fairs aggressively confounded.

The World's Fair engagements gave the 'Isawa still other opportunities to exhibit their talents within what cultural historian Simon During calls the European *magic assemblage*, "a loose cluster of entertainment attractions based on effects, tricks, dexterities, and illusions" (2002: 215). After the fair closed in 1889, they remained in France for some time, appearing at the Théâtre Dicksonn, a Parisian illusionist's eponymous magic theater, as headliners of a largely North African review.[9] Ironically, Dicksonn had managed Robert-Houdin's own Paris theater, the Théâtre des Soirées Fantastiques, for several seasons, but after falling out with Robert-Houdin's daughter-in-law, opened his rival venue just steps away in the Passage de l'Opéra (Dif 1986: 220). Whether booking the 'Isawa had some significance in his personal quarrel with Robert-Houdin's successors is unclear. Dicksonn went on to lecture against charlatanism, publishing anti-humbug tracts (e.g., Dicksonn 1927) without further mention of the Sufi brotherhood.[10]

The colorful poster from the 'Isawa's engagement at Dicksonn's theater (figure 15) bills them as "The famous troupe from the Universal Exhibition of Paris," and as "HOWLING DERVISHES" (presumably in reference to their vigorous devotional cries). Reprising the iconographic strategy of sensationalistic segmentation, it depicts their legendary marvels (along with two other, adventitious, acts) in captioned individual images (from right to left): "Balances on the blade of a sword"; "Lying belly-down on the blade of a sword"; "Fire Eater"; "The Belly Dance"; "The Gladiators"; "Pops out his eyes with sharp nails"; "Drives spikes in his mouth and arms"; and "The Snake Eater." This attention-grabbing poster is remarkable evidence of how the machinery of show business could absorb the 'Isawa's intensely physical displays of religious devotion to manufacture a commoditized, spectacular sensation.

In addition to Paris, the 'Isawa also performed in London, appearing in 1867 at London's Egyptian Hall, a theater famous for its magic acts. An English reviewer warned that the "performing Arabs" would "drive the strongest spectator to brandy-and-water" (*Fun* 1867). In 1889, they would return to London for an engagement at St. James Hall, playing to mixed reviews. A column in the *Era* (1889) described the show as "several brown-skinned individuals in Oriental costume" performing, "with a vast amount of 'moping and mowing,' roaring and tomfoolery, tricks which are most of them familiar to the patrons of the penny shows at country fairs, and others which, if they were really performed—which is doubtful—were simply disgusting and not at all dangerous." The reviewer complained that the French impresario who brought the 'Isawa to London "must have sanguine notions of the 'gullibility' and bad taste of the British public to believe that an entertainment of so tedious, unnovel, and repulsive a nature can be foisted on

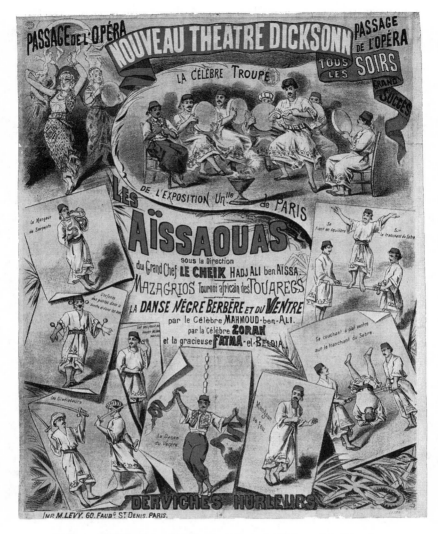

Figure 15. Poster advertising 'Isawa at illusionist Dicksonn's Paris magic theater, circa 1889. Réunion des Musées Nationaux/Art Resource, NY.

Londoners by the accompaniment of hideous tambourining, extravagant pantomime and pretended hypnotism."

As the reaction of the *Era*'s critic suggests, it was not difficult for European audiences to equate the 'Isawa with other cultural offerings on the contemporary stage. For centuries, there had been European entertainers specializing in extreme physical feats, as Harry Houdini describes in his book *Miracle Mongers and Their Methods* (1920), tellingly subtitled *A Complete Exposé of the Modus Operandi of Fire Eaters, Heat Resisters, Poison Eaters, Venomous Reptile Defiers, Sword Swallowers, Human Ostriches, Strong Men, etc.* What's more, European spectators could associate the 'Isawa with the vogue for "Oriental" acts by magicians from India and China, and the burgeoning field of Europeans impersonating them (Dadswell 2007; Goto-Jones 2014; Stahl 2008; Steinmeyer 2005).[11]

In a particularly rich parallel with the case I am describing, historian Peter Lamont (2005) offers an engrossing account of the extraordinary elaboration surrounding Indian illusionism—and, in particular, the mythical "Indian Rope Trick"—in British colonial culture. In Victorian Britain, he writes, "Indian jugglers . . . would become one of the most prominent images of India . . . presented as evidence of a native tendency towards deceit on the one hand, and credulity to the other. Victorians read how these devious jugglers deceived a susceptible native population" (17). Indeed, after attending a hadra, one French traveler in Algeria complained that the 'Isawa were "scarcely up to middling jugglery in France," and could certainly not compare "with the Indian [magician] who, without clothing, without music, without accomplices, without preparation, transforms a dry stick into a flowering bush, a bead into a terrestrial globe, a terrestrial globe into a bead, who knots poisonous snakes around his neck and suspends himself in the air on an iron cane!" (Maire 1883: 537).

As exotic stories about the brotherhood continued to spread in metropolitan France, the 'Isawa's performances became increasingly popular tourist attractions in North Africa itself. Trumbull explains that, by the 1890s, 'Isawi "ceremonies became . . . more spectacles than demonstrations of religious faith," prompting tourists to portray the order as *"emblematic* not only of Islamic mysticism, but of Algeria" (2009: 135). "By 1906, the tourist spectacles proliferated to such a degree" that local administrators imposed a ban on public performance: the 'Isawa's "shocking displays . . . menaced public order and hence demanded a political response" (141). Similarly, Spadola describes how, in colonial Morocco, the 'Isawa's public rites similarly "captured the gaze of European visitors and Moroccan commoners," portrayed in photographs that could be "commoditized, mechanically reproduced," and made "to speak on Morocco's behalf" (2008: 123). Moroccan nationalists and "reformists were well aware of French colonial exploitation of popular rites," and in the 1930s sought to ban public performances by the 'Isawa, particularly with an eye on controlling the global circulation of images of what they regarded as Sufi excess.

Analogical Resonance

Ideological determinations certainly shaped the selection of entertainment magic as an analogue in descriptions of the 'Isawi hadra, and ideological resonances gave analogical ridicule broader cultural currency in French colonial culture. From a range of possible readings, nineteenth-century French depictions of the hadra consistently emphasized unfavorable comparisons with stage magic in a way that maximally distanced the symbolic and religious content of Isawi ritual practices. Of course, the selection of illusionism as the source domain for this ethnographic analogy was ideologically overdetermined. Wiener (2003: 140) argues that, within a colonial framework, "the 'irrationality' of native superstitions and practices was necessary to demonstrate the rationality of modern European institutions." French discourses accordingly seized upon the foil of illusionism, making an invidious comparison between an indigenous ritual system caricatured as pathologically enchanted, and a European entertainment genre figured as normatively disenchanted.

In the context of emergent racialist paradigms (Conklin 2013), popular depictions of the 'Isawa as fanatical charlatans served to substantiate and extend negative French stereotypes of North African Arabs. The exhibitionary and representational strategies I have discussed in this chapter were part of a vast multimedia apparatus that mobilized imagery of colonial Otherness for a variety of intersecting purposes. "The exhibitions, expositions, news media, and other popular outlets disseminated information contrasting all that was rare, curious, strange, different, and unhabitual with Europe's rational construction of the world," write Lemaire and Blanchard (2014: 96). "These visual media publicized alterity. Over time it familiarized the French with the foreign, but in such a way as to confine the Other to the negative space engendered by European normativity."

The tropes articulated during this period have proven long-lived. They continue to resonate in France today, as, in the words of Mayanthi Fernando (2014: 7), "the distinct iteration of Muslim alterity in the postcolonial present . . . draws on earlier, colonial configurations of the Muslim 'native.'" Muslims and people of North African descent in France today endure patterns of symbolic and physical racist violence that are deeply rooted in the violent colonial past (Hannoum 2010; Fassin 2015; Terrio 2009). Even as Islam in France takes forms that are distinctively, natively French (Bowen 2010; Davidson 2012), symbols of Muslim devotion remain legible to French non-Muslims as threats to state authority and separation from national identity (Keaton 2006: 184).

Scholars argue that Islamophobia and anti-Arab racism in contemporary France are only the most recent expressions of attitudes tracing back to the colonization of Algeria. Promoters of French colonial projects mobilized racist depictions of Arabs, emphasizing inherent qualities of both zealotry and indolence that legitimized colonization and simultaneously called into question the very possibility of its purported goals (Scott 2007: 46; Silverstein 2004: 45–51). Nearly two centuries later, "the paradox of a civilizing mission aimed at the uncivilizable continues. Even if the characteristics attributed to French North Africans have changed over the years, the stigma of their origin still attaches to them" (Scott 2007: 88).

In recent years, anthropologists of France have taken Islamophobic discourses as evidence that the denigration of Muslims is not a spontaneous outgrowth of *laïcité*, the French replication tradition of militant secularism.[12] Quite the contrary, secular republicanism has often been "a placeholder for racism" (Chamedes and Foster 2015: 3), and seems to require embodiments of non-normative alterity—be they Catholic, Jewish, or Muslim—to define itself. Thus, Silverstein (2004: 32–33) argues that "the French national imagery of republican universalism" should be viewed as "a historical product of colonialism," with "its definitions of 'nation,' 'nationality,' and 'citizenship'" being "themselves historically linked to a series of ongoing exclusions of particular peoples and cultural features." Similarly, Fernando (2014: 192–93) shows that the simultaneous exclusion of most colonial subjects from citizenship on the basis of uncivility and "selective assimilation" of "a few exceptional individuals who demonstrated French cultural competence" underscores how both excluded and assimilated Muslims have not been "ancillary to republican rule but integral to its operation."

Islamists and jihadis may have displaced Sufi mystics as embodiments of the most radically unassimilable Muslim subjects in the postcolonial French imagination, but the same synecdochial relation to Islam remains. Indeed, in light of recent events, it is difficult not to view many nineteenth-century depictions of the 'Isawa as an early episode in a long and flourishing iconographic tradition of French Islamophobia. As Hannoum (2015: 22–23) writes, "The type of 'humour' generated by *Charlie Hebdo* was not new and was itself an effect of a larger cause: the colonial legacy of the French state . . . The caricatures of the Prophet were only one example in a system of racist symbols that extend the themes of an entire vulgar repertoire of colonial racism." In this context, even representations of 'Isawi practices that strive for some degree of artistic sensitivity nevertheless participated in and contributed to sensationalizing Islam and Othering colonial subjects.

There is one particular feature of 'Isawi performance practices that strikes me as particularly significant in light of the scholarship on common French stereotypes of Islam: their physicality. Davidson (2012: 18) writes that, in the eyes of French critics and admirers alike, "what marked Islam as irrevocably different from secular French civilization . . . was their belief in Islam's immutable physicality and in the embodied nature of the Muslim everyday experience." This is, in turn, linked with what Fernando (2014: 7) calls "the tension between abstract universalism and embodied particularism that has historically been entrenched in republican citizenship." The intense physicality of the 'Isawa's devotional practices did not only facilitate the circulation of mass-reproduced imagery, but may have in some way contributed to emerging understandings of Muslim faith as more problematically embodied—and more disturbingly linked to insensate bodily excess—than a normatively disembodied secularism.[13]

Conclusion

The kind of sustained disanalogy between French magic acts and 'Isawi ritual practices that I have examined has ambivalent implications for illusionism as a source paradigm. On the one hand, this skein of analogies positions magic as a synecdoche of modernity, and professional magicians themselves played an active role in elaborating invidious comparisons with putatively premodern or antimodern charlatans to burnish their own image as paragons of modern virtues: rationality, transparency, progress. On the other hand, these analogies, in the hands of colonial ethnographers like de Neveu and Rinn, seem to have a particularly contemptuous bite because entertainment magic may have already been culturally tainted by triviality. When Robert-Houdin and Raynaly position themselves as crusading against primitive unreason, it is precisely to counteract illusionism's associations with childish enchantments or rustic amusements (recall that de Neveu's specific comparison in *Les Khouan* is to fairground mountebanks). Disenchantment was also a strategy of legitimization.

Less intuitively, I will argue in the following chapter that this analogy, which in the context of French colonial culture appears entirely negative, may have had equivocal implications for the 'Isawa themselves. At the very least, the presence of Algerian 'Isawa on metropolitan stages indexes their resourceful and agentive adaptation to new performance opportunities.[14] In the Maghreb, 'Isawa regularly staged public processionals (Doutté 1900) and offered private performances for Muslim patrons (Rinn 1884: 331). While this may have facilitated their performances for European publics, one wonders how 'Isawi performers approached touristic, commercial, and theatrical performances, and how new, co-constructed forms and meanings may have emerged from these intercultural encounters.[15]

Consistent with the pervasive thematic emphasis on artifice, some contemporary commentators were certainly concerned with how the 'Isawa may have adapted their techniques to these intercultural conditions. As George Trumbull argues, some members of the French public grew convinced that, however authentic the 'Isawa might once have been, they had descended into charlatanism in an effort to satisfy European audiences. For these observers, "the incessant repetition of spiritual tests—in tourist ceremonies—stripped the rites of their mystical meaning, of authenticity," transforming the 'Isawa "from exemplars of the exotic into charlatans, living testaments to colonial bastardization" (Trumbull 2009: 139). Trumbull quotes an unnamed colonial administrator who, in 1895, wrote: "The order loses . . . every day its true character to transform itself into a school for jugglers or fetishists" (140). These assessments, which Trumbull likens to romantic salvage anthropology, represent a surprising inversion, blaming the prurient European gaze for the 'Isawa's lapse into trickery.

Conceptual and institutional associations with spectacle, however denigratory, also allowed some 'Isawa to cultivate new performance possibilities as far afield as colonial metropoles, addressing displays of skill and devotion to ever wider audiences. In the next chapter, I show how some French audiences favorably received these performances, albeit through the lens of positively valenced analogies that carried their own potential for distortion and misapprehension. During the period under consideration, the 'Isawa attracted sustained attention from members of French esoteric movements—Mesmerists, Spiritists, and Occultists—who hailed them as veritable scientific marvels and aggressively disputed allegations of trickery.

Challenging the authority of modern magicians and positivistic ethnographers, these groups contested the analogy with illusionism. The articulation and enactment of this analogy provided powerful evidence of the cultural role of magic in constituting what I call the normative ontology of Western modernity—a set of assumptions about the material nature of reality and physical limits of human perception that received widespread support in the scientific and scholarly institutions of post-Enlightenment Europe. Likewise, disputing representations of the 'Isawa as tricksters was a means for heterodox intellectuals to assert alternative ontologies. Debates about artifice and authenticity locked Western intellectuals in a framework that left little room for considerations of how 'Isawa themselves understood the significance of their ritual practices. Eventually, more nuanced ethnographic understandings of 'Isawi ritual would come to displace questions about the truth or falsity of their effects.

FOUR

Counteranalogy

À l'école, nous, vautours, contre l'albatros de Baudelaire.
—LA CAUTION, "Thé à la menthe"

With the 'Isawa touring the European magic circuit, the process set in motion by Robert-Houdin's 1856 trip would appear to have come to a logical conclusion. Even if the whole business clearly confounds any simple distinctions between enchantment and disenchantment or ritual and entertainment, dominant interpretations aligned with the basic ideological premises of colonial culture. The 'Isawa's performances on metropolitan stages enacted an apparent similarity with Western illusionists, confirming suspicions of charlatanism. In the process, they substantiated French perceptions of Algerian Muslims as irrational fanatics.

There were, however, dissenting voices. The most sustained critique of deflationary representations of the 'Isawa as lapsed magicians came from an unexpected quarter: esotericism. As I describe in this chapter, several heterodox intellectual and religious movements seized upon the 'Isawa as evidence of claims about the undiscovered potential of occult powers. Framing any parallelism between stage magic and 'Isawi ritual as a *misanalogy* (Shelley 2002a: 485), they proposed competing interpretations in the form of what Shelley calls a *counteranalogy*: "an alternative hypothesis that happens to be analogical. In other words, it is an analogical explanation that shares the explanandum of its model but employs a different source analog" (487). In this case, the revised source analogue was not to be the Western entertainment magician, but rather the controversial figure of the Western medium.

Likening the 'Isawa to mediums capable of channeling unknown human abilities, these esotericists sought to popularize this counteranalogy through publications and public debate and to explore its implications through a variety of research activities. Nevertheless, the analogy with entertainment magic largely dictated the terms of the 'Isawiyya controversy, spawning ceaseless argumentation over authenticity and fraud. Enactments in print and performance, from artistic renderings to ethnographic exhibitions, continued to reinforce the fittingness of this analogy, assimilating the 'Isawa into the modern magic assemblage. As I will show, even as esoteric movements involving performances of mediumship (such as Mesmerism and Spirtualism) sought to challenge the implications of this analogy, their counteranalogies reinforced its essential analytic focus on explanation rather than interpretation.

Beyond the Illusionist's Art . . .

As powerful as discourses equating the 'Isawa with illusionists were, they did not gain unanimous support—far from it. An uncanny spectacle involving intense displays of religious devotion and virtually indisputable acts of self-mutilation, the hadra was, for many French observers, deeply unnerving and impossible to write off as *only* trickery. Highlighting that analogy with entertainment magic was not ineluctable, a number of authors (e.g., Bellemare 1858; Lenôtre 1890; Rinn 1884) drew analogies between the 'Isawa and the convulsionaries of Saint-Médard, a mid-eighteenth-century Parisian sect famous for séances involving cataleptic trances (Kreiser 1978) and brutal mortifications—beating, stabbing, burning, and eventually even crucifixion (Maire 1985).

A number of commentators stressed that legerdemain alone could not possibly account for the phenomena they observed during a hadra. Others went further still, denying the involvement of any artifice at all. One was Théophile Gautier, the Romantic literary chronicler of nineteenth-century life. In 1845, the same year that de Neveu published *Les Khouan*, Gautier took his first trip to Algeria, where he witnessed a hadra ceremony outside Blida. The account of this experience, published in *Revue de Paris* five years later, helped establish the 'Isawa as a commonplace in North African travel literature. It is an extraordinary example of literary Orientalism, conveying a sense of the hadra as both sublime and grotesque, and utterly overpowering.

In stark contrast to Robert-Houdin, who portrayed his participation status in terms of detached analysis, Gautier depicts himself as supremely susceptible to the 'Isawa's trance practices. As the 'Isawa performed, he writes, "my vision blurred and my reason clouded . . . The singular sympathy that makes your jaws slacken when someone yawns, caused me to have involuntary spasms on my carpet; I shook my head mechanically and I felt—me too—a mad desire to scream" (Gautier 1851: 181). Whereas the illusionist writes of himself as a cool and dispassionate observer, Gautier is sucked into the performance as a more or less unwilling participant. There are entirely different regimes of authentication at work in these two texts: Robert-Houdin and de Neveu assert textual authority through willful repudiation; Gautier through helpless capitulation.[1]

For all his exoticism, Gautier exerts tremendous effort to portray the hadra as *real*. Before describing its characteristic repertoire of mortifications (intended, he indicates, to "perpetuate the memory" of Ibn 'Isa's miracles), Gautier addresses the reader: "I beg my readers to believe literally everything that I am about to say. My narrative does not contain any exaggeration, exaggeration being impossible in the painting of a monstrous delirium that leaves the visions of Smarra and the Caprichos of Goya . . . far behind" (182). In a hyperbolic Orientalist gesture, Gautier stresses the profoundly disturbing *reality* of 'Isawi monstrosity in respect to merely fictional works—a gothic novelist's vampire tale and a gothic printmaker's grotesqueries. (He also thereby stresses his own literary prowess as a producer of representational texts.) Years later, Antonin Artaud would seem to be working in this same vein in *The Theatre and Its Double*, outlining a "theatre of cruelty" that would use "violent physical imagery" to "pulverize and hypnotize the spectator's consciousness," inducing a "state of trance . . . like the 'Isawa produce trances" (1964: 128).

The visceral impact of the 'Isawa's performances themselves conferred potency if not always authenticity. Some French spectators, like Gautier, emphasized susceptibility; others, imperviousness, for different rhetorical ends. Trumbull (2009: 137) points out that tourist narratives often framed the hadra "as a kind of performative challenge . . . a litmus test for French stoicism and power." Writers described the 'Isawa as so disturbing to watch that spectatorship itself became a performance of masculine prowess. One observer recalled:

The feats of incomprehensible piety were about to begin . . . A shudder passed through the crowd, and our blood ran cold. Two [European] women decided—with good reason—to stop watching. From the pallor of their faces, it was easy to tell they were on the verge of fainting. Incidentally, this wasn't surprising for women at this kind of event; many men can't stay much longer. Only one woman, sitting in the first row of Europeans, kept watching, without flinching. Some seemed to admire her proud courage. Others, on the contrary, described her singular coolness with another term. (Ravet 1888: 394)

Here, one Frenchwoman's ability to watch the hadra is framed as a non-normative, for insufficiently delicate, performance of femininity.

At the same time as it constituted an emotional challenge for Europeans, the hadra also represented an intellectual challenge, an opportunity to gain firsthand experience and to formulate opinions about such controversial performances. In this regard, it is important to recall that, during this time, in Paris and beyond, novel modes of performance, exhibition, and publicity were developing in relation to new spectating publics eager for marvelous diversions (Schwartz 1998), which often involved displays of embodied dexterity, prowess, or endurance. Entertainers and impresarios on both sides of the Atlantic—most famously P. T. Barnum—were learning how to make increasingly sophisticated use of newspapers and advertisements to arouse controversy about their marvels and curiosities. As historian James Cook beautifully argues, by inviting members of the public at large to adjudicate controversial claims for themselves, popular entertainments created new arenas for democratic discourse. In an era of social changes and protean identities, he writes, "tricksters provide . . . the indeterminate object, the uncertain image, the morally suspect act—an engaging assortment of cultural deceits with which an eager public gauges its moral and aesthetic thresholds, defines itself" (Cook 2001: 259–60).

Many popular nineteenth-century texts about the 'Isawa reflect a conscious intention to produce knowledge by vigilantly detecting fraud, as both an enactment of virtuous spectatorship and a guarantee of representational authenticity. One writer says, "we saw everything in bright light, very close, and determined to resist any illusion . . . I can't explain what happened except in terms of the intervention of an occult and unknown power" (Nouvellet 1887: 442). In a reversal of the magician-as-debunker story, a journalist for L'Illustration reported that he took Chinese magician Arr Hee (who was presumably on tour in Algeria) to see the 'Isawa in 1873, "hoping I could get from him the explanation of some of their tricks" (Ney 1881b: 87). Not only was he unable to explain the Isawa's feats, but the terrified Arr Hee allegedly fled the performance, convinced they received help from the devil himself. This anecdote invites multiple interpretations. Perhaps the illusionist's bafflement vindicates the 'Isawa, or perhaps it suggests that the Chinese illusionist, despite his professional credentials, was himself revealed as a credulous or effeminate Other by his inability to explain away—or at least valiantly withstand—the ceremony. Any squeamishness is surprising, considering Arr Hee's own act featured a routine called "Impaling a Man Alive" (figure 16).

Figure 16. Poster (*detail*) for "real" Chinese magician Arr Hee and his troupe, featuring "World-renowned Chinese Sword Swallowers" and the "Marvellous Feat" of "impaling a man alive," circa 1870. Harry Ransom Center, The University of Texas at Austin.

Other commentators found ways to concede the illusionary artifice that European skeptics saw in the 'Isawa's public performances, but without altogether discounting the authenticity of the hadra. They did this by shifting the locus of authenticity from the public exhibition of marvels to other, private occasions or to other dimensions of the ceremony. For instance, Davasse (1862: 33) suggests that the 'Isawa perform simulated miracles for Europeans, reserving authentic feats for private ceremonies. He quotes a French librarian in Algiers who attributes "divergences in European opinions on the 'Isawiyya" to "different circumstances of observation." He maintains that there is a "vast difference" between ceremonies performed for tourists and "those the 'Isawa organize spontaneously for themselves," where "the reality of facts" and the "seriousness of the manifestations" is clear. Lucien Rabourdin drew a distinction between the leaders of the 'Isawiyya order—"nimble jugglers who can do dangerous exercises with impunity" (1881: 118)—and the mass of faithful followers "who really fall into anesthesia and often hystero-epileptic convulsions" (119–20).

. . . And Beyond the Laws of Nature

If the figuration of the 'Isawa (and, by extension, maraboutism) as charlatanic complemented France's colonial interests and largely received official support, other constituencies with different agendas endorsed competing interpretations. In particular, followers of nineteenth-century esoteric movements like Mesmerism, Spiritism, and Occultism hailed the 'Isawa as exemplifying human potentialities unknown to the West. As detailed in several excellent studies (Brower 2010; Lachapelle 2011; Monroe 2008), all of these movements shared a common concern with cultivating undiscovered human abilities such as spirit communication, telekinesis, or extrasensory perception at a moment of intense excitement about new scientific discoveries and technological breakthroughs.[2] In France, "this emergent interest in the occult occurred in the context of a growing fascination with the East," and "the exoticism and aura of mystery associated with distant lands" piqued curiosity (Lachapelle 2011: 36). Acolytes of the modern paranormal were immediately interested in the 'Isawa and challenged the dismissive comparisons of the hadra to Western illusionism.[3]

Mesmerism had a long tradition as an alternative therapeutic practice using "animal magnetism" to unblock the circulation of patients' "universal fluid" (Monroe 2008: 67). *Magnetizers*, as Mesmerist specialists called themselves, could also use animal magnetism to induce "magnetic sleep" or "somnambulism," a trance state that "usually entailed a dramatic diminution or augmentation of perceptual or cognitive abilities" (68).[4] For Mesmerists, these phenomena were not miraculous, but rather connected to natural human faculties that academic science had yet to comprehend. The *Journal du magnétisme*, the dominant mid-century periodical of Mesmerism, published several articles on the 'Isawa in the 1850s. In 1854, the journal reproduced an article by Prince de la Moskowa describing a hadra ceremony observed in Constantine. To prepare themselves "for eating snakes, scorpions, broken glass, swords, and a multitude of other indigestible objects," the prince writes, "they put themselves in a kind of somnambulistic state" through music and dance (quoted in du Potet 1854: 353). The editor, Baron Jules du Potet de Sennevoy, comments that the prince is a "partisan of magnetism . . . Researching with care everything relevant to this science, he thinks that the phenomena he observed himself in Africa can be explained without recourse to the miraculous, and we agree that they are a part of the class of magnetic phenomena" (355). Here, du Potet establishes the relevance of the hadra for Mesmeric research; the Mesmerist critique of discourses equating the 'Isawa with European magicians would develop several years later in the pages of the same journal.

As Monroe (2008) explains, the advent of American Spiritualism divided French Mesmerists in the 1850s. Spiritualist mediums claimed the ability to communicate with deceased spirits, and to produce bizarre spirit manifestations like eerie noises, moving furniture (especially turning tables), and ectoplasmic excretions. While Mesmerists were generally receptive to evidence of "the mind's power to act outside the body," the attribution of the effects produced by Spiritualist mediums to deceased spirits created a rift (66). Among the Mesmerists who cautiously embraced Spiritualism, André-Saturnin Morin also greeted the 'Isawa with enthusiasm. In 1857, he published a long article in the *Journal du magnétisme*, attacking skeptical views of the hadra. In particular, his criticism centers on an eyewitness account of the ceremony by Émile Carrey published the previous year. "The author," Morin (1857: 258) writes, "certifies the facts of his arresting account, but, far from sharing the admiration of other onlookers, describes them as one would a fairground spectacle, as if they were simply well executed sleight-of-hand tricks." Morin's criticism focuses particularly on Carrey's explanation of the Isawa's feats, which he quotes verbatim:

> In regards to explaining these things, *the youngest doctor of the smallest village can do it better than me*. I will say only that the cactus doesn't hurt; that, under certain conditions well known to chemists (such as moistness, etc.), fire doesn't burn; that the skin of southerners, and particularly negroes, is

much more porous and sweaty than that of northerners; and that in South America, I have seen negroes hold hot coals in their hand to light their own cigar or their master's; that the blades of a sword and even a razor do not cut when placed upright; that the human eye can be popped from its socket and reinserted without danger; and that—with apologies to the followers of 'Isa— their ceremonies, as far as I'm concerned, are perfectly explicable. There's nothing divine about it. (260–61)

Morin sneers at this demystification. "I seriously doubt," he writes, "that a single doctor, from the city or even the country, would accept Mr. Carrey's supposed explanation" of the 'Isawa's eyeball feat. "Without a doubt, the eyeball, removed from its orbit, can be reinserted; what I deny is that this double operation can be performed for pleasure, and that any man *in an ordinary state* could make a habitual sport of it, without a display of suffering or emotion." For Morin, writing off the 'Isawa's performances as sideshow charlatanism is arrogance verging on willful ignorance: "That there's no miracle, fine. But what happens is beyond everyday reality, and should excite the attention of everyone interested in deepening human nature. This is a mystery that could put us on the path of an unknown or poorly understood law" (261). Morin explains that Mesmerists can induce comparable states of heightened resistance to pain and physical harm, but that ethical considerations have prevented sustained experimentation. The example of "fanatical" sects like the 'Isawiyya, he writes, "persuade me that, by augmenting the force of magnetism, we could arrive at similar effects." He concludes by asking whether the "extraordinary power" the hadra reveals, "instead of giving rise to vain and barbarous entertainments, could be instead applied to produce salutary and grandiose effects, great works to benefit all of humanity. But it is inexcusably flippant to regard these bizarre phenomena with disdain instead of reason, as nothing but juggling tricks" (262). It is clear that Morin's rejection of the analogy between the hadra and a magic act does not arise from any sympathy toward the 'Isawa themselves, but rather from what he considers the imperative of scientific objectivity.

The publication of Robert-Houdin's memoirs—and at least one personal interview with the author—brought Morin back to the subject of the 'Isawa. In an 1859 article, Morin describes Robert-Houdin as "the prince of the conjurors, the master of his art . . . gifted with prodigious dexterity [and] a fecund imagination," who "knew how to apply scientific discoveries to prestidigitation" (213). He reviews Robert-Houdin's deflationary account of the 'Isawi hadra, which he describes as "very persuasive": "because the same effect can be produced by different causes, it seems likely that if the supposed miracles of the 'Isawa aren't accomplished using the recipes [Robert-Houdin] provides, they involve analogous, equally natural, methods" (219). However, he recalls the rapturous ritual of chanting and dance through which the 'Isawa enter a state of "ecstatic exaltation" (220) in preparation for the feats of self-mortification. He suggests that the hadra therefore should be seen as a "combination of conjuring tricks and phenomena of a magnetic sort"—an interpretation he claims Robert-Houdin himself endorsed in private conversation.

For figures like Morin, engaging in debates about the 'Isawa was a means for advancing the intellectual prerogatives of Mesmerism. In this, Robert-Houdin, then at the height of his cultural authority, was a potentially powerful ally, whose support crusaders on both sides of the Spiritualist controversy sought. Earlier in 1859, Paul d'Ivoi appealed publicly to the magician in the pages of the *Messager*, asking him to debunk French esotericists:

> Robert-Houdin . . . has toppled the sorcery of the 'Isawa and the marabouts of Algiers . . . It would be a crying shame if the idiocy of civilized peoples were more difficult to vanquish than the superstition and ignorance of savages. But it wouldn't surprise me. Whatever the case, when Mr. Robert-Houdin decides to, I am sure that he can accomplish all of the miracles that spiritists, mediums . . . magnetizers, somnambulists and other magicians want us to believe in. Mr. Robert Houdin must only will it, and it would be a great service to his contemporaries. (quoted in Morin 1859: 221)

Morin dismisses d'Ivoi's "attempt to explain everything by legerdemain" as "a self-evident exaggeration." Many Spiritualist phenomena—the telekinetic movement of objects, the apparition of phantom members, and human levitation—could never, according to Morin, be produced through trickery: "whatever opinion one has about the reality of these phenomena, we must admit that they are beyond the illusionist's art, and may even affirm that they are beyond the currently known laws of nature." Morin therefore invites Robert-Houdin to subject Mesmeric and somnambulistic phenomena to careful scrutiny: "the control of illusionists . . . can be the touchstone for distinguishing gold from glittering fakery; conscientious magnetizers will not shrink from any mode of verification, persuaded that a severe examination can only profit the cause of truth" (222).

Mesmerists were not the only esotericists interested in the 'Isawa. In 1867, an anonymous editor from the *Revue spirite*, the flagship journal of the Spiritist movement, went to observe the 'Isawa firsthand at the Parisian Exposition. Spiritists believed that trained mediums could communicate with dead souls, who revealed cosmological insights and moral verities. Like Mesmerists, they had a scientistic outlook, equating the medium as "an innovative religious instrument" with "the innovative scientific instruments that characterized the modern laboratory" (Monroe 2008: 108). They did not regard spirit manifestations as miraculous, but rather as "direct consequences of human physiology," maintaining that "spirit phenomena appeared to transgress the laws of nature only because human beings did not yet understand the manner in which the body and soul . . . collaborated in their production." In the 'Isawa, the *Revue spirite* saw evidence of Spiritist understandings of the dynamic relationship between matter and mind, body and soul:

> I attended one of the 'Isawa séances myself, and I can say . . . that it was not a matter of legerdemain, simulacra, or jugglery, but rather of positive facts, physiological phenomena that derail the most mundane scientific notions . . . Since these phenomena are neither miracles nor tricks of prestidigitation, we must conclude that they are natural effects with an unknown cause, but one that is not unknowable. Who knows if Spiritism, which has already given us the key to so many misunderstood things, might not give us this one as well? (*Revue spirite* 1868: 22–23)

This author's mediumistic counteranalogy denies that 'Isawa's feats are magical "tricks," asserting instead that they are scientific "facts" that reflect natural law. The emphasis remains firmly on explanation, not interpretation—determining how the feats are performed, rather than seeking to understand what (or even how) they might mean.

In 1900, the 'Isawa's appearance at the World's Fair again attracted esotericists. That year, the short-lived magazine *L'Echo de l'au-delà et d'ici-bas*, published by the French Occultist Charles Bartlet, produced a sympathetic booklet on the 'Isawa, profiling members of the order then performing in Paris, and giving their names as Ounnas Hadjz Abdel Kader, a manuscript illuminator; Choula el Hadj Mohamed, a coffee-shop owner; and Noubia Mohamed ben Ali, a cobbler. In order to control for imposture, the editors assembled modern photographic equipment, along with two medical doctors and "over thirty" other observers "familiar with the trickery of mediums, the subtleties of prestidigitators, and the dexterity of conjurors" (*L'Echo . . .* 1901: 6). Such an insistence on scientific methods was crucial for advocates of mediumism: "Since fraud was frequently uncovered at séances, control was essential for those interested in formulating scientific explanations of the phenomena witnessed. Authenticity could be confirmed only once the participants had eliminated the possibility of conscious or unconscious fraud by the medium" (Lachapelle 2011: 108).

Satisfied by the authenticity of the phenomena they observed, the editors enlisted the help of spirit mediums to shed light on the 'Isawa's superhuman feats. "Fontenelle" and "Julia," disembodied spirits communicating through female mediums, attributed the 'Isawa's powers to the assistance of spirit beings they identified as "Elementals" (*L'Echo* . . . 1901: 61–69). The editors also consulted a psychic, who corroborated the involvement of Elementals, which he traced to a sub-Saharan African origin. After the conquest of Senegal, he said, the Elementals had grown hostile and potentially harmful to the French. He continued: "In using them . . . for religious and often humanitarian purposes, and particularly in employing them among us, the 'Isawa help protect us from . . . malefic danger" (71). Inverting depictions of the 'Isawa as religious fakes obstructing France's civilizing mission in Algeria, this psychic shockingly construed them as vital intermediaries between incursive Europeans and protective spirits of the African continent.[5]

Among the esoteric movements that flourished in nineteenth-century France, Mesmerism, Spiritism, and Occultism all seized upon the 'Isawa to substantiate claims—both natural and supernatural—about extraordinary human abilities and paranormal powers. These North African mystics were not dangerous, but rather distinguishing doubles for the Western mediums these groups lionized. It is important to remember that esotericists themselves often faced accusations of charlatanism in the mainstream press and from the scientific establishment. In the eyes of psychologists who studied and pronounced authoritatively on mediumistic phenomena, for instance, "mediums, stigmatics, and visionaries were patients, and spiritism joined possession, visions, and spiritual delusions as the latest expression of dangerous delirium" (Lachapelle 2011: 61).

In challenging the representation of the 'Isawa as *mere* magicians, members of these groups also sought to vindicate their own intellectual positions. That modern magicians disagreed with them about the authenticity of 'Isawi marvels is not surprising. Beginning with Robert-Houdin, challenging charlatanism and superstition became one of modern magicians' central vocational prerogatives (During 2002; Hess 1993; Lachapelle 2015; Lamont 2004, 2006; Mangan 2007). Crusading against mystics, mediums, fakirs, psychics, and other exponents of the paranormal, illusionists sometimes blurred the line between public service and publicity stunt. Disagreements over the 'Isawa thus reflected a growing metaphysical schism that would pit modern magicians and esotericists as adversaries to the present day, often in a gendered and/or racialized dynamic whereby magician-debunkers are white men and their adversaries, female and/or ethnically Othered mediums (see, for instance, Beckman 2003; Young 2014).

Just as the analogy between the 'Isawa and stage magic "reprojectively" (Jones 2014a: 201) illuminates the analogical source domain of Western illusionism, counteranalogies with mediumism reveal central concerns of Western esotericists. Mediums were dangerous doubles for magicians, but the reverse is also true. Natale (2013: 95) shows that

> spiritualist mediums in the Victorian age had much in common with professional performers. Their séances were often presented on the stage, in theaters and public halls, before a paying audience. Like performers in the show trade, they hired managers, toured countries and advertised in the press. Their séances mingled entertainment with religious beliefs, and frequently offered some spectacular manifestations of spirit presence.

Just as modern magicians defined themselves in opposition to mediums, it was imperative for mediums to define themselves in opposition to modern magicians, to whom they often bore a disconcerting resemblance.

Establishing authenticity was key to the production of value in mediumistic performances, for, as Natale (2011: 246) puts it elsewhere, "testing the truth of spirit communication was the principal activity of sitters in all spiritual séances." Thus, the counteranalogy with mediumism (which, as a cultural category, itself already contained, embedded within it, an implicit comparison to magicians' artifice) in many ways only reinforced the dichotomizing debates surrounding the truth or falsity of the 'Isawa's performance. Drawing on Lamont (2006), Natale makes a vitally important point: because Victorian audiences could potentially view séances in theatrical terms, as little more than a magic act, trance functioned as an index of authenticity, situating the medium as a passive conduit for communications from beyond rather than an active agent in producing spirit manifestation (2011: 250). Thus, "one of the key arguments deployed by spiritualists to demonstrate the authenticity of spiritualist phenomena was the naivety of spirit mediums . . . Their ignorance, ingenuity, and inexperience were often underlined as further evidence that the hypothesis of trickery and fraud" was untenable. Consequently, mediumistic powers were often identified in women and children. Similarly, the feminized or infantilized status of ethnic Otherness may have also factored into the reception of the 'Isawa as authentic mediums, often described as primitive rustics even by their staunchest defenders.

There could be a way to put a somewhat more positive spin on esotericists' reception of the 'Isawa: Green (2015: 383) argues that the modern "occult" is "an inherently bicultural and transcultural channel of religious creativity and connectivity." Connections between the 'Isawa and esotericists seem to have been generative for both sides, expanding receptive audiences for the former's devotional displays and giving the latter further evidence in favor of a contentious scientific position. Still, as the Comaroffs (2012: 6) argue, even when modernity is seen as an inherently "north-south collaboration," its process of production is "a sharply asymmetrical one." In even the esotericists' most favorable responses to 'Isawi ceremonial performances, signifying content was inevitably bracketed off as cultural fiction, in favor of asserting the facticity of paranormal manifestations.

Analogical Horizons

Competing interpretations of the 'Isawa always seemed to return to a single, vexed, question: Were these Algerians charlatanic impostors, as French illusionists and colonial ethnographers contended, or did they have extraordinary abilities transcending trickery, as Mesmerists, Spiritists, and Occultists maintained? Regardless of the answer, it is clear that the all-consuming preoccupation with adjudicating the authenticity of the 'Isawa's marvels eclipsed efforts to interpret how those marvels may have functioned as complex signifiers within a conventionalized field of ritual communication. Whether positively or negatively valanced, analogy and counteranalogy functioned as not only a means of cross-cultural comprehension, but also a modality of ideological capture that limited analytic possibilities based on observers' argumentative agendas.

Michael Taussig (2003) identifies a similar insistence on falsification in ethnographic representations of shamans worldwide who employed legerdemain. Branding the shamans "frauds," European observers reinscribed an Enlightenment opposition between *tricks* and *reality* under the "assumption that there [was] some other world out there beyond and bereft of trickery" (278). In *Defacement*, Taussig provides a brilliant discussion of the analytic difficulties occasioned for European ethnographers by all kinds of performances involving masks, artifice, or the exhibition of prodigious abilities. Taussig shows how, in many ethnographies focusing on the performative display of initiatory secrets, the "question keeps recurring as to who knows what and how much, and what the heck is 'belief' anyway in this maze of deceit" (1999: 203).

Taussig suggests that the best way to "understand the fraudulent" aspects of such performances is to recognize them "as not only true but efficacious, the trick as technique" (2003: 281). He suggests substituting "for the word *fraud* the word *simulation* or *mimesis*. This has remarkable fallout poetically as much as philosophically and is uncannily resonant with the ethnographic record" (282). I do not have the kind of unadulterated historical evidence that would be necessary to develop fully the implications of this suggestion for the nineteenth-century Algerian 'Isawa, nor is providing an ethnohistorical reassessment of their ritual practices my intention in writing this book. Nevertheless, recent anthropological research among contemporary North African 'Isawa does suggest that a shift in focus from fraud and trickery to simulation and mimesis certainly does promise to yield substantially greater insight into the kinds of local meanings and interpretive conventions associated with their controversial ritual marvels.

Perhaps more important, it can help us see what colonial ethnographers may have gotten wrong, and how their assumptions and analogies may have led them astray. Such a view would advance my central project: to explore the role of popular forms of magical entertainment in supporting the normative ontology of Western modernity by providing a model for thinking about certain kinds of ritual practices as empirically falsifiable. In particular, the frequent invocation of entertainment magic as a cross-cultural frame of reference points to a modern, Euro-American tendency to evaluate ritual feats in truth-functional terms—as a vector of false belief—at the expense of other analytic strategies. In short, the beguiling analogy with illusionism renders other meanings invisible. By examining what it occludes in the realm of ethnographic description, we will be in a better position to understand the particular cultural expectations associated with Western magic as a form of entertainment.

Alongside accounts focused on the veracity of the 'Isawa's effects, there was also a current of more culturally sensitive ethnographic writing about the order.[6] For instance, Le Chatelier (1887: 102), while acknowledging that the 'Isawa hadra had become a spectacle and tourist attraction, emphasizes how the rite functions to "annihilate the individuality of the adept through his absorption in the essence of God," and to evoke the holiness of the founding saint "through the imitation of his practices such that, through an interplay of creator and creation, he becomes the object of personal adoration." Idoux (1898) narrates the hadra from the performer's point of view, occluding any critical perspective. Émile Dermenghem, a government archivist and amateur ethnographer, published a study of maraboutism arguing for an explanation of 'Isawi ritual marvels in terms of their psychological efficacy as visible evidence "that the limits of the self have been surpassed in [the mystic's] submersion in a universe of passion and love" for God (Dermenghem 1954: 312).

The anthropologist Sossie Andézian's extraordinary monograph *Expériences du divin dans l'Algérie contemporaine* (2001) represents the culmination of this tradition, offering a perspective on the 'Isawa's performance practices that contrasts sharply with accounts focalizing exclusively on ritual effects. Although she describes ceremonial performances closely resembling those de Neveu and Robert-Houdin reportedly witnessed nearly a century and a half earlier, her widely divergent interpretations—based on three years of ethnographic fieldwork at the 'Isawiyya zawiya in Tlemcen and in-depth interviews with participants—demands a thorough reappraisal of previous depictions.

Andézian explains that, as is evident from the very inception of the ethnographic record, the hadra comprises two clearly demarcated sequences— the *dhikr*, the initial musical component, and the *la'b*, the passage into religious ecstasy and trance, involving dramatized self-mortifications.[7] "Ibn 'Isa," Andézian explains, "is said to have subjected his disciples to dangerous acts rendered innocuous by his hypnotic powers: ingesting snakes, scorpions, and glass; handling sharp instruments; and walking though flames. Having become myths of the brotherhood, these incidents are reproduced during the la'b sequence of the hadra by entranced disciples" (98).[8] For Andézian, the la'b is not miracle-working thaumaturgy, as French observers originally assumed, but rather mimetic representation of prior miracles: "it is considered by the affiliates of the brotherhood to be a theatrical staging (*mise en scène*) of the prodigious feats attributed to their spiritual ancestors, intended both to perpetuate their memory and to bear witness to the efficacy of the founding saint's baraka" (107).

Early French observers appeared to inadequately appreciate the representational, simulative properties of the 'Isawa's performative wonders and also to misrecognize their ritual functions inextricable from the experience of trance. During the course of the la'b, the (exclusively male) 'Isawi performers and many members of the audience (especially women) lapse into trance. Although "represented as an unexpected event that transpires abruptly," the state of religious ecstasy is, in fact, carefully "planned, codified, conduct" (191). Andézian's 'Isawi interlocutors describe trance as direct communion with divinity, and the entranced person is regarded as a conduit for divine blessing or baraka that benefits all members of the community (198).[9]

Inducing trance therefore takes the form of a coordinated effort between 'Isawi performers and their audience that presupposes a shared system of belief and convergent spiritual training. For the performer, in particular, this training provides a structured framework for the mystical experience of trance: "Under the effect of religious emotion, the adepts play a range of roles, identifying themselves completely with the characters they portray. Their gestures, calculated in advance, help to contain the emotions liberated by the trance" (114). According to this interpretation, the rehearsed and carefully choreographed nature of the ritual that magicians like Robert-Houdin and Raynaly found so repugnant is not necessarily antithetical to religious sincerity. It is integral to the way the ritual accomplishes its purpose.

The objection might be raised that it is impossible to reinterpret the historical accounts of the hadra in light of Andézian's more recent 'Isawi ethnography: might not years of scrutiny from colonial authorities and Islamic reformers (Gellner 1981; Goodman 1998; Hadibi 2004; McDougall 2006; Merad 1967; Prochaska 1990a; Spadola 2008, 2014; Zarcone 2009) have led the 'Isawa to embrace a more explicitly self-reflexive stance toward their ritual practices, emphasizing simulative properties and downplaying miraculous charismata? Andézian (2001: 101) herself argues not only for the long-term continuity of cultural practice at the particular site of her study but also that, since the 'Isawa shunned all forms of political involvement during both the colonial and postcolonial period, they were largely spared the repression that other Sufi brotherhoods endured (25, 97).[10]

I am aware of the potential fragility of the ethnohistorical reassessment I am proposing here, given that contemporary 'Isawa may well have internalized outside critiques. Still, Andézian's account is consistent with the work of earlier scholars who rejected the view of the 'Isawa as essentially charlatanic. It is also important to recall how consistent her perspective is with the findings of anthropologists working on other magico-religious traditions: ritual trance consistently involves extensive training and careful coordination (Lewis 1989), and local understandings almost invariably accommodate what Robert Weller (1994: 105) calls "the accusation that tends to accompany professional mediums anywhere—faking."

On Faking It

In a fascinating recent study, the German anthropologist Martin Zillinger shows how contemporary Moroccan 'Isawa (and Hmadsha) mediums use digitally reproduced video recordings of trance performances to "mediatize ritually produced *baraka* for their clients across time and space" (2014: 43). In addition to circulating these media throughout the Moroccan diaspora, "the brotherhoods maintain trance media archives in which films, photos and objects are kept" for purposes of documentation, analysis, publicity, and promotion (44). Zillinger (2015a) goes on to argue elsewhere that these digital mediations are not secondary or external to 'Isawi ritual practices, but rather fully domesticated within a set of activities that are always already about mediations of baraka. "In these particular rituals," he writes, "media do not move into the background as if operating beyond mediation. Rather, the recordings emphasize the visibility and the mediation of the mediators used for integrating the ritual actors across time and space: vestments, photos, and cell phones are held up to the camera, and their ritual use serves to enhance the ritual's efficacy" (99).[11]

This emphasis on mediation helps explain not only Algerian 'Isawa's use of techniques of enchantment (Gell 1998) within a ritual frame, but also their apparent willingness to perform for foreign audiences—who are thereby incorporated, mobilized as allies whose mediations (narratives, texts, images, films, etc.) enhance the efficacy of ritual practices. In a talk at Harvard, Zillinger (2015b) explained that, according to 'Isawi theories of mimetic behavior, trance is a way of making baraka detectable through a state of patienthood; because video can reproduce trance and make baraka perceptible, the 'Isawa value it as a means of mediation. Technical means of reproduction extends the state of baraka through a processes of intermediation. "The more mediated trance-mediumship is," he said, "the more real it becomes."

During his talk, Zillinger screened incredible documentary footage he and Anja Dreshke had filmed among Moroccan 'Isawa. He showed us scenes of an 'Isawi raptly watching videos of himself slashing his head and torso while in a state of trance—which is impossible for entranced adepts to remember—and commenting on the performance to his nephew and the anthropologist. I was sitting beside an eminent continental philosopher, who at one point whispered to me, "I don't understand what the point of all this is supposed to be. How do we know it means anything? How do we know he wasn't just *faking* it? Even the medium admitted that he used special techniques to handle the blade." I immediately switched from an anthropologist taking notes on a scholarly presentation to an ethnographer taking field notes. I had before me precisely the kind of native I'm writing about in this book: an heir to what Taussig (2003: 289) calls the Enlightenment "way of looking at human and social phenomena that comes with a disenchantment of the world" and according to which supernatural phenomena "are to be explained rather than providing the explanation."

In the sweeping essay *Ritual and Its Consequences*, Seligman et al. (2008) contrast two pervasive modes of organizing experience: ritual and sincerity. "Enlightenment thought and sentiment," they say, emphasizes the sincere expression of authentic interiority and regards "ritual acts and practitioners" as "hypocritical because they give external signs for an internal state that may not be present" (113). They go on to argue that "what we usually call the 'modern' period . . . should instead be understood in part as a period in which sincerity claims have been given a rare institutional and cultural emphasis. As a consequence, ritual has come to be seen from the perspective of sincerity claims" (181).

In the nineteenth-century 'Isawiyya controversy, we can see precisely how this dynamic unfolds, as French intellectuals came to understand a Sufi ritual complex positively or negatively, depending on whether they viewed its participants as acting sincerely and authentically. And if a contemporary European philosopher's reaction to images of 'Isawi trance is any indication, the motif of sincerity remains every bit as resonant for cynically framing perceptions of ritual as a form of artifice with downright conspiratorial potentials: *Perhaps the 'Isawi was faking not only his trance, but also all that blood—where could he have hidden it? A bladder in his mouth? A reservoir in the knife? And then, feigning amnesia, how he hoodwinked the anthropologist (a sucker is born every minute!) into thinking it all was real. Maybe the nephew was in on it too!*

This paranoiac stance toward artifice gives trickery an altogether inordinate analytic significance, consuming everything around it: symbolism, tradition, affect, experience. My contention is that entertainment magic has historically enabled this style of reasoning. In part, it has done this by heightening awareness of simulation as a mechanical process, suggesting that marvelous feats could, in fact, be only tricks. More importantly, by amplifying cultural emphases on sincerity and authenticity, the genre insinuates that marvelous feats should be analyzed as tricks before all else—explained rather than interpreted.

I have argued that entertainment magic has historically constituted a vital framework for articulating—and, for that reason, also contesting—the master narrative of modern disenchantment. Nineteenth-century French reactions to the 'Isawa are a microcosm of European efforts to conceptualize cultural differences in terms of an evolutionary schema of cognitive hierarchies. In this sense, they provide a useful case study on habitual connections between magic (in every sense of the term) and mentation circulating in European intellectual culture. The formalization of these ambient associations into a coherent—albeit problematic—system would await the work of anthropologists.

In the following chapter, I explore in greater detail how the cultural patterns of performance and reception associated with European illusionism came to figure into anthropological theories of magic. I shift from discussing the place of magical artifice in the tradition of French colonial ethnographies of North African Sufism to a broader consideration of the place of artifice within anthropological efforts to theorize magical thinking. The analytic disputes surrounding the 'Isawa hovered relatively close to the ethnology of North Africa, but the implicit line of theoretical development that emerges from the analogization of entertainment magic and religious ritual found perhaps its most general and influential statement in the work of Edward Burnett Tylor, a founding father of cultural anthropology.

FIVE

An Anthropologist among the Spirits

In 1855, Ira and William Davenport, a pair of brothers from upstate New York—the epicenter of North Atlantic Spiritualism—began staging a sensational new kind of séance. In their performances, the boys had themselves bound tightly with ropes and closed inside a large mahogany cabinet that contained a cowbell, a tambourine, a guitar, and a violin. As soon as the doors shut, the instruments struck up a devilish cacophony. From a curtained aperture, phantom members appeared and objects projected toward the audience. Whenever the cabinet doors were opened, however, the Davenports were found still tied firmly in place. As a further feat, they sometimes brought a spectator into the cabinet with them and mysteriously removed his coat. After ten years of performing in the United States, they struck off on a tour of Europe in 1864 (figure 17).

While they never directly claimed to be true mediums, the taciturn pair didn't present themselves as illusionists either, coyly leaving it to the public at large to hash out the significance of their controversial séances. For During (2002: 154–55), "the spirits invoked by the Davenports seemed less interested in communication from beyond the grave than in spectacle here and now . . . The Davenport brothers effectively transformed the presentation of spiritualist phenomena into an illusion show." While Spiritualists on both sides of the Atlantic hailed them as holy figures, skeptics and detractors were equally vocal. Audiences met their performances with riots in Paris and several English cities (Christopher 2006: 202–3; During 2002: 155).

The brothers began performing at a moment when Spiritualism had aroused intense curiosity in Europe and North America alike about the possibility of communicating with deceased spirits, provoking what Lamont (2004) calls a "mid-Victorian crisis of evidence" that would shake the foundations of the scientific establishment. In essence, the Davenports capital-

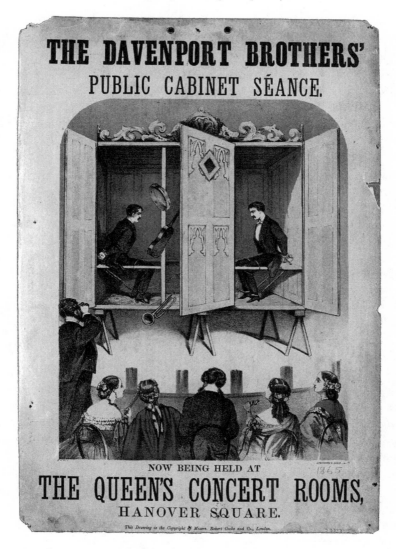

Figure 17. 1865 poster advertising the Davenport Brothers' Public Cabinet Séance at the Queen's Concert Rooms in London. © Victoria and Albert Museum, London.

ized on public curiosity about paranormal phenomena, exhibiting uncanny mental and physical abilities that they invited the public at large to pay for an opportunity to assess for itself. To scale the sitting-room séance up to high-capacity theaters required some ingenuity. Master inventor of magical stage illusions and magic historian Jim Steinmeyer shows what a crucial role their famous cabinet played. It "was just a large wooden box of a specific size," he writes, "but it meant the performers could standardize the rope tying, control the sequences, and carry the 'darkness' with them—the headline-making subject of Spiritualism could take the stage and be exhibited before hundreds of people at a time" (Steinmeyer 2003: 57).[1]

The Davenports' equivocation about Spiritualism provoked moral indignation among stage magicians. The elder statesman of French magic, Jean-Eugène Robert-Houdin, who saw them perform in 1865, published a long article the following year debunking the Davenports' spirit manifestations. Still, he hailed the brothers as ingenious performers:

> I attended their séances several times, and amused myself as I have when watching well-executed sleight-of-hand tricks; because I knew what to make of the spirit manifestations of the two brothers, I often laughed at the brazenness with which they presented themselves as passive intermediaries for spirits from another world. Let us loudly declare: the Davenports weren't anything but skilled prestidigitators, who, to give their performances more appeal, found it fitting to attribute supernatural intervention to their purely physical exercises. From an economic standpoint, they were abundantly right to do so, as . . . they brought in enormous box office revenues. (Robert-Houdin 1877: 229–30)

Note the marked difference in tone between Robert-Houdin's reactions to the Davenport Brothers and to the 'Isawa. He considered both to be charlatans and seized upon the opportunity to explain away their phenomena as an "enactment of expertise" (Carr 2010). Still, he could not but grudgingly admire the Davenports' ingenuity, pluck, and business acumen, placing the blame much more squarely on the credulous public for failing to appreciate the performances at their true value. The diagrams accompanying Robert-Houdin's explanation of the quick-release knots that he believed the mediums to use (figure 18) visually emphasized that their feats were "purely physical," as he put it.

In England, a young Nevil Maskelyne, who would become Victorian Britain's leading illusionist, launched his career by replicating the Spirit Cabinet phenomenon then explaining the legerdemain involved (Christopher 2006: 156–57; During 2002: 156). Soon, entertainment magicians on both sides of the Atlantic were featuring anti-Spiritualist demonstrations in their stage acts, as much to discredit the Davenports' charlatanism as to themselves capitalize on a faddish sensation. Still, magicians could not seem to vanquish the mediums—nor did they necessarily want to, since a lengthy and

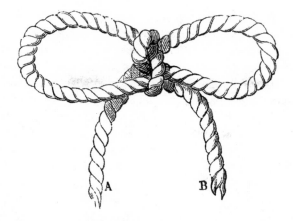

Figure 18. Diagram exposing the Davenport Brothers' slipknot, from Robert-Houdin's 1877 *Magie et physique amusante*. Bibliothèque Nationale de France.

strident controversy was mutually beneficial to all parties. As Lamont (2006: 29) explains, when "Maskelyne and other stage conjurors duplicated the Davenport brothers' spirit cabinet act, spiritualists claimed that such performances were not accurate duplications." When Spiritualists did accept the legitimacy of duplications, they could still discount debunking discourses, arguing "that the conjuror's feats were themselves the result of the spirits."

Thought Experiments

The Davenport Brothers also provoked moral indignation among anthropologists, particularly Sir Edward Burnett Tylor, the towering figure of the British anthropological establishment. Although he never attended university, Tylor was elected fellow of the Royal Academy in 1871, and the University of Oxford conferred on him an honorary doctorate in 1875. At Oxford, he became keeper of the University Museum, then reader, professor, and the first-ever Chair of Anthropology. He was, by all accounts, a tall, imposing, high-spirited figure who attracted many admirers. One of his followers, the ethnologist R. R. Marett, wrote of Tylor, "Great as was his science, the man himself was greater. To look as handsome as a Greek god, to be as gentle at heart as a good Christian should, and, withal, to have the hard, keen, penetrating intelligence of the naturalist of genius—this is to be gifted indeed; or, as they would say in the Pacific, such a man has *mana*" (1936: 8).

A leading exponent of social evolutionism, Tylor maintained that universal faculties of intelligence would propel all human populations to progress along similar lines of development, if at variable rates determined by historically contingent local circumstances. Tylor viewed culture unilineally according to what he saw as relative stages of development, distinguished, among other things, by dominant modes of understanding how the world works. In his view, primitive magic and modern science were linked as dangerous doubles. "The great characteristic of magic," Tylor wrote (1883: 200), "is its unreality," with its "old precepts . . . handed on by faithful but stupid tradition, from age to age. When the test of practical efficacy comes in upon the magic art, it is apt to destroy it utterly or transform it into something more rational, which passes from supernatural into natural science." Over the course of evolutionary progress, "the vague and misleading parts which could not be thus transformed were left behind as occult science, and thus the very reason why magic is almost all bad is because when any of it becomes good it ceases to be magic" (207). Given his objective of establishing the discipline of anthropology on what he repeatedly calls an "analogy" (Tylor 1873: 8, 23) with perpetually advancing natural science, Tylor's account of occult science—that is, magic—as intellectually stagnant (and stagnating) frames it as the antipode to his own knowledge practices.

Tylor's influence in anthropology stems not only from the position of institutional prominence that he achieved, but also from his role as a systematizer of previous generations' casual ethnographic observations. He argued that it was possible to take "a statement as to customs, myths, beliefs, &c. of a savage tribe" as evidence even when it depends "on the testimony of some traveller or missionary, who may be a superficial observer, more or less ignorant of the native language, a careless retailer of unsifted talk, a man prejudiced or even willfully deceitful" (Tylor 1873: 9), when accounts "agree in describing some analogous art or rite or myth" among people in different countries or at different times. In this coherentist epistemology, cross-cultural analogy served as both a control on the validity of observations and as a source of theoretical ideas, risking an ultimately fatal problem of logical regress. Thus, Tylor formed concepts like "magic" by using analogies to sort cross-cultural examples into often predetermined analytic categories—a practice that came to be known, somewhat misleadingly, as the "comparative method" (see Boas 1896).

It is not clear whether Tylor ever saw the Davenport Brothers perform, but he certainly commented on their act at some length, lumping it together with a number of apparently similar shamanic rituals. In a pivotal passage of *Primitive Culture*, he situates the Davenports alongside reports, which in some cases date back centuries, from European travelers in Greenland and

Siberia of eerie performances by tightly bound indigenous mediums. Before the spread of Christianity, Inuit shamans called *angakot* (singular, *angakok*) performed clairvoyant séances in the dark, making drums beat wildly and strangely speaking spirit manifestations brush against audience members, remaining all the while tied up with leather thongs. While missionaries condemned these performances as diabolical, many European observers wrote them off as crude trickery (for a complete discussion, see Flaherty 1992; Holm 1914).

Prior to European contact, the angakok séance-form appears to have spread through Algonquin-speaking North America, giving rise to the closely related Shaking Tent oracle (Hultkrantz 1967). In this tradition, a bound medium is placed inside a hide-covered wood-frame edifice that shudders violently to indicate the presence of spirits who address spectators' questions in distinct, sometimes humorous, voices. Even when the medium was tied at the fingers, hands, wrists, elbows, toes, ankles, and thighs, with his neck tethered to his knees, then bundled in a leather hide tied round with sinew, instruments would still play inside the tent, and the tent itself would shake violently, before the medium emerged fully untied at the end of the séance.[2] Europeans were not sure how to classify these performances, variously referring to Shaking Tent operators as *necromancers, nigromancers, sorcerers, wizards, conjurors*—and, most commonly, *jugglers*.[3] Seventeenth-century Jesuit missionaries wavered between classifying the ceremony as malicious charlatanism or a real supernatural feat accomplished with diabolical assistance.[4]

Pointing to its parallels with circumpolar shamanism and the Native North American Shaking Tent ceremony, Tylor refers to this entire category of performances—if category it indeed be—as "the trick of the Davenport Brothers" (1873: 144). In *Primitive Culture*, he writes, "the untying trick performed among savages is so similar to that of our mountebanks [the Davenports], that when we find the North American Indian jugglers doing" it, "we are at a loss to judge whether they inherited [this feat] from their savage ancestors, or borrowed [it] from the white men" (1873: 154). Any borrowing was assuredly in the other direction—indeed, according to tradition among entertainment magicians, the Davenport Brothers' policeman father got the idea for their act after seeing a demonstration of the Shaking Tent ceremony by indigenous people (Steinmeyer 2003: 54).

In any event, Tylor's principal concern was clearly not the particulars of cultural diffusion. "The point is not . . . the mere performance of the untying trick," he continued, "but its being attributed to the help of supernatural beings. This notion is thoroughly at home in savage culture." This observation pointed to a potentially fatal flaw in Tylor's system: if it is the correct explanation of the trick in terms of purely manual methods that distinguishes modern spectators from credulous savages, why were so many of his own contemporaries convinced that the Davenports had help from supernatural beings?

Tylor fashioned the theory of *survivals* (also *revivals*) to account for the persistence (or recrudescence) of practices—most specifically, Spiritualism— that he associated with more primitive stages of cultural development in more advanced stages. The belief in communication with disembodied spirits, promoted by the theatrics of entertainers such as the Davenport Brothers, fell squarely into this category. "It appears," he wrote dryly, "that the received spiritualistic theory of the alleged phenomena belongs to the philosophy of savages" (1873: 155). At this juncture in *Primitive Culture*, he proposes a thought experiment that exemplifies the role of trickery in his approach to primitive magic:

> Suppose a wild North American Indian looking on at a spirit-séance in London. As to the presence of disembodied spirits, manifesting themselves by raps, noises, voices, and other physical actions, the savage would be perfectly at home in the proceedings, for such things are part and parcel of his recognized system of nature . . . Do the Red Indian medicine-man, the Tatar necromancer, the Highland ghost-seer, and the Boston medium, share the possession of belief and knowledge of the highest truth and import, which, nevertheless, the great intellectual movement of the last two centuries has simply thrown aside as worthless? (155–56)

For my purposes, this thought experiment itself is an object of interest in its own right, offering clear evidence of how the ability or inability to interpret paranormal effects as tricks according to normative standards enunciated by stage magicians and embraced by Victorian anthropologists could become the definitive diagnostic for developmental progress.

Tylor positioned himself as a prominent opponent of Spiritualism, and his hostility fundamentally shaped the social theory he produced (Masuzawa 2000; Pels 2003b, 2008; Stocking 1971). The apparent resurgence of magical thinking in the midst of modern civilization posed a major problem for his teleological model of cultural development according to which magical modes of thought should progressively dissipate. This, of course, had to be addressed. On a somewhat deeper level, however, Peter Pels (2003b: 245) shows that Tylor's debates about the veracity of Spiritualism with

Alfred Russel Wallace—an anthropologist, natural scientist, co-originator of the theory of evolution, and himself a Spiritualist devotee—also enacted divergent visions of "the proper *publicity* of science: in Tylor's case, a public revelation of progress on the basis of a certain kind of exclusive expertise, and in Wallace's, one that situates it in a more democratic and domestic interior."

Wallace mobilized testimony from several observers who claimed to have closely scrutinized the Davenports under carefully controlled experimental conditions. One, the extraordinary scholar and adventurer Sir Richard Francis Burton, was said to have seen the Davenports "under the most favourable circumstances, in private houses, when the spectators were all sceptics, the doors bolted, and the ropes, tape, and musical instruments provided by themselves" (Wallace 1875: 98). Burton went on to give the following written report:

> I have spent a great part of my life in Oriental lands, and have seen there many magicians. Lately I have been permitted to see and be present at the performances of [entertainment magicians] Messrs. Anderson and Tolmaque. The latter showed, as they profess, clever conjuring, *but they do not even attempt what the Messrs. Davenport . . . succeed in doing.* Finally, I have read and listened to every explanation of the Davenport "tricks" hitherto placed before the English public, and, believe me, if anything would make me take that tremendous leap "from matter to spirit," *it is the utter and complete unreason of the reasons by which the manifestations are explained.* (quoted in Wallace 1875: 98)

Spiritualism constituted an almost ineluctable "shared stance object" (Du Bois 2007: 115), in respect to which members of the British intelligentsia and of particular interpretive communities like anthropology staked out social and professional identities. Robert Weller draws an analogy with the chemical condition of saturated solutions to describe historical moments like this when competing interpretations abound. "Saturated events are thick, overflowing with dissolved possibilities," but with energy and effort they can be made to yield "precipitated interpretations" that are "thin and easier to analyze" (Weller 1994: 23). Interpretive communities can enforce and sustain precipitated interpretations, Weller argues, if they can gain sufficient institutional purchase. In the case of the nineteenth-century mediumship controversy—which embroiled the 'Isawa, the Davenports, and others—the skeptical interpretations promulgated by modern magicians and anthropologists faced considerable opposition from heterodox esotericist viewpoints, with both sides claiming, irresolvably, the authority of science.

Almost certainly as a result of the debate with Wallace (Pels 2008: 276), Tylor set out, in 1872, to conduct two weeks of ethnographic fieldwork on the London Spiritualist scene, mingling with the movement's proponents and detractors, and attending a number of séances. George Stocking (1971) discovered Tylor's unpublished field notes from this research in the archives of the Pitt-Rivers Museum and published them in *Man*. Reading over these notes suggests that, unlike the kind of fieldwork a contemporary ethnographer might undertake, the purpose of Tylor's inquiries was not so much to evenhandedly document the cultural practices surrounding Spiritualism, as to partake in the Victorian crisis of evidence and assess close up the nature and extent of the mediums' trickery. The field notes conclude as follows:

> Returned home. What I have seen & heard fails to convince me that there is a genuine residue[. I]t all might have been legerdemain, & was so in great measure[,] except that legerté is too complimentary for the clumsiness of many of the obvious imposters. The weight of the argument lies in testimony of other witnesses . . . But it has not proved itself by evidence of my senses, and I distinctly think the case weaker than written documents led me to think. Seeing has not (to me) been believing, & I propose a new text to define faith[:] "Blessed are they that have seen, and *yet* have believed." (quoted in Stocking 1971: 100)

In Tylor's account, there is little indication that, beyond the truth or falsity of its alleged manifestations, Spiritualism as a religious movement held any cultural significance or scholarly interest whatsoever. If it was only clumsy "legerdemain" operated by "obvious imposters," why should it require an interpretation at all rather than simply being explained away? A more robust interpretive approach to Spiritualism, attending to the ways the movement had created a generative expressive idiom for subaltern subjects to contest dominant religious, political, and scientific viewpoints, would have to await the advent of feminist, queer, and postcolonial turns in cultural historiography (e.g., McGarry 2008; Owen 2004).

As with Robert-Houdin, the issue of trickery was, for Tylor too, inevitably also bound up with issues of sincerity. He conceptualized primitive magic as an edifice of illusion maintained by the connivance of clerics mainly interested in protecting their positions of prestige. In this, maybe the implicit analogue of the self-aggrandizing showmen like the Davenports also entered into his reasoning. When Tylor asks how the "whole monstrous farrago" of magic, with "no truth or value whatever . . . could have held its ground, not merely in independence but in defiance of its own facts" (1873: 133), he places the blame first on willful deceivers:

> Often priest as well as magician, he has the whole power of religion at his back; often a man in power, always an unscrupulous intriguer, he can work witchcraft and statecraft together, and make his left hand help his right. Often a doctor, he can aid his omens of life or death with remedy or poison, while what we still call "conjurors' tricks" of sleight of hand, have done much to keep up his supernatural prestige. (134)

Tylor seemed to imagine occult magic as a symptom of a larger problem: the contamination of traditional authority in primitive society by secrecy, manipulation, and opacity. Still, he viewed the primitive magician as an almost tragicomic figure, fooled by his own deceptions. "At once dupe and cheat," these false magicians combined "the energy of the believer with the cunning of a hypocrite" (121).

Historians of anthropology point to Tylor's Quaker upbringing as the source of a particular aversion to manifestations of magico-religious belief in material or ritual form (Engelke 2012). Tricks spell trouble in a Tylorian framework that considers any materialization of belief to be a liability, particularly if the signifying materialities or signifying agents could be suspected of intentional deceit. As Pels (2008: 276) puts it, "Tylor described the materiality of the séance as a human construction: as the result of either fraud or hysteria, as voluntary or involuntary deception." The materiality of spirit manifestations was simply incompatible with the dematerializing tendency of a Tylorian anthropology that "valued [its] subject matter the more it shed the taint of human hands," in Pels's words.

Tylor's theory of social evolution, clearly suffused with colonial chauvinism about the cultural superiority of Western modernity, makes telling use of magic as a marker of cognitive differences. Under Tylor's influence, psychologists also began formulating distinctions between primitive and modern mentalities with respect to perspectives on trickery. The American psychologist Norman Triplett wrote that "primitive conjuring was the deceptive performances of priests" made "miracle by the religious superstitions of a deluded people" (1900: 447). Driven by "the acquisition of power, veneration and obedience," primitive magicians used "all the resources of legerdemain" to "form a veil of mystery and . . . to paralyze the critical faculty of minds not too acute in that naïve age" (449). Triplett's contemporary, Joseph Jastrow (1900: 111–12), took up Tylor's evolutionary system wholesale, emphasizing the difference between conjuring tricks presented, on the one hand, by "the ancient priest or . . . the savage medicine-man . . . as miracle" or "as proof of spirit agency by the modern spiritualistic medium," and, on the other, "by the stage performer for entertainment."[5]

If the discussion of the untying trick plays such a prominent role in Tylor's and, following him, psychologists' theorization of magical thinking, I argue that it is in part because the industry of show business had so successfully commodified religious and metaphysical controversies as popular entertainment. More specifically, Tylor's use of audiences' attitudes toward illusionary performance as a signifier of cultural and cognitive differences would probably not have been possible if contemporary European illusionists had not so thoroughly discredited the Davenports and, more importantly, modeled a normative way of framing and appreciating paranormal effects as products of natural human ingenuity. Moreover, the Spiritualist controversy into which Tylor plunged headlong would not itself have gained such cyclonic proportions if unorthodox performers operating squarely within the magic assemblage had not so aggressively provoked public debates about the status and meaning of their weird effects.

Tricks as Traps

In the wake of Tylor's attacks on artifice, anthropologists have been working for some time to sort out the relationship between magical thinking and magic tricks, and in the process, to disenchant the magical/rational dichotomy that Tylor formulated partially in reference to practices of responding to tricks.[6] Tylor's disciple—and, later, critic—Andrew Lang was an early advocate of approaching paranormal phenomena in a way that would do away with terms like *primitive* and *modern*, proposing something that anticipates Latour's (1993b) notion of a "symmetrical anthropology" of the paranormal. For Lang, this also involved overcoming entrenched disciplinary biases.

In the preface to the second edition of his book *Cock Lane and Common-Sense*, Lang (1896) complained that "anthropologists will hear gladly about wraiths, ghosts, corpse-candles, hauntings, crystal-gazing, and walking unharmed through fire, as long as these things are part of . . . savage belief. But, as soon as there is first-hand evidence of honourable men and women for the apparent existence of any of the phenomena enumerated," they "refuse to have anything to do with the subject" (ix). Meanwhile, Lang reproached the discipline of psychical research—what we might now call paranormal investigation—for "anxiously examining all the modern instances" of paranormal phenomena while entirely neglecting "that evidence from history, tradition, savage superstition, saintly legend, and so forth" (x).[7]

The problem, Lang rather ingeniously argues, is that both anthropologists and paranormal investigators were operating with inherent social biases: anthropology, starting from a conviction that paranormal beliefs are false, could not accept the prevalence of comparable beliefs among people too much like anthropologists themselves; paranormal research, starting from a conviction that paranormal beliefs are true, could not accept the prevalence of comparable beliefs among people too much unlike psychical researchers themselves. Indeed, Stocking (1971: 101–2) shows that the real crisis Tylor faced in his research on Spiritualism was how to deal with secondhand evidence for Spiritualist marvels coming from people of high social standing to whose perspectives he was inclined to defer.

Lang proposes to treat paranormal inquiry in a more symmetrical fashion, abolishing arbitrary distinctions between fieldsites and disciplines. Doing so arguably generates a much more robust research program than Tylor's paint-by-numbers comparativism. "On every side we find, as we try to show, in all ages, climates, races, and stages of civilisation, consentient testimony to a set of extraordinary phenomena. Equally diffused we find fraudulent imitations of these occurrences," Lang (1896: 5) observes. "It is a question whether human folly would, everywhere and always, suffer from the same delusions, undergo the same hallucinations, and elaborate the same frauds."

Working with the same evidence as Tylor, but doing away with the problematic notion of "survivals" (which he pretty handily savages), Lang poses an entirely different set of questions about the cross-cultural prevalence of the untying trick:

> We have to decide between the theories of independent invention; of transmission, borrowing, and secular tradition; and of a substratum of actual fact. Thus, either the rite of binding the sorcerer was invented, for no obvious reason, in a given place, and thence reached the Australian blacks, the Eskimo, the Dene Hareskins, the Davenport Brothers, and the Neoplatonists; or it was independently evolved in each of several remote regions; or it was found to have some actual effect—what we cannot guess—on persons entranced. (Lang 1896: 36)

Implicit in Lang's question about the origination of the untying effect is a very different way of dealing with materiality. Instead of focusing on the trick as an explanatory challenge revealing spectators' cast of mind, he

Figure 19. 1894 poster for illusionist Harry Kellar's rendition of the Davenport Spirit Cabinet, featuring occult iconography of spirits, imps, devils, and skeletons. New York Public Library.

emphasizes the performative substance of the effect itself: what indeed is it about our human constitution that would make an effect of this nature so apt to be widely diffused and/or independently generated? To explore this line of questioning, Lang thought it important to enlist the assistance of real (though congenitally unreliable) experts: illusionists. He reports private conversations with Maskelyne, and repeatedly invokes the authority of his American contemporary Harry Kellar. Assisting in anthropological fieldwork, Lang thought illusionists "might detect some of the tricks, though Mr. Kellar, a professional conjurer and exposer of spiritualistic imposture, has been fairly baffled (he says) by Zulus and Hindus" (1896: 54). Lang explains the parenthetical "he says" in a later footnote: "As a professional conjurer, and exposer of spiritualistic imposture, Mr. Kellar has made statements about his own experiences which are not easily to be harmonised" (1896: 78).

Lang was not wrong to mistrust a trickster like Kellar, who had learned his profession at the knee of none other than the Davenport Brothers. As a young man, Kellar worked for two years as general manager and understudy for the Davenports, learning their act so well that he eventually struck out on his own as an exhibitor of Spiritualist phenomena (Cook 2001: 206–8; Steinmeyer 2003: 166–67). He toured widely (figure 19), and later wrote a picturesque travel memoir that included a chapter on the feats of East Indian magicians, which he alternately portrayed as baffling and ludicrous (Lamont 2005: 90–92). When he introduced a high-tech new levitation illusion in 1904, he called it "The Levitation of Princess Karnac," and peppered audiences with outlandish stories about learning the effect from an inscrutable Hindu magician along the banks of the mystical Ganges (Steinmeyer 2003: 174–76). Clearly, a magician like Kellar was at least as interested in the entertainment value of his myriad mystifications as in the scientific value of anthropological investigation.[8]

In any event, Lang, acknowledging that representatives of the magic assemblage might not always be the most reliable collaborators, entertains the possible implications of Kellar's stories, if they were true: "if we admit the theory of intentional imposture by saints, *angakut*, Zulu medicine-men, mediums, and the rest, we must grant that a trick which takes in a professional conjurer, like Mr. Kellar, is a trick well worthy of examination" (Lang 1896: 77–78). Even if ritual marvels are tricks, Lang argues, that trickery itself could provide an anthropological window into human intelligence, rather than being taken as a reflection of human stupidity. This line of reasoning puts Lang much closer to the perspective on artifice eventually developed by Alfred Gell (1988: 7): "Superior intelligence manifests itself in the technical strategies of enchantment . . . The manipulation of desire, terror, wonder, cupidity, fantasy, vanity, an inexhaustible list of human passions, offers an equally inexhaustible field for the expression of technical ingenuity."

From a Gellian perspective, magical effects might exhibit independent but convergent evolutionary patterns because they are a *technical* solution to a *technical* problem: given the cognitive and perceptual capacities of an audience along with the physical and expressive capacities of a performer, the possibilities for producing enchanting paranormal effects may be "inexhaustible" but they are not limitless in variety—in fact, magicians themselves generally number the categories of effects somewhere in the range of six to nine (Lamont and Wiseman 1999: 2–6).

Gell (1996) characterizes enchanting artifice as a cognitive "trap" designed to captivate spectators and enmesh them in the artificer's agenda. No technique of enchantment exhibits this property quite so perfectly as the conjuring trick.[9] But the idea of the trick is also an analytic trap associated with a strictly truth-functional stance toward artifice, as if truth could only obtain in the absence of trickery. The more one resists the cognitive trap set by techniques of enchantment, the more this analytic trap seems to tighten. As we have seen, when observers are most convinced that they can explain 'Isawi or Spiritualist effects, they feel least compelled to exert any effort interpreting what those effects might mean. One way of loosening the hold of this analytic trap has been rewiring the analogy between primitive and modern magic.

Alexander Goldenweiser, another early proponent of a more symmetrical anthropological approach to magic, suggested preserving an analogy between entertainment and occult magician, but repolarizing it in ways that would unsettle any easy dichotomization between primitive and modern cosmologies. In a chapter on occult magic, he describes "the great popularity of modern magicians . . . in the midst of a matter-of-fact world" as a form of "latter-day supernaturalism" (1937: 212–14). He imagines a detractor of this view asking, " 'But what bearing has this on magic? . . . Surely everyone knows that these magicians are merely tricksters.' " To this, Goldenweiser replies, "True enough; but we do not know how they perform their tricks" and during a magic show we accept our "visual experiences . . . as facts, not tricks. It is to this that our amazement is due." Recasting the Tylorian narrative of linear (but troubled) disenchantment, Goldenweiser portrays entertainment magic as a rather positive, playful form of persisting enchantment or of reënchantment.

This *persistence view* of enchantment, as we might call it, has appealed to many scholars, particularly outside anthropology in fields such as performance and cultural studies, who have posited some degree of historical continuity between primitive and modern magical practices. Kirby (1974: 6), for instance, argues that "many popular entertainments may be traced back to this single source—the rituals of shamanism" and that "illusionism like that of the stage magician was originally proof of the shaman's supernatural control over death" (8). Rogan Taylor (1985) intricately argues that "show business as we know it has derived directly from the performances of the ancient shamans" (44), in which " 'the show' was created by taking those elements of the healing séance most suited to becoming merely entertainment, and *inflating* them disproportionately. The most suitable bits for this purpose" included "lots of tricks and stunts, *legerdemain*, feats of escapology," and so forth (56). In a particularly Tylorian turn of phrase, the cultural historian Simon During (2002: 26) suggests that "magic's survival [as entertainment] in the current era signifies a residual irrationality."[10]

Hubert and Mauss offer an intriguing variation on this motif, framing the figure of the magician as an archetype for the formation of social relations. They classify entertainment magicians, along with ventriloquists and jugglers, as types of "persons who attract public attention, fear and mistrust because of . . . extraordinary dexterity" (Hubert and Mauss 1902–1903: 23), and hence become objects of (occult) magical belief. The approach to the ritual artifice of magical practices that they go on to articulate set an interpretative standard in cultural anthropology, followed by Lévi-Strauss (1963), Taussig (1999, 2003), and others. Hubert and Mauss focus on what they call "the moment of prestidigitation," when a shaman uses "cunning legerdemain" to extract from a sick person's body "a small pebble that he claims is the spell causing sickness" (1902–1903: 124). From their perspective, the trick is a communicative strategy to represent the otherwise invisible cure and, moreover, model the healing process.[11]

Note that Hubert and Mauss use a term here, "prestidigitation," that strongly connotes modern theatrical entertainment (see Pels 2014: 235), and furthermore refer to onlookers as "impassioned spectators, immobilized by the spectacle, absorbed and hypnotized." Crapanzano (1995) shows that whatever the illusions the ritual magician creates are, for Hubert and Mauss, they must also be Durkheimian collective representations: "it is because society gestures that magical belief imposes itself and because of magical belief that society gestures," they write (Hubert and Mauss 1902–1903: 135). By this view, the conjuring trick becomes not only a vital means for establishing intersubjectivity, but also the quintessential expression of human sociality.[12]

If one symmetrizing gesture involves positively recasting the figure of the modern magician as a persistently enchanted heir to shamanic mysteries, another has been to recast shamanic performers as predecessors of modern magicians' disenchantments, valued indigenously as quasi-secular entertainers as much as religious figures. We might call this a *precedence view*. For instance, one of the few anthropologists to ever observe the Shaking Tent ceremony, Irving Hallowell, was struck by the entertainment value it manifestly held among the Berens River Saulteaux community in Manitoba. "I believe that the Saulteaux themselves are not insensible to the esthetic qualities in these performances," he wrote (Hallowell 1942: 87).[13] "The Indians appear to *enjoy* a performance where there is a great variety of [spirits] present, where the spirits are well characterized and where there are funny things said. This requires considerable artistic skill on the part of the conjurer" (88).[14] Clearly a correlate of this view is also attributing a much higher degree of reflexivity to non-modern, non-Western spectators than Tylor could have countenanced. Along these lines, Rasmussen (1938: 125–26) portrays Eastern Greenlanders as great admirers of the angokot's amazing skills, but who are nevertheless curious and knowledgeable about techniques of trickery, and retain an attitude of deep skepticism.

From Lang onward, there have been a number of efforts within anthropology to preserve an analogy between enchanted occult magic and the disenchanted modern magic assemblage. These efforts have sought to acknowledge the types of recurrent cross-cultural patterns that this analogy could be useful for revealing, while chipping away at the evolutionist framework that made Tylor's comparisons so invidious. Still, whether they emphasize the enchanted qualities of modern secular magic or the disenchanted qualities of primitive occult magic, it appears difficult for advocates of a more symmetrical approach to magic to ever fully escape the dualism of the magical/rational binary. Inevitably, the persistence of enchantment and the precedence of disenchantment views seek to subvert a dichotomy by inverting it, but an implicit antinomy remains.

Specters of the Past

The storied legacy of the Spirit Cabinet effect in Western magic continues to this day. Harry Houdini, perhaps the most famous magician of all time, distinguished himself by performing Davenport-inspired feats of untying and unbinding, resignified in terms of singular physical prowess (Silverman 1996: 41–42). In 1910, Houdini succeeded in tracking down the one remaining Davenport, Ira, in Mayville, New York (figure 20). "As Houdini sat, notebook in hand, Ira took a long piece of rope and divulged to him, thrillingly, perhaps the best-kept secret in modern magic"—the rope-tie that the brothers used to slip quickly out of—and, more importantly, back into—their knots in the Spirit Cabinet (Silverman 1996: 170).

Houdini was a paradoxical repository for this secret. On the one hand, he wielded his fame and professional credibility as an illusionist as a weapon against Spiritualism. He made the exposure of mediums a personal crusade, attending séances in disguise to confront mediums face to face, and writing a book-length exposé, *A Magician among the Spirits* (Houdini 1924). Some modern magicians even contend that he was assassinated by Spiritualist operatives (Kalush and Sloman 2006). On the other hand, his feats of unbinding and escape have mystical, even shamanic resonances in the eyes of many scholars (e.g., Mangan 2007: 145–50; Taylor 1985). Some have read his performances through the lens of class conflict, arguing that the muscular physicality of his escapes from prison cells, bank vaults, and straitjackets expressed the wishes of working people to cast off the shackles of carceral capitalism (Cook 2001: 257–58; Mangan 2007: 155–56).[15] Perhaps Houdini's equivocal status as both myth-buster and myth-maker made him the perfect recipient for the Davenports' secret. His renown also gave him a place in the anthropological record: whereas Tylor had referred to the unbinding component of the Shaking Tent complex as "The Davenport

Figure 20. Mediumistic sensation Ira Davenport (*left*) meets admiring illusionist
Harry Houdini (*right*), 1910. Library of Congress, LC-USZ62-66398.

Trick," by the mid-twentieth century, an anthropologist like Cooper (1944:
66) would be calling it "the Houdini trick."

Today, the Spirit Cabinet has become a standard stage magic effect,
which I saw performed at least a dozen times during my fieldwork, often
in a burlesque register, playfully suggesting a homoerotic sexual situation
between a male volunteer invited into the "cabinet" (a more easily portable curtain is generally used nowadays) and the male magician-medium.[16]
Some performers made tongue-in-cheek allusions to Hollywood horror
movies, framing the performance as a supernatural spoof. Alain, the Afro-
Antillean magician I mention in the introduction, accompanied his rendition of the effect with quips about "Island voodoo," playing with French
audiences' stereotypes about the Caribbean.

Ultimately, the ironic, playful, and fundamentally skeptical stance toward the paranormal implicit in these contemporary renditions of the Spirit Cabinet by Parisian illusionists seems to starkly contrast with the way that anthropologists traditionally imagined the solemnity of rituals like the Shaking Tent. But, as my discussion of Tylor and his commentators shows, the self-reflexivity of the modern magic assemblage has been a foil against which anthropology has historically constructed ideas about the enchantedness of ritual and fallacy of artifice. So much so that it can be difficult to infer from the ethnographic record what the Shaking Tent once might have been without the imposition of the adventitious analogue of stage magic. In the next chapter, I describe in greater detail how the discipline has contended directly and indirectly with this beguiling analogy, reworking theories of magic while, in the process, developing new approaches to cross-cultural comparison.

SIX

The Magic of Analogy

On January 5, 1894, leading American anthropologist Daniel Brinton presented his extensive research on the esoteric powers of Mesoamerican *naguals*—shape-shifting shamans—to the American Philosophical Society in Philadelphia. A self-proclaimed "Americanist,"[1] Brinton depicted what he called "the cult of nagualism" as a regionally pervasive institution, and identified its "powerful though hidden hand" in every indigenous revolt "against the Spanish domination during the three centuries of its existence" (1894: 39). After presenting detailed ethnohistorical and ethnolinguistic evidence from numerous Mexican and Central American tribes, Brinton took a step back to situate his account of nagualism in a global, comparative frame: "All who have any acquaintance with the folk-lore of the world are aware that the notion of men and women having the power to change themselves into beasts is as wide as superstition itself and older than history" (67). He then asked a deceptively simple question: why?

"It will not do to take the short and easy road of saying" that the marvelous accounts of shape-shifting sorcery "are all lies and frauds," Brinton told his audience (1894: 68). "The evidence is too abundant for us to doubt that there was skillful jugglery among the proficients in the occult arts among those nations" where such sorcery was reputed. "They could rival their colleagues in the East Indies and Europe, if not surpass them." The "colleagues" Brinton was referring to were entertainment magicians, or illusionists. Here, the otherwise fastidious scholar presented neither corroborating evidence nor supporting citations. He didn't need to. By that time, Euro-American intellectuals could largely take it for granted that many non-Western peoples were kept in the thralldom of primitive magical thinking by ritual experts adept at conjuring tricks—tricks not so different from those they could themselves see illusionists, white or less frequently Asian, performing in the popular theatrical venues of their day.

Why, that very same year, a young Harry Houdini was touring the American vaudeville circuit with his first breakout illusion, "The Metamorphosis"—a title quite explicitly suggesting shape-shifting transformations. After inviting a committee of volunteers to laboriously tie his hands with rope, seal him in a cloth sack, and lock him inside a trunk, the magician would almost instantaneously reappear onstage, completely liberated, in the same spot where his wife and partner, Bess, had just been standing. He would then dramatically reveal her tied up and imprisoned in his place.[2] It was a visually arresting effect, perfectly epitomizing stage magic's heyday: easy to marvel at, virtually impossible to explain. Although they called it "Metamorphosis," technically speaking what the Houdinis really presented was an effect of transposition, not transformation;[3] most of their publicity materials emphasized the ability to "exchange" places "in 3 seconds" or less (figure 21). Highlighting the short time interval needed for the partners to switch places called attention to precisely the things the Houdinis wanted credit for: skill and dexterity, not supernatural power.[4]

Brinton and Houdini may well have crossed paths a year earlier at the 1893 Chicago Columbian Exposition, where the anthropologist was delivering three lectures—including the International Congress of Anthropology's presidential address (see Hinsley 2016)—and the magician was performing on the midway, presenting an early version of "The Metamorphosis" with his brother Theo as an assistant. Of course, Brinton wouldn't have needed to actually see a performance by Houdini or any of the untold other illusionists crisscrossing North America at the time. The widely publicized feats of these entertainers could be known by reputation alone. Brinton reasoned that naguals and their shamanic counterparts in other cultural traditions used tricks—jugglery, as he puts it—that could rival and surpass the likes of the man who would become the world-renowned "Handcuff King." Given how deceptive we know illusionists' tricks to be, Brinton asked, "is there anything incredible in the reports of spectators" (1894: 68) who attribute marvelous abilities to indigenous shamans no doubt employing similar artifice?

Brinton's use of the term *spectators* in place of, say, *observers* or *witnesses*—much less *participants*—suggests that he was doing more with the glancing comparison to illusionism than just characterizing the types of effects he thought naguals might produce. He was importing a conceptual model of spectacle and applying it to a system of ritual, displacing what Tambiah calls an orientation of "participation" with an orientation of "causality" that "involves a particular kind of distancing, affective neutrality and abstraction

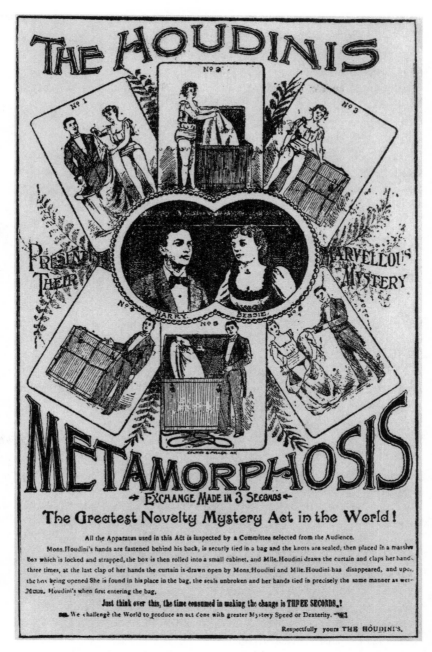

Figure 21. Advertisement for the Houdinis' Metamorphosis effect, circa 1895.
"Exchange Made in 3 Seconds." Library of Congress, LC-USZ62-112438.

to events in the world" (1990: 105). In the process, he also changed registers and scales. His methodical areal comparisons between Aztec, Maya, Mixtec, and Zapotec nagualism gave way to a more audacious comparative leap from indigenous shaman to Western showman, connoting a contrast between dangerous charlatanism and harmless entertainment. This invidious comparison set in motion a flurry of additional associations:

> The tricks of cutting oneself or others, of swallowing broken glass, of handling venomous reptiles, are well-known performances of the sect of the Aissaoua in northern Africa, and nowadays one does not have to go off the boulevards of Paris to see them repeated. The phenomena of thought transference, of telepathy, of clairvoyance, of spiritual rappings, do but reiterate under the clear light of the close of the nineteenth century the mystical thaumaturgy with which these children of nature were familiar centuries ago in the New World . . . So long as many intelligent and sensible people among ourselves find all the explanations of these modern phenomena inadequate and unsatisfactory, we may patiently wait for a complete solution of those of a greater antiquity. (Brinton 1894: 68–69)

Brinton was bringing together a wide range of cross-cultural examples that he considered to share a common element with nagualism: trickery, real or imagined, professed or imputed. In so doing, he wove a skein of conceptual associations between a variety of ethnographic cases and the Western settings in which illusionists, Spiritualists, and even the 'Isawa ("Aissaoua") had come to exhibit their marvelous talents, During's *magic assemblage*, that "loose cluster of entertainment attractions based on effects, tricks, dexterities, and illusions" (2002: 215) that reached a kind of cultural apogee around the time Brinton was writing.

As I have shown in previous chapters, in part because of the notoriety they achieved, the 'Isawa and Spiritualists attracted the attention of both Western illusionists keen to debunk their supernatural feats and Western anthropologists keen to explain how forms of magic they classed as "primitive" could gain such sway in their own "modern" culture—"under the clear light of the close of the nineteenth century," in Brinton's words. Both illusionists and anthropologists largely concurred: all the associated paranormal effects were products of charlatanism, but in the Barnumesque logic of show business (Cook 2001), of course any critical attention could only bring the performers greater notoriety.

In hindsight, we may find it easy to dismiss Brinton's analogy between the modern magician and the Mesoamerican nagual, overdetermined as it was by his fervently racialist and evolutionist outlook (see Stocking 1982). Brinton, however, was traveling a well-worn intellectual track. Myriad nineteenth-century ethnographers and anthropologists had already established conceptual connections between non-Western religious practices that they classified as primitive magic and Western entertainment magic, which came to figure implicitly as a correspondingly modern alternative.

Operations of analogy were key to the way the magic assemblage and its diverse and sundry attractions came to factor into anthropological accounts of primitive magic. Moreover, anthropology's modernism hinged on a conviction that analogical reasoning was a crutch that any real science would ultimately transcend. To better understand both how analogy functioned in constructing anthropological representations of magic, and the ineluctable role that it continues to play in anthropological reasoning in spite of discredited positivisms, requires further anatomizing its cognitive features. For this, I turn to the elegant and influential model developed by cognitive psychologist Dedre Gentner (1983) and her colleagues.[5]

According to Gentner's model, people make analogies by mapping structural patterns from a familiar domain (the *base*) onto a novel domain (the *target*). Analogies convey "that two situations or domains share relational structure despite arbitrary degrees of difference in the objects that make [them] up" (Gentner and Markman 1997: 46). As I show in figure 22, those common relational patterns can be abstracted away from specific analogical mappings, giving rise to concepts that can be applied in new contexts (Gentner and Namy 1999). Structural alignment not only helps identify relational similarities across disparate cases; it can also make differences salient; Gentner and Markman (1997: 49–50) argue that the most salient differences are the ones they call *alignable* in respect to a close structural correspondence between matching systems. In my view, this "disanalogy" (Shelley 2002b) or "negative analogy" (Hesse 1967) can, like positive analogy, also powerfully contribute to concept formation.[6]

I have shown how modern stage magic became a vexed base domain in ethnographic analogies with ritual practices such as the 'Isawi hadra, Native North American Shaking Tent, or Mesoamerican nagualism as their targets. In analogies connecting the Western magic assemblage and various magico-religious ritual traditions, cosmological outlooks of non-modern enchantment and modern disenchantment emerge as alignable differences. Just like a positive analogy, this ideologically charged disanalogy, sustained across multiple cases, yielded an abstraction, or rather a set of nesting abstractions. At the narrowest ethnographic scale, it constituted a "structured representation" (Markman and Gentner 1997: 363) of particular non-Western peoples

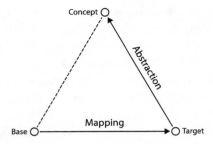

Figure 22. Gentner's model of analogy. Illustration by Insil Choi.

or magico-religious traditions as cognitively deviant; more broadly it provided a basis for anthropological conceptualizations of primitive magic in terms of erroneous explanations and false causal beliefs (Tambiah 1990).

In this chapter, I describe this conceptualization and trace some of its lingering intellectual consequences. Moreover, I show how the anthropological magic concept has evolved in tandem with changing understandings of how analogy should ideally function in mediating cross-cultural comparisons. The style of reasoning that anthropologists like Brinton and Tylor engaged in—using cross-cultural analogies to build a category that paves the way for further analogy-making—remains an essential, albeit epistemologically fraught, feature of anthropological argumentation. Even as anthropologists have become much more circumspect about the kinds of analogies they draw, I argue that the concept of magic continues to bear traces of an earlier history of analogical mappings connecting it with the Western magic assemblage.

Disciplining Magic

Tylor's methodological statements accorded a prominent place to analogy. What he called "the similarity and consistency" (1873: 6) of human nature made a correspondence of patterns inevitable across superficial ethnic or cultural differences, both horizontally, between comparably developed peoples, and vertically, between differentially developed peoples. Horizontally, culture could "be studied with especial fitness in comparing races near the same grade of civilization. Little respect need be had in such comparisons for date in history or for place on the map." Vertically, "even when it comes to comparing barbarous hordes with civilized nations, the consideration thrusts itself upon our minds, how far item after item of the life of the lower races passes into analogous proceedings of the higher" (6–7). Thus, in the category of "intellectual culture," magic, religion, and science play analogous explanatory roles, but at different "grades of civilization."

Tylor fit his account of differential reactions to the "untying trick," from primitive credulity to modern incredulity, into an evolutionary framework using relationships of both analogy and disanalogy. On the one hand, the analogy between Western Spiritualists and Native American Shaking Tent operators provided the basis for his theory of survivals. On the other, the disanalogy with normative entertainment magic substantiated a vision of progress in terms of the kind of rationalization and disenchantment that make illusionists' tricks harmless fun. The way entertainment magicians provoked audiences to seek explanations for their mystifying tricks helped provide a model for theories of false causal belief as the essence of instrumental, ritual magic. Evans-Pritchard (1965: 20) calls these "intellectualist" theories of magic that take "it for granted that primitive man is essentially rational, though his attempts to explain puzzling phenomena are crude and fallacious."

Continuing in this intellectualist vein, James Frazer wrote that "the fatal flaw of magic lies not in its general assumption of a succession of events determined by law, but in its total misconception of the nature of the particular laws which govern that succession" (1900: 62). From this intellectualist perspective, the explanatory practices of science, which entertainment magic had emulated and absorbed, constituted a principal base domain for analogical comparisons with ritual magic. Like Tylor, Frazer posited a disanalogy between the way scientists and occult magicians drew analogies: "the principles of association," he wrote, are "absolutely essential to the working of the human mind. Legitimately applied they yield science; illegitimately applied they yield magic, the bastard sister of science." Tylor and Frazer's intellectualist account of instrumental magic as the corruption of causal reasoning by contaminating analogies established the framework in which subsequent generations of anthropologists would address the topic and amend the concept (Tambiah 1990: 45–46).[7] It also reflected a style of argument by analogy that anthropologists would soon widely reject.

Intellectualist approaches relied on analogies with Western practices such as science and stage magic that emphasized explanation via cause-and-effect reasoning. If these analogies were merely dubious, they could be easily revised or exchanged for others. But, insofar as intellectualism emerged from a paradigm itself committed to a particular kind of cross-cultural comparison, the problems ran deeper. Franz Boas devastatingly showed that, when they were able to "find an analogon of single traits of culture among distant peoples" (1896: 901), social evolutionists moved too quickly to the assumption that they were dealing with examples of the same thing. Evolutionists, he argued, committed themselves to the fallacious premise that "the same ethnological phenomena are always due to the same causes" (903). Because of the deductive style of evolutionist research, in which cross-cultural examples populated categories predetermined by the researcher's theoretical priorities, it was simply too easy to mistake superficial resemblances between the objects making up different domains for analogies in terms of deep relational structures. But Boas did not stop there, attacking "the wider generalization that the sameness of ethnological phenomena found in diverse regions is proof that the human mind obeys the same laws everywhere" (903). Boas had exposed the vicious circularity involved in so many evolutionist arguments: without the assumption of universal human nature, comparisons of the sort that Tylor and Brinton drew suddenly seemed lacking for warrant. They were no less chimerical than the evolutionists alleged magic to be.

Boas did not, however, rule cross-cultural comparisons entirely out. Rather, he cautioned that "before extended comparisons are made, the comparability of the material must be proved" (904). Just because cultures share superficial resemblances between objects (institutions, practices, beliefs, etc.), it does not necessarily follow that those objects are enmeshed in the same underlying relational patterns of meaning or value. The only way to ensure comparability would be through intensive ethnography that carefully documented the place of particular objects—ritual magic, say—in the overall skein of a culture, with careful attention to the locally specific forms that human nature itself might take. The paradigm shift to Boasian cultural relativism coincided with a growing emphasis on long-term fieldwork by theoretically trained ethnographers as the standard form of anthropological knowledge production, ushering in a new era of holistic, monographic ethnography.

The gradual development of the anthropological magic concept in the twentieth century mirrored these trends. As researchers came to focus more on the place of instrumental magic in specific cultural systems, observing firsthand how it was integrated into the flow of everyday life, intellectualism gradually receded from favor. Freed of procrustean models of progress, ethnographers found ways to account for magic as productive rather than merely harmful. Malinowski (1948: 2) argued that "Tylor's view of primitive religion, important as it was . . . made early man too contemplative and rational. Recent fieldwork, done by specialists, shows us the savage interested" in practical activities "rather . . . than brooding" over supernatural phenomena. Drawing on his work in Melanesia with Trobriand Island sea-farers and gardeners, Malinowski (1922, 1935) proposed a functionalist account of magic, arguing that magical practices do not substitute for scientific or technical knowledge, but rather fulfill emotional and psychological needs alongside practical know-how. Soon after, Evans-Pritchard (1937) described the way magic regulated social order among the Sudanese Azande. In his structural functionalist account, witchcraft accusations were a way of policing deviance, and control over the oracular systems used in adjudicating those accusations served as a basis for political power.

For Malinowski and Evans-Pritchard, magical practices were not fundamentally antithetical to rational thinking, but rather coexisted with rationality and responded to psychological and social problems beyond strictly intellectual/cognitive considerations. By the 1980s, any vestiges of the idea that instrumental magic was somehow "primitive" seemed to be radically overturned by ethnographers—Jeanne Favret-Saada (1980) in France and Tanya Luhrmann (1989b) in England—showing that magical practices and beliefs in contemporary Europe conformed to functionalist and structural functionalist models previously developed in Melanesia and Africa.

Participant observation also created new forms of knowledge and evidence about magical practices and beliefs. Methodologically, it became standard for ethnographers to not only observe magical practices firsthand, but to a greater or lesser extent, also take an active part in the magical systems they studied. For instance, Evans-Pritchard (1976: 244) reported, "when I was among the Azande, I got to accept their ideas about witchcraft . . . In their culture, in the set of ideas I then lived in, I accepted them; in a kind of way I believed them . . . I had to act as though I trusted the Zande oracles and therefore to give assent to their dogma of witchcraft, whatever reservations I might have . . . If one must act as though one believed, one ends in believing, or half-believing as one acts." In contrast with the intellectualist contempt for magic, these newer studies, grounded in ethnographic fieldwork, came titillatingly close to embracing native viewpoints, though often within the reassuring frame of liminally "suspended disbelief" (Kapferer 2001) on the part of the researcher and, by extension, the reader. Evans-Pritchard (1976: 244) makes it clear that he left any credence behind in the field: "In my own culture . . . I rejected, and reject, Zande notions of witchcraft."

By contrast, Jeanne Favret-Saada's (1980) classic monograph on witchcraft in rural France hinges on the researcher herself getting "caught," as she puts it, in the system she studies, principally as a terrorized victim of witchcraft, but also as a potential unbewitcher, from whom bewitched people seek support. She registers the shock and trauma of an ethnographer inextricably implicated, stripped of disciplinary dispassion and fully exposed to the "spiritual insecurity" (Ashforth 2005) of witchcraft.

More recently, Favret-Saada (2015: 97) has written that this work on witchcraft "gradually led [her] to reconsider the notion of affect and the importance of exploring it, both as a way of addressing a critical dimension of fieldwork (the state of being affected)" and "as a way of rethinking anthropology itself." She contrasts this approach to canonical anthropological projects that depict witchcraft as incapable of affecting anthropologists—because it is not real, and because they do not, therefore, participate in it. "And so these anthropologists . . . engaged in an absurd attempt to recreate the Great Divide between 'Us' and 'Them' ('we' also believed in witches but that was three hundred years ago, when 'we' were 'them'), and thereby to protect the ethnologist, this acultural entity whose mind only contained true propositions, from contamination by his object" (101).

Favret-Saada invokes Evans-Pritchard as both an inspiration and an opponent, arguing that his work was still beholden to evolutionist premises. Nevertheless, she situates her work in a lineage that he mediates as an antecedent, which therefore traces its way back to intellectualism. It is in this same sense that Evans-Pritchard credits Tylor and Frazer for setting the anthropology of magic in motion by propounding theories, "thereby inviting logical analysis of their contents and the testing of them against recorded ethnological fact and in field research" (1965: 122). The work of subsequent ethnographers gradually "disciplined" (Bazerman 2012: 261) the concept of magic, working to purge the kind of "spontaneous" (ibid.) cultural associations—most pertinently, the conceptual connection with the magic assemblage—that had seeped into Victorian intellectualism. By taking part in magical practices, working more closely with local categories of what counted as magical, situating magical practices in the context of other activities, and identifying comparable practices in Western settings, they gave the anthropological magic concept a much higher degree of theoretical precision.

Paradoxically, the increasing precision with which anthropologists discussed magic did not necessarily contribute to building a more general theory.[8] By the mid-1960s, Evans-Pritchard could write that "to try to understand magic as an idea in itself, what is the essence of it, as it were, is a hopeless task" (1965: 111). He argued that magic could only become "intelligible when it is viewed not only in relation to empirical activities but also in relation to other beliefs, as part of a system of thought," and "the system itself making sense only in relation to other institutional systems, as part of a wider set of relations" (112).[9] Although magic remained a topic of vital concern, like many anthropological concepts, it now occupied a liminal status, hovering between the specificity of highly detailed ethnographic cases and the generality of an ever-elusive overarching theory.

Middle-Range Magic

Balancing competing commitments to cultural relativism and cross-cultural comparison, anthropologists after Boas came to adopt an approach of cautious generalization via qualified analogies, otherwise known as *middle-range theory*. Expounding on this approach, Clifford Geertz writes that anthropology "progresses conceptually" when ethnographers "take a line of theoretical attack developed in connection with one exercise in ethnographic interpretation and employ it in another, pushing it forward to greater precision and broader relevance" (1973: 25–26). These lines of attack are distilled or encapsulated in concepts—symbol, revolution, ritual, and culture itself are Geertz's examples, but we can easily add magic to this list. Such "theoretical ideas," he continues, "are not created wholly anew in each study" but rather "adopted from other, related studies, and, refined in the process, applied to new interpretive problems" as long as they remain useful (27).

Sociologist Robert Merton seemed to have something slightly different than this in mind when he coined the phrase "theories of the middle range" to describe "theories intermediate to the minor working hypotheses evolved in abundance during the day-by-day routines of research, and the all-inclusive speculations comprising a master conceptual scheme from which it is hoped to derive a very large number of empirically observed uniformities of social behavior" (1949: 5). Merton maintained that relying on middle-range theory was a necessary step for a relatively young discipline such as sociology moving toward the ultimate goal of generating master conceptual schemes. "Perhaps sociology is not yet ready for its Einstein because it has not yet found its Kepler," he wrote (7).

For a time, this Mertonian ideal of theoretical progress appealed to cultural anthropologists as well (Eggan 1954: 748). But Geertz's cynicism about progress proved a bellwether. Eschewing the positivistic, natural science model in favor of a humanistic, hermeneutic approach, Geertz writes, "Anthropology, or at least interpretive anthropology, is a science whose progress is marked less by a perfection of consensus than by a refinement of debate. What gets better is the precision with which we vex each other" (1973: 29). At the same time that anthropologists seek to identify recurrent patterns of behavior across cultural differences, they also search for disconfirming cultural examples that thwart efforts—their own, but also those of other disciplines—to make universalizing claims, precisely as Malinowski and Evans-Pritchard amended and ultimately overturned the intellectualist theory of magic.

To connect together case studies from different cultural contexts in order to make generalizations or to reveal the limits of generalizability, anthropologists need mediating concepts like "magic," which serve as the frame and conduit for cross-cultural comparison.[10] How exactly are concepts "adopted" from one case, "applied" to another, and "refined in the process," in the Geertzian conception of middle-range theory? Essentially what is at play here is the production of analogies between different case studies via concept-mediated comparison. These analogies may emerge dyadically, as "the relation that the anthropologist builds between two cultures," in Roy Wagner's (1981: 9) terms. This relation results in "an analogy, or a set of analogies, that 'translates' one group of basic meanings into the other." When these analogies work, Wagner says, they serve the ethnographer "as a kind of 'lever,' the way a pole vaulter uses his pole, to catapult his comprehension beyond the limitations imposed by earlier viewpoints" (12).[11]

In addition to their own native categories, ethnographers also mobilize comparative analogues in the form of ethnographic exemplars. As Marilyn Strathern puts it, "the deployment of analogy" is "very much a part of the repertoire of comparative methods," and anthropologists "carry around in their heads examples from 'elsewhere,' using the images and languages of one thing to talk about another" (2008: 30). That elsewhere may be the ethnographer's own backyard, or it may be another ethnographer's fieldsite with which one has become vicariously acquainted. Psychologist Kevin Dunbar (1995: 386) finds that more experienced scientists make "both more analogies and more productive analogies" because "it is much easier for [them], for whom the deep features are obvious" to "map these features onto other domains." Anthropologists read widely in global ethnography precisely to achieve this facility; ethnographers trained in the discipline scan constantly for comparative analogues in cultures other than their own, both as a means of generalization and as a mode of reflexivity—the effort to make oneself aware of inadvertent distortions arising from the conscious or unconscious use of exogenous analogues.

While cautious about exaggerating the resemblance between intrapersonal and interpersonal processes of analogy-making, I am particularly interested in the role of concept-driven analogy in anthropology as a collective activity functioning as a system of distributed cognition (Hutchins 2012) largely mediated by textual artifacts. In the words of Charles Bazerman (2012: 259), texts are a primary medium by which individuals articulate and share their concepts within disciplines and professions and by which epistemic communities negotiate, deploy, and store their most elaborated concepts, linked within the conceptual systems of communal intellectual projects. Those inscribed social marks then are available for others to make sense of and internalize as they become cognitively enculturated into the epistemic community.

Anthropologists work collectively, as participants in a co-constructed disciplinary enterprise, to elaborate patterns of analogy shared among themselves as concepts that can be de- and recontextualized, and then entextualized (Bauman and Briggs 1990) in ethnographic writing.

The development of concepts over time through continued reapplication in successive studies yields conceptual composites that embed manifold cross-cultural comparisons. These concepts not only allow individual ethnographers to perform analogistic "pole vaults," in Wagner's terms, but they also allow groups of ethnographers to talk with each other about shared theoretical preoccupations that transcend the concrete ethnographic particulars of their individual fieldsites (Small 2009). Henrietta Moore describes how terms like "global, gender, the self and the body" function as "a kind of conceptual shorthand . . . They are domain terms that orient us towards areas of shared exchange" (2004: 73). Ultimately, these concepts, whose meanings are necessarily underspecified, allow anthropologists to connect cases, serving "to facilitate comparison, to frame contexts, levels or domains within which data—however defined—can be compared for similarities and differences" (75–76).[12]

Concepts also mediate social relationships among anthropologists, indexing intellectual kinship and lineage. Because they generally circulate with the names of their originators and principal exponents attached, using concepts is a way of mobilizing allies (however unwilling) and displaying allegiances (however wishful), not just predicating something about an ethnographic case. This leads Falcone (2013: 125) to analogize anthropological concepts and reciprocal exchange valuables, describing the hopeful italicization that writers often apply to a novel middle-range concept as a kind of *giftwrapping*, "a suggestion that the reader ought to take it, use it, and refer to its hau through citation."

Through citational recontextualization, concepts develop via what Snow, Morrill, and Anderson (2003: 187) call "extension," which "focuses on broadening the relevance of a particular concept or theoretical system to a range of empirical contexts other than those in which they were first developed or intended to be used. In this sense, theoretical extension preeminently involves the 'transferability' of theory between at least two contexts."[13] Charles Sanders Peirce offers a useful encapsulation of how analogy facilitates the process of extensional conceptual development in cross-cultural research. "In science," he writes, "a diagram or analogue of the observed fact leads on to a further analogy" (Peirce 1991: 196). Furthermore, "the relations of reason which go to the formation of such a triple relation need not be all resemblances" because contrasts and comparisons entail the same sorts of relations.[14]

From an anthropological standpoint, this process unfolds either through the comparison of two or more ethnographic cases, or through the extension of one conceptual composite to a new case (which is a mediated comparison). This constitutes a triadic relationship between a previous case (the analogical base), a new case (the analogical target), and the resulting conceptual abstraction that anticipates further mappings onto additional cases (Gentner and Smith 2012: 113; Markman and Gentner 2001: 235). By Peirce's account, discovering the limitations to theoretical extension (the unextendability of one's concepts to new cases) can also lead to conceptual refinement, hence theoretical development.

This process would look something like figure 23, which depicts what I call an *analogical ladder*. Each step of the ladder represents an individual ethnographic case study that incorporates an analogical mapping from a prior case or previously synthesized conceptual composite, and generates an abstraction, contributing to the development of a middle-range concept via stepwise extension. The upward vector on the left does not necessarily indicate *progress* in the sense of concepts becoming more accurate or true, but it does indicate, at the very least, a concept's increased use/usefulness, as manifest by extension (to new fieldsites) and circulation (among additional anthropologists).

Because ethnographic studies are richly textured skeins of association, there would be a variety of longer and shorter ladders like this, with steps of different intervals, converging toward any ethnographic text from multiple directions (and also potentially radiating from it). The diagram is simply an ideal typic visualization of relationships between ethnographic texts that inter-refer within a particular tradition of conceptual development. In this sense, the ladder of analogies I have traced in describing the development of the anthropological magic concept is merely adumbrative, privileging a few key, representative texts, and making irregular connections between them.

Key to the transferability of concepts across contexts is the operation of positing analogistic resemblance between those contexts, all the while maintaining a crucial element of disanalogy. Anthropological "analogies both conserve and extend" but "the power of thinking one thing through

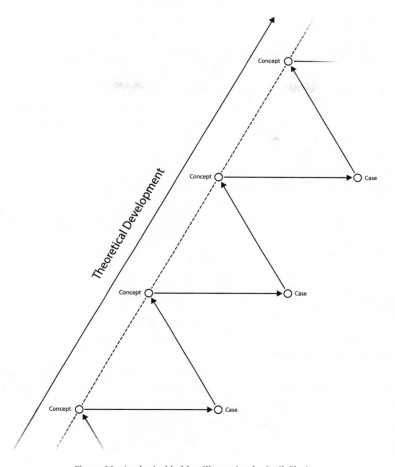

Figure 23. Analogical ladder. Illustration by Insil Choi.

another" requires "keeping their ancestry apart" (Strathern 2007b: 91). As a result, along with conservation, there must also be dissipation: to compare similarities across fundamentally different cases inevitably entails disregarding certain features of earlier cases, whether or not they are mappable. For instance, Beidelman (1990: 623) faults Luhrmann's only partial use of Evans-Pritchard's Zande study as a base domain in her research on contemporary British witchcraft: "Luhrmann appears fond of citing Evans-Pritchard and draws heavily on some of his ideas. Yet nowhere does she mention that Evans-Pritchard also demonstrated how Zande beliefs . . . enable some to exploit, dominate, and intimidate others." Perhaps, but Luhrmann's

Persuasions of the Witch's Craft remains a historic achievement because of the way it extended the anthropological magic concept to strikingly new ethnographic contexts. As new ethnographic analogies conserve some relational patterns, they inevitably allow others to fade away.

Diverging slightly from Peirce's remarks on scientific analogy, my diagram of an analogical ladder begins in the lower left-hand corner with concept rather than a case. On one level, I do this to emphasize the continuity of conceptual development in the form of a dotted line—an issue of particular concern to anthropologists, who, like members of any discipline, often envision the intellectual history of their field in such terms. On a deeper level, I do this to illustrate an argument that theorists of qualitative methods have made about conceptual origination: however much ethnographers may idealize the discovery of entirely new concepts as the supreme act of theoretical development, it is exceedingly rare (Snow, Morrill, and Anderson 2003: 186–87; Timmermans and Tavory 2012: 168). I won't go so far as to say that it is impossible, but I want to emphasize how common it is for concepts—in the form of theoretical concerns—to precede the first case in any analogical ladder. As Emerson, Fretz, and Shaw (2011: 198) write, "data are never pure but, rather, are imbued with, and structured by, concepts in the first place." Maxwell (1992: 287) concurs, "all observation and description are based on theory, even if this theory is implicit or common sense."

Poole (1986: 429) calls the cultural factors that impact the kinds of analogies anthropologists draw and the base domains they select as relevant for comparison *prefigurations*, "those often diffuse assumptions, interests, images, and theories that shape what we find to be intriguing, important, puzzling, or problematic, and, thus, central to our analytic concerns in probing the significance of particular aspects of cultural, psychological, and social phenomena." According to this perspective, all cross-cultural analogies are prefigured somehow or other, whether they are drawn by casual ethnographers (such as colonial officials) or academically trained participant observers, overdetermined by prejudicial ideology or anthropological theory.[15] In this sense, the way I have chosen to depict the relationship between ethnographic cases and theoretical concepts, with the former following the latter, is more true to the actual practice of qualitative research, with all its prefigurational peril.[16]

If analogies are to produce real knowledge, they must be carefully scrutinized. Wagner writes that if an ethnographer "intends his analogies to be no analogies at all, but an objective description of the culture, he will make every effort to refine them into a closer and closer approximation of his experience" until his "analogies seem more appropriate or 'accurate'" (1981: 18–19).[17] An ideal of analogies that asymptotically converge with natives' concepts is the logical upshot of Boasian relativism. In previous chapters, I have mostly been concerned with patterns of analogy-making that did not aspire to this standard. Detailing some of the prefigurations that preceded and accompanied qualitative research on primitive magic in Western anthropology, I have particularly focused on situations where scientific objectives appeared to be subsumed within the broader ideological agenda and racialist rationale of Euro-American colonialism. These prefigurations created a kind of conceptual inertia, which persisted even as intellectualism was ultimately overturned.

Presto! Theory!

Even as we move along an analogical ladder leading decisively away from an intellectualist theory of magic (and the analogies with stage magic that I suggest helped shape it), the anthropological concept of magic continues to bear traces of its early ancestry, its prefigurations. For instance, Hubert and Mauss, who otherwise categorically broke with the basic premises of intellectualism, nevertheless asserted that "magic is essentially a practical art, and magicians have carefully used their know-how, sleight-of-hand, and manual dexterity. It is the domain of pure production, *ex nihilo*, accomplishing with words and gestures what technique accomplishes through labor" (1902: 143). Even if magic is a technique of sorts, "it is always the easiest technique. It avoids effort, because it successfully replaces reality with images. It does nothing, or next to nothing, but it makes people believe everything."

We might call this a "Presto!" theory of magic.

Emphasizing elements of trickery, Hubert and Mauss suggest a strong resemblance between the ritual magician and the stage magician, who, with a wave of the wand and a quasi-cabalistic utterance, effortlessly pulls a rabbit from a hat. *That* kind of magic, magic assemblage magic, is what Roland Barthes describes as "the aesthetic form of work," a particularly modern "fantasy that erases all brutality from labor" culturally attuned to the conditions of industrial capitalism (1957: 177–78).[18] But is that *really* what *real* magicians do, or just the role that Robert-Houdin (himself a clockmaker-craftsman by training who married into a wealthy family of bourgeois industrialists) thought illusionists should play?

From Malinowski we know that Trobriand magic rituals, for instance, far from being the effortless production of something from nothing, require significant investments of resources, time, and ostentatious labor. He explains that "magic is a systematising, regulating, and controlling influence in garden work," which "also imposes on the tribe a good deal of extra work, of apparently unnecessary, hampering taboos and regulations" (Malinowski 1922: 60). It also requires "exact remembrance of a spell, unimpeachable performance of the rite, unswerving adhesion to the taboos and observances which shackle the magician" (Malinowski 1948: 65). And yet, almost a century later we find another brilliant Melanesianist, Alfred Gell, espousing a similar version of the "Presto!" theory. "The defining feature of 'magic' as an ideal technology," he writes, "is that it is 'costless' in terms of the kinds of drudgery, hazards and investments which actual technical activity inevitably requires. Production 'by magic' is production minus the disadvantageous side-effects, such as struggle, effort, etc." (Gell 1988: 9).

The concept of "magic freezes inquiry, by tricking us into thinking we know what we are dealing with," Wiener (2013: 507) writes. This is certainly true, but the same could be said of any, if not all, anthropological concepts. The history of magic is a reminder that the concepts anthropologists use are often not entirely of their making. Anthropologists may arrive belatedly to a conversation, only to find the tenor of talk not much to their liking. However they may choose to redirect a topic, contours of the original dialogue may remain embedded in the very terms of discussion. As Bakhtin puts it, "Language is not a neutral medium that passes freely and easily into the private property of the speaker's intentions; it is populated—overpopulated—with the intentions of others. Expropriating it, forcing it to submit to one's own intentions and accents, is a difficult and complicated process" (1981: 294).

In the arc of time, originary analogies and their ideological prefigurations may recede toward the historical horizon and the margins of relevance. But the abstractions they generate persist as concepts. Concepts are malleable, changing as they are readapted to new analogical applications. As much as a concept can be disciplined, it can never be entirely purged of the kinds of refractory connotations that give the "Presto!" theory its enduring appeal. This is all the more so because a concept such as magic has the messy semantics of a natural language category.

Given all the problems with keeping prefigurational associations out of concepts as seemingly indispensable as magic, it seems fair to ask whether this kind of theoretical development though middle-range concepts—which always come culturally loaded—is really the best way to go about doing anthropology. Eduardo Viveiros de Castro offers what, at least on the surface, appears to be a radical critique of this entire modus operandi. Although he maintains that "comparison is . . . our primary analytic tool" (2004: 4), he is critical of comparative approaches in which "anthropological knowledge" emerges "as the result of applying concepts that are extrinsic to their object" such as "social relations, cognition, kinship, religion, politics," and so forth

(2013: 477). Instead of viewing "each culture or society as embodying a specific solution to a generic problem—or as filling a universal form (the anthropological concept) with specific contents," Viveiros de Castro emphasizes "the prospect of the problems themselves being radically diverse." In other words, instead of assuming that a handful of concepts can analogize the full spectrum of beliefs, practices, and institutions, what if anthropologists began with the assumption that no analogies might apply to a given culture?

From the perspective of the discipline as a whole, Viveiros de Castro mounts a provocative challenge. It seems to me that he isn't so much imagining that concepts shouldn't be developed and extended analogically, but that they should in the first instance originate from indigenous ways of thinking. Some have rightfully asked if this isn't just a shimmeringly reformulated version of Boasian relativism (e.g., Kelly 2014: 264). At the very least, Viveiros de Castro sounds a powerful cautionary note about the challenges of determining analogizability in cross-cultural comparison. His assertion that anthropologists should focus on "determining the problems posed by each culture, not finding solutions for the problems posed by [their] own" (Viveiros de Castro 2013: 477), strikes a particular chord for an anthropologist of Europe such as myself engaged in a project of critical intellectual history: what is it about accounts of primitive magic that has made them such a good "solution" to particular "problems" posed by the cultures of Euro-American ethnographers?

From Doubles to Dichotomies

Anthropologists have, in many ways, heeded Evans-Pritchard's warning about the anthropological magic concept, applying it with cautious circumspection to other cultures. But even as they have disciplined the concept in some areas, they have also eagerly engaged in proliferating its use in others. With time, anthropologists found their own societies teeming with magic, which seemed to pervade every paradigmatically modern institution, even science itself—not as a residual survival or occult revival, but as an integral element.

For convenience, we may again trace this tendency to Malinowski. In an offhand passage of *Coral Gardens and Their Magic*, Malinowski observes that the hopeful repetition of optimistic metaphors in the Trobriand Islanders' magical incantations closely resembles the way modern, Western advertising firms use language to sell products—even if, he jokes, "the language of Trobriand magic is . . . more direct and more honest" (1935, vol. 2: 238). With this framing, Malinowski makes it possible to perceive a parallelism between the extraordinary expectations associated with both Trobriand magic spells and European advertisements that link fetishized commodities with fantasizes of personal fulfillment. By using his conception of verbal magic to compare two seemingly incommensurable cases, Malinowski demonstrates how widely generalizable his own theory of magical language can be. And, like many ingenious cross-cultural comparisons, his argument paradoxically subverts seeming cultural differences while also reinforcing them through a kind of ironic inversion apparent, for instance, in his characterization of political propaganda as "modern savagery" (ibid.).[19]

Is advertising really an "example" of magic? A number of influential scholars have certainly agreed with Malinowski that it is (Gell 1988; Wagner 1981; Williams 1960), but how are we to know whether this isn't just an anthropological curlicue? In the words of Marilyn Strathern, "where systems appear analogous and comparison becomes feasible, the possibilities bifurcate . . . between substantive comparisons that elucidate the effects of similar practices in different contexts and metaphorical illuminations that deploy concepts derived from the study of one ethnographic arena in another" (2007a: 127). How can we tell the difference? Put differently, are these comparisons more like the kinds of analogies Tylor and Frazer attributed to modern scientists or the kind they attributed to primitive magicians? Does *that* distinction even matter?[20]

Anthropologists have found magical associations within virtually every institution distinctive of high modernity: the state (Taussig 1997), bureaucracy (Herzfeld 1992; Graeber 2015), science (Gusterson 2004; Pels 2013), the corporation (Arnould and Cayla 2015; Hagen 2015; Lépinay 2011), the fashion industry (Moeran 2015), and so forth. *Magic and Modernity*, a collection of essays edited by Birgit Meyer and Peter Pels (2003), offers a panoramic view of the myriad entanglements modern culture maintains with the magical enchantments it so vehemently disavows.[21] Consider just one example in this tradition, Laura Nader's analysis of the culture of American energy science through the lens of Malinowski's functionalist theory of magic. "While Malinowski challenged the dogma that primitive man was characterized by irrationality," she questions his assumption that "science and scientists are characterized by rationality" (Nader 1996: 273). Just as "Malinowski found magic, science, and religion demarcated among the Trobrianders; among energy experts," she finds, "reason and desire intermingled."

In characterizing modern institutions as magical, an analysis like this creates an analogy with an earlier account of magic as fundamentally nonmodern, if not primitive, and uses a stark contextual difference to impel theoretical development. In comparing Trobriand magic and Western physics,

Nader draws a maximally "distant" analogy (Lamond 2014) between cases that, on the surface, seem to bear little resemblance. In contrast to authors claiming that "theoretical 'transferability' is more likely the greater the similarity between two contexts," Snow, Morrill, and Anderson argue that "there is a curvilinear relationship between theoretical development and contextual similarity. More explicitly, the likelihood of theoretical development is greatest under conditions of either pronounced contextual similarity or dissimilarity" (2003: 194). In other words, the starkness of the difference between science and magic—the disanalogy—amplifies the theoretical value of revealing a conceptual commonality between the contexts—the analogy.

More often than not, efforts to apply the concept of magic ethnographically to modern contexts involve invocations of a few canonical authors. Michael Brown goes so far as to say that an "impediment to debate on the meaning of magic is that it has taken place in the long shadows cast by Malinowski and Evans-Pritchard. Few areas of contention in anthropology have been so thoroughly dominated by only two ethnographic accounts" (1997: 131). The problem is that an over-reliance on these canonical sources may not add much to the concept of magic, other than illustrating its extensibility to novel domains. Instead, we might ask whether the extensibility of the anthropological concept of paradigmatically primitive magic to paradigmatically modern contexts suggests that these analogies were already somehow present in the canonical sources. In other words, perhaps Malinowski's comparison of Trobriand garden magic to Western advertising already presupposed a comparison in the other direction.

In the previous chapters, I have shown how analogies (and, of course, disanalogies) with the Western magic assemblage shaped ethnographic accounts of magico-religious ritual practices that used reactions to tricks as indicators of cognitive sophistication. This analogy, with all its prefigurational apparatus, thus figured into one of the most influential formulations of one of the most pivotal dichotomies in anthropological history—magical versus rational thinking—where magic epitomizes primitiveness and rationality stands for modernity. Like all anthropological dichotomies, this one too functions as a binary concept, with the term on either side available for independent theoretical extension through analogical mappings onto new case material (figure 24). The resulting diagram of this operation looks like a pair of analogical ladders beginning at the same point, but traveling stepwise in opposite directions.

A dichotomy expresses a culturally conspicuous relationship of disanalogy, a comparison involving dominant negative analogy and subordinate positive analogy. Once formulated, these comparisons remain embedded within both dichotomic concepts. Even when the concepts "magic" and

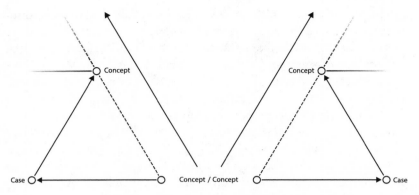

Figure 24. Bifurcating theoretical development of conceptual dichotomy. Illustration by Insil Choi.

"rationality" are employed independently, a comparison between the two remains an implicit feature of any subsequent application. Doubleness persists, even across dichotomous divides. As Zhan (2009: 95) puts it—focusing especially on Malinowski and Evans-Pritchard—anthropologists of magic have "long battled along the lines of 'rational and 'irrational,' " but "in so doing," they have "reinscribed these lines even while contesting along them." It is as if the concepts exhibited a form of the quantum entanglement that links pairs of elementary particles even when they are subsequently separated—what Einstein called "spooky actions at a distance" (see Kaiser 2011: 30). In this way, it is not surprising that the key insight of anthropological research on rationality has been how gol-danged magical it is, and that the key insight of the anthropological research on occult magic has been how gol-danged rational it is. In either case, the magical/rational dichotomy and its potential to generate paradox enters almost prophetically into ethnographic analysis even as explicit cross-cultural comparisons recede from view: studies on rationality will always have to reveal magical inner workings and vice versa if they are to represent a legible contribution to disciplinary knowledge.

It remains to be seen whether anthropology can ever truly overcome the asymmetrical relations inbuilt to magic as one of its core concepts to achieve Latour's (1993b) vision of a "symmetrical anthropology." Latour (2007: 20) writes, "if it is true that it was the Europeans who invented modernity, it is important that they are able, if I dare say, to 'uninvent' it, or more precisely, to 'recall' it, just as industries recall defective products." Insofar as European anthropologists conspired in elaborating the idea of modernity, Latour says that the first task for "any symmetrical anthropology" is "to finally write its own history." In part, this book seeks to recall (in both senses) the anthropological magic concept, which played such a central role in efforts to define modernity (or, more precisely, what modernity isn't), by critically examining the place of magic tricks in its historical genesis.

While anthropologists themselves may be more disciplined in their use of "magic" as a comparative concept, the early intellectualist emphasis on false causal belief as its essence—reflective of the analogy with illusionism—continues to resound in the discipline's seemingly unending problems with the status of belief (Asad 2011). Perhaps this is one reason why, for contemporary cultural anthropologists, no double seems more dangerous than the Tylorian social evolutionist—the theoretically and methodologically primitive Other against which the enlightened field defines its relativistic identity.

"How does it happen," Byron Good (1994: 20) asks, "that 'irrational beliefs' becomes the central, paradigmatic issue" for all of anthropology? Largely, he concludes, because of patterns that congealed around debates about magic. Nancy Scheper-Hughes (1993: 21) concurs: "the study of magic," she writes, established "the issue of divergent rationalities" as the discipline's core concern, providing "a springboard for anthropological analyses designed to reveal the internal logic that made magical thinking and practice a *reasonable*, rather than an irrational, human activity." Insofar as primitive magic is *the* paradigmatic object of cross-cultural anthropology, we might even view it as a synecdoche for the *other* Other of rationality: culture itself.

Could anthropology, seeking to settle the issue of belief, ever move beyond its problems with magic? There are sharply conflicting views on this question. Arguing that "anthropologists have been remarkably complacent about accepting the notion that the label is cross-culturally valid," Michael Brown holds that "anthropology awaits a bold reformulation that banishes 'magic' from analysis altogether" (1997: 122). Susan Greenwood espouses a diametric position: "for any transformation of anthropological understanding to occur, magic has to be recognized as a legitimate form of knowledge" (2009: 4). For reasons I have begun to explore in this chapter, it might be profoundly difficult for anthropologists to either utterly banish magic or utterly rehabilitate it without entirely rethinking the discipline, with its organizing conceits of revealing irrational practices as fundamentally rational and rational practices as fundamentally irrational.

How would they proceed without those tricks?

SEVEN

Meta-Analogy, or,
Once More with Meaning

I recall suggestions about the anthropology of primitive magic being a relatively regular (if not entirely frequent) occurrence during my fieldwork among French illusionists, or magicos, but looking back over my field notes now, I see that I almost never jotted them down. When magicos explicitly suggested anthropological citations on primitive or occult magic, I nodded along but secretly dismissed them as mostly irrelevant to the kind of project I thought I was doing. When they contrasted the rational outlook of audiences who (correctly) understood that magic should be nothing but trickery with the perspectives of non-Western or non-modern people who "*still* really believe" in it, I blanched at what seemed to me to be an implicit evolutionism. For me, these kinds of exchanges were something of an embarrassment.

For instance, during one audio-recorded interview, the deeply philosophical illusionist Jacques Delord rhapsodized about his extensive experiences performing throughout Africa as a cultural ambassador for the Alliance Française. "Over there, I'm not an actor, I'm an event. I'm a *ma-gi-cian*," he said, drawing out this last word with exaggerated pomp. "Of course it's a mistake. I tell them that I'm not a magician, that I'm French and that in France we've lost . . ." Here, Delord trailed off. "I tell them, '*You* have magicians. *You* are magicians. Us? We're rationalists, and we *imitate* magic because we've forgotten its secrets.' They understand very well, but when they see me do my tricks, they say, 'You little white man, you *know* how to do something! You're lying to us when you say it's just a trick!'"

At this point in the recording, I laughed along with Delord, but conversations like this put me in an awkward position. On the one hand, I was moved to hear how deeply Delord had been affected by his years of touring in Africa (as well as Asia and Latin America) and the friendships he formed along the way. Moreover, I was curious about the adaptation and reception of his performances in such a wide variety of intercultural settings. I had no doubt that his stories about some spectators misconstruing him as something other than a mere entertainer contained many elements of truth, though I suspected that added contextual information would yield a more complicated interpretation. In these postcolonial contact zones, I reasoned, there was just too much room for mutual misapprehension, however smart and sympathetic an observer like Delord might have been.

Delord was not inventing this interpretation *ex nihilo*, either, but rather assimilating his own experience to a preceding analytic frame that had crystallized at least as early as the nineteenth century. A deep admirer of Robert-Houdin, Delord reanimated in this interview the Founding Father of Modern Magic's definition of the illusionist as "an actor playing the role of a magician" (Robert-Houdin 1868: 54). Delord's stories about African audiences miscategorizing his "tricks" for the real supernatural magic they purportedly "imitated" had an almost mythical cast, like the legend of the ancient artist Zeuxis who painted such realistic grapes that birds tried to eat them. Delord's telling of these stories was equivocal, at once criticizing and celebrating his African audiences. As he wrote elsewhere, "perhaps they are primitive, but to that I say: long live primitives, for they maintain something of an original purity" (1990: 19).[1] Delord, in this sense, inverted and resignified Robert-Houdin's contrast between real and theatrical, imitative magic, casting the former in an idealized light of premodern enchantment. Still, even a romantic dichotomization between the enchanted, authentic magic of "primitive," "traditional" people and the disenchanted, simulated magic of "modern," "rational" people, as he described it, put me ill at ease—however experientially valid it might have been for him, or self-evidently credible for other magicos.

I prided myself as a sensitive fieldworker, adapting my positionality as a participant observer to align with native categories.[2] But, at least concerning magicos' interest in the topic of primitive magic, my disciplinary conditioning got in the way. At stake were my analogies. I did not want to approach modern magic as in any way an analogue to the kind of instrumental magic enshrined in anthropological literature. For reasons that should now be clear enough given the foregoing chapters, that analogy seemed far too problematic. I preferred other analogues, mobilizing middle-range concepts like "art world" (Becker 1982), "subculture" (Becker 1991), and "community of practice" (Lave and Wenger 1991) to characterize the nature of relationships among magicos and to insert my ethnography along a very different set of analogical ladders. A partial consequence of avoiding comparisons with anthropological research on instrumental magic was bracketing off the cosmological concerns so central to that tradition, with its recurring questions about belief. Eschewing the methods and theories of symbolic anthropology, I focused primarily on analyzing social relationships and symbolic interactions among magicos rather than on interpreting the content of their performances as theater or ritual.

In many ways, *meaning* and *symbolism* were not among magicos' most salient categories either, and focusing instead on their principal everyday concerns—practices of producing, circulating, and displaying secret skills—seemed to be a culturally consistent ethnographic choice at the time. I mostly spent my time in the field listening to sleight-of-hand artists discuss the minutiae of techniques for revealing a spectator's chosen card or making a coin seem to pass from one hand to the other—and the intellectual property claims attendant upon variants of such trade secrets. I modulated my research questions accordingly.

In studying Brazilian capoeira, Greg Downey came to a similar conclusion, moving from an approach that "treated it as a performance to analyze, as if the game were a symbolic text," to a phenomenological approach emphasizing "what was most important to practitioners: learning it, teaching it, and developing their abilities" (2005: 17). Still, the ineluctable cultural significance of capoeira as a contested medium of both Afro-Brazilian nationalism and post-racial Brazilian nation-building permeates the practice—and the pages of Downey's ethnography.

Similarly, although skillful practice and performance were magicos' central preoccupation, this did not preclude abiding concerns with what magic meant, even if they did not always agree on how to talk about meaning among themselves, much less with an anthropologist. Indeed, magicos constantly complained to each other that, too often, illusionists presented magic tricks as mere puzzles for the spectator to solve by trying to explain how the illusion was produced. They craved more—illusions that would signify something beyond the mechanics of their own production, illusions that *meant* something, be it personal, political, social, or metaphysical, which also required that audiences seek to interpret their effects rather than merely explain them. I now understand that one of the ways they thought about not just what kinds of meanings that might be but also about the ability of magical illusions to mean anything at all was through analogies with the dangerous but also distinguishing double of primitive magic.

My problem was that magicos' native analogies between primitive and modern magic violated, I thought, my anthropological reluctance to analogize those domains, and my commitments to other, seemingly less problematic, comparisons. Rather than viewing this native analogical pattern as background noise that needed to be filtered out so that I could attend to the signals that interested me at the time, I now wonder what I would have found if I trained my attention all the more carefully upon it as an ethnographic object par excellence. Magicos' interest in analogizing the modern magic they perform with primitive magic as known to them mostly via ethnographic representations was a crucial datum, offering insight into not just the practice of illusionism but also its deeper symbolic resonances. My argument certainly is not that currents of racism pervade French magic any more so than the surrounding society, nor even that evolutionist ideas about progress play much of a role in shaping what Euro-American magicians do onstage. Instead, I seek to uncover why it is that, when they do pause to reflect on the historical origins of modern magic, the evolutionist linkage with primitive magic should present itself with such fittingness.

The prevalence of this native analogy also says something about the way that ethnographic representations circulate beyond anthropology's disciplinary confines in a social context like contemporary France, just as my initial aversion to this analogy says something about anthropology's desire to monopolize control of ethnographic representations. Anthropological theories constitute part of the cultural repertoire of many of the people that anthropologists study today (e.g., Helmreich 2001).[3] Even when we, as anthropologists, don't share the same theories, it is crucial to engage them. In my case, I now recognize that, by expressing their fascination with potential linkages between modern illusionism and images of primitive sorcery that both attracted and repelled them, magicos were telling me something vitally important about the cultural constitution of their expressive practice and its vexed association with European modernity.

Ethnohistorical Reflexivity

In the past several decades, the elaboration of an anthropological approach to economic and political centers of power in Northwestern Europe has had a crucial role to play in parallel projects of "decolonizing anthropology" (Harrison 1997) and "provincializing Europe" (Chakrabarty 2000). Recent ethnographies like Lilith Mahmud's (2014) *The Brotherhood of Freemason Sisters* and Mayanthi Fernando's (2014) *The Republic Unsettled* explore tensions and contradictions at the very core of the cultural, political, and philosophical construction of hegemonic European identities. Such studies fulfill the radical promise of Europeanist anthropology in two ways. First, they reveal how Western liberal universalism is produced and reproduced through living legacies of exclusion based on race, gender, religion, and class. In the process, they implicitly also reveal how humanistic anthropology has traditionally produced its subject matter by epistemologically rehabilitating subjects normatively excluded from embodying ideals of liberal universalism (albeit outside Europe).

It is not uncommon that Europeanist ethnographers are led to confront, through their fieldwork, intellectual traditions closely related to anthropology itself. For instance, Dominic Boyer found that the East German journalists he worked with in the years following German reunification were steeped in a mode of dialectical social reasoning in many ways akin to his own anthropological training. He ended up "studying German philosophy with analytical strategies and frameworks that were themselves borrowed from German philosophy, inconveniently blurring the emic/etic, frame/content distinctions upon which we, as anthropologists, tend to rely" (Boyer 2007: 39).

Some Europeanist works incorporate European anthropology itself as data, along the lines of what I do in *Magic's Reason*. In *After Nature*, Strathern (1992a) uses classic (mostly Africanist) studies of kinship in British social anthropology as ethnohistorical evidence of characteristically English cultural norms. "In thinking about what English kinship was to become, I propose to use British anthropological kinship theory and English kin constructs as mutual perspectives on each other's modernisms," she writes (Strathern 1992a: 8). British anthropology helped create "the idea of Englishness" by theorizing African kinship in a way that made English kinship appear distinctive: "Its recognisable components included the idea that kinship was the cultural construction of biological (natural) facts, that one studied society as a set of conventions external to and internalised by the individual, that Western kinship systems were cognatic or bilateral in nature, and that what was peculiar to the English was their individualism" (139).

No work exemplifies this approach more forcefully than Michael Herzfeld's classic *Anthropology through the Looking-Glass*. Herzfeld uses the ethnography of modern Greece, "a society that brings together the stereotypes of the exotic and the European" (1989: 1), as a foil for anthropological theory, highlighting "the symbolic character of anthropology as the exploration and expression, not of exotic societies, but on the contrary of the cultural identities of those globally dominant societies that themselves created the discipline."[4] He argues that contemporary Greeks confront a crisis of national identity as both *the* prototypical Europeans, living heirs to classical antiquity, and underdeveloped, subaltern Others, peripheral to the northern centers of cultural, economic, and political power. Turning to traditions of ethnographic writing about Greece, Herzfeld finds similar tensions between scholarly approaches that emphasize either Greeks' commonalities or differences with the rest of Europe. He brilliantly mobilizes this literature to evidence the cultural predicament of Greek identity, while also using the ethnography of Greece to illuminate the theoretical predicaments of anthropology as a discipline torn between conflicting impulses to universalize and exoticize.

"All ethnography," Herzfeld writes, "is in some sense an account of a social group's ethnocentrism," and "as a European-originated discipline . . . anthropology cannot evade the Eurocentric character of its criteria of comparison" in spite of the "potent yearning to escape the constraints of bias" (18). Methodologically, he takes what he calls an "etymological" approach to subject the "roots of our own disciplinary vocabulary and practices to . . . critical analysis" (23). Just as "folk" etymologies often feature into ethnographic accounts, Herzfeld argues, treating scholarly concepts themselves as European "folk" categories is an essential part of "turning anthropology into an ethnographic object." Herzfeld's approach, then, is to "use etymological comparisons between anthropological theory (or at least part of it) and a specific body of ethnographic material" (195).

This is very similar to the approach that I will take with magic in this final chapter, comparing the anthropology of "primitive" magic to the ethnography of "modern" magic to show how Western anthropology and Western illusionism culturally converged in their approaches to defining magic in respect to modern/primitive, rational/irrational binaries. To do this, I situate the analogical ladder I have described in the foregoing chapters—one that repeatedly links ethnographic accounts of instrumental magic through implicit comparisons with entertainment magic—as itself a case study in a second-order analogical ladder (figure 25). Here, the development of the anthropological concept of "primitive" magic, represented as the first-order ladder, is embedded as a historical case in a second-order analogical ladder leading to my current ethnographic case: "modern" Euro-American magic, which I apprehend principally, but not exclusively, from the vantage point of Parisian magicos. I call this approach of enfolding the intellectual history of a Euro-American anthropological concept into the ethnography of an interdependent Euro-American cultural system *ethnohistorical reflexivity*.

Technically speaking, the current case in this diagram should also show a telescoping first-order analogical ladder, since my main ethnographic

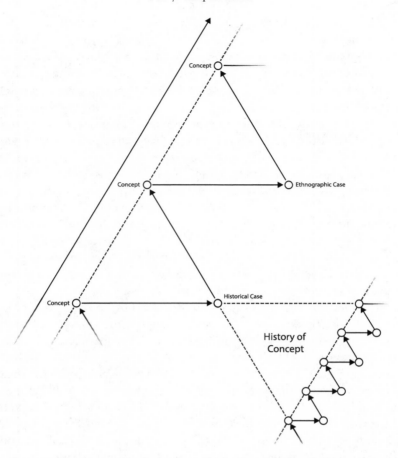

Figure 25. Ethnohistorically reflexive theoretical development. Illustration by Insil Choi.

focus in this chapter is the way that modern magicians—like modern anthropologists—elaborated a tradition of drawing analogies between "modern" and "primitive" magic. What I am really comparing are two practices of analogy-making, and arguing that they are culturally codependent. This kind of reflexive ethnohistory thus gives rise to a meta-analogy: a comparison of analogy-making practices in two different, but interrelated, domains, cultural anthropology and entertainment magic. But for simplicity's sake, and to accentuate my own frame of reference here as an ethnographer, I have designed this diagram to highlight the insertion of the intellectual history of European anthropology into a Europeanist ethnography of entertainment magic.

Native Evolutionism

In this concluding chapter, I return to the bibliography that I first described in the introduction—a reading list on the anthropology of primitive magic, given by a contemporary illusionist to an anthropologist engaged in an ethnography of modern magic. What would it be like to travel down the intellectual pathway that it seems to unfurl? There is no better place to begin than with the most explicitly elaborated and ethnographically pertinent item on the reading list, Max Dif's (1986) *Histoire de la prestidigitation*. A mass-market publication inevitably on the bookshelf of any magicos remotely interested in the history of illusionism, this book was recommended to me by a clerk in a Parisian magic shop just a few days into my fieldwork. It occupies the status of a go-to reference work similar to Milbourne Christopher's (2006) *The Illustrated History of Magic* in the English-speaking world. As I show below, the two books (both initially published in the mid-1970s and subsequently reissued) are also largely convergent in the accounts they provide of primitive magic.

Dif's first chapter, entitled "The Savage Era" (*Les ages farouches*), begins with a description of "prehistoric man's absolute ignorance of the world in which he lived," which "condemned him to superstition. Everything around him was the subject of surprise and dread" (1986: 9). To deal with this abject condition of primitive terror, Dif explains, "man invented, little by little, an entire series of rites, acts of humility, sacrifices, glorifications and offerings in honor of the Unknown. From the imagination of man, magic was born" (10). To substantiate these claims, Dif points to cave paintings putatively depicting the deeds of sorcerers. The following chapters focus on ritual magic in antiquity, from Pharaonic Egypt and biblical miracles to the special effects of pagan temples.

By placing this discussion of prehistoric and ancient ritual magic at the beginning of a book that chronologically details the history of entertainment magic, Dif establishes an originary connection between the two domains. He returns to this theme in several places, notably in a chapter on "Magic at the Ends of the Earth," chronologically situated to coincide with early modern European expansion. There, he argues, for instance, that "the magic of indigenous Americans, like that of primitive people, was before all else, instrumental" (Dif 1986: 90), contrasting it with entertainment magic. Another chapter, "The Legend of the Orient," addresses the controversial topic of fakirism, notably beginning with the 'Isawa, magic history's canonical embodiments of self-mortifying trickery.

The final chapter, "Back to the Beginnings," brings the connection between primitive and modern magic most sharply into focus through a discussion of magic in contemporary Africa. Dif writes, "More than in the Orient, where the magic of legerdemainists has hardly any hold on the jaded and more or less indifferent autochthones, the African continent, and particularly Black Africa, seems to constitute the most fertile soil for sorcery, magic and superstition" (Dif 1986: 349).[5] He relays stories from Western illusionists who, like Jacques Delord, traveled and performed in sub-Saharan Africa. According to one, for Africans, "prestidigitation does not exist. There are things that they understand and things that they don't understand. They consider everything they don't understand to be controlled by spirits, and the Black sorcerers use this to their advantage, reinforcing their power and authority" (350). According to another:

> The African does not draw a clear line between trickery and what he thinks real magic to be; he remains in a vague middle-ground between these two concepts . . . The African views simulated magic from the perspective of his knowledge, experience, and environment. The European does likewise, but because the points of departure are fundamentally different, the resulting attitudes are deeply divergent. Finally, let us not forget that the reactions of Africans today resemble those of people in the Middle Ages, Antiquity, and certainly Prehistory. (351–52)

Dif concludes that contemporary African "fetish doctors" and the prehistoric sorcerers depicted in European cave paintings are essentially equivalent, analogously primitive magicians. Both, in turn, resemble modern magicians in terms of the contact they maintain with mysterious forces, although they diverge by making claims of real powers that modern magicians disavow—and abhor. These arguments could be straight from E. B. Tylor. They reflect what Johannes Fabian (2002: 32) famously terms "allochronism," a style of framing cultural differences in temporal terms. In the work of social evolutionists like Tylor and his successors, Fabian argues, allochronism "denies coevalness" to non-Western people, who are treated as living fossils of modern Europe's own past.

Like most historians of magic, Dif was an "organic" intellectual, an entertainer—he at one point performed an "oriental" act under the stage name "Chang"—before becoming a writer. His views reflect shared assumptions among magicos about what magic is and where it comes from. That modern magic derived from primitive magic, and that primitive magicians are charlatanic impostors, were truisms among magicians I worked with, and many of the accounts they produced about the history of magic reflect these ideas. For instance, one wrote in an essay on the history of illusionism, "in pre-history, we can image that a number of individuals scattered around the world discovered that they had the talent of making suckers out of their peers. They became the first *magicians* or *sorcerers* . . . or *healers*," combining medical knowledge with "the ability to trick either orally . . . or visually" (Stone 2006: 42).[6]

The prevalence of native evolutionism and the preoccupation with figures of non-modern alterity among illusionists provocatively parallels the primitivism that Susan Terrio found among French chocolate-makers and connoisseurs. In that luxury market, "France's colonial past . . . informs the construction of the exoticized discourse of consumption and the eroticized images of people of color who stand in for chocolate as a substance that retains the seductive power of its 'wild,' 'natural' origins outside France and Europe" (Terrio 2000: 260).[7]

These primitivist ideas are by no means isolated to illusionists in France, circulating internationally as a widely accepted origin story for professional entertainment magic. American magic theorist Eugene Burger points out that they are pervasive in histories of magic penned by Anglophone illusionists as well, most notably Milbourne Christopher. Burger calls this view

> an essentially *economic-political interpretation* of the place of magic in early cultures. Early conjuring is here seen as the story of the smart people (temple ritualists, shamans, etc.) using religion, bolstered by trickery and deception, to get power over the common ("superstitious") herd. This grab for political power seeks wealth ("bountiful sacrifices"), which the awe-struck superstitious handed over to the crafty deceivers. (2009a: 28–29)

After astutely detailing a number of empirical problems with this line of reasoning, Burger wonders why modern magicians themselves would promulgate such a factually questionable—but more importantly, tonally negative—origin story about their own expressive practices. "Do you think there might be a connection between this picture of the early magician as an unscrupulous scoundrel and the character or persona adopted by many contemporary magicians when they perform?" he asks (Burger 2009b: 69). "Much contemporary conjuring is performed as little more than a power struggle between performer and spectators. The ultimate aim of this endeavor is for the performer to deceive the spectators and thereby win the battle."

For Burger and his coauthor Robert E. Neale, the popularity of an economic-political interpretation of the origins of modern magic in shamanic charlatanism points not so much to a historical truth, as to a cultural conception of the paramount significance of deceptive trickery among modern magicians themselves. Neale speculates that the more modern magicians have come to emphasize their own power to produce deceptive illusions, the less meaningful those illusions have become. "Maybe, just maybe," he writes, "it is degeneration of belief that gives rise to more spectacular magic effects and more subtle methods for achieving them. Perhaps our Western conjuring history is remarkable for its progress in mechanics and sleight-of-hand. If so, perhaps our loss of meaningful magic is related" (Neale 2009: 53).

I cannot say whether there is truly an inverse correlation between technical progress and a decline of meaning in the history of Western entertainment magic. It is an elegant argument, but it retains an evolutionist cast, pointing backwards to shamanic deceptions—conceptualized as mimetic representations of supernatural realities in a manner not inconsistent with contemporary anthropological norms (Crapanzano 1995; Kapchan 2007; Taussig 2003)—as the ultimate, prelapsarian form of meaningful magic. For instance, Neale writes that, even though the effect of the Ojibwa Shaking Tent was almost certainly produced through tricks that performers "lied" about,

> these conjurors played an important role in their society, important to themselves and important to their people. And every time the shaking tent occurred, these roles and their supporting beliefs were strengthened. The magicians validated the basic understandings of the society about the meaning of life, maintained connections between their daily lives and the spirits, upheld the moral code of the group, and provided security and confidence in individual and group crises. To themselves and their people, they were not impostors and charlatans. (Neale 2009: 51)

In essence, Burger and Neale seek to maintain an equivalence between primitive and modern magicians, but to make the former a distinguishing rather than a dangerous double of the latter—similar to the inversion Jacques Delord seemed to have in mind. By emphasizing the primitive plentitude of meaning that the economic-political theory occludes, they repolarize the analogy, and seek to provide a charter for modern magicians to try to make their performances once again meaningful on the model of shamanic rituals.[8] In the preceding chapters, I have argued a somewhat different, but still complementary, position, namely that Western illusionists, in their self-conscious preoccupation with disenchantment, do indeed play a significant ritual function, mediating the cosmological values of secular modernity. It is precisely by emphasizing "mechanics" over "meaning"—to use Neale's terms, which are interestingly also Bruno Latour's (1993b: 35)—that they do so, concatenating magic performance and scientific demonstration.

What is important for me to retain from Neale's hypothesis is not how historically accurate it may be, but rather how *plausible* it seems within cultures of contemporary magic.[9] During the course of almost two years of fieldwork within the flourishing magic subculture of contemporary Paris, I was perpetually amazed by the cunning artistry of the magicians with whom I worked, as I watched them draw gasps of astonishment from admiring spectators, or listened to them expound on the sophisticated technical details of their deceptions. At the same time, I was surprised how difficult it could be to elicit insights into the *meaning* of particular tricks or of magic in general from these accomplished performers or, for that matter, their audiences. Some of my interlocutors actively disavowed the possibility that magic *meant* anything beyond the sheer delight (or, perhaps, bewilderment) their tricks occasioned.

In many ways, Gregory Bateson's offhanded comment about modern magic is ethnographically spot-on. "Conjurers," Bateson writes, "concentrate upon acquiring a virtuosity whose *only reward* is reached after the viewer detects that he has been deceived and is forced to smile or marvel at the skill of the deceiver" (1972: 182, emphasis mine). Magic tricks are self-referential insofar as effects accrue significance by calling attention to the secret, inscrutable, methods of their own production—the locus of magicians' deceptive skill. In this sense, magic recalls Alfred Gell's characterization of virtuosic works of art and performance as indexical signs that point to the originating agency of the skilled artists or performers who create them. According to Gell (1998: 71), the enchantment "produced by the spectacle of unimaginable virtuosity . . . ensues from the spectator becoming trapped within the index because the index embodies agency which is essentially indecipherable. Partly this comes from the spectator's inability mentally to rehearse the origination of the index from the point of view of the originator, the artist." As Bateson saw, secular entertainment magic emphasizes the enchantment spectators feel in the face of the effect/index whose method/ agency lies irretrievably beyond their grasp as the principal justification for performance.

The problem is that many magicos were profoundly dissatisfied with a status quo that locks them into a battle of wits with spectators struggling to explain effects that they design to be inexplicable rather than working collaboratively to co-construct interpretations. It is as if there were a kind of normative vacuity built into modern magic as a genre whose performances conventionally signify through indexical self-reference rather than through the kinds of symbolic or iconic representation that can be more easily associated with meaning in a discursively elaborated sense. The irony is that the magicos I know constantly strive to counteract the undertow of referential or representational meaninglessness by emphasizing what they call "presentation," the theatrical embellishment of their effects, for instance, by weaving elaborate storylines around their tricks.

Still, generic conventions make it difficult for them to avoid an almost ineluctable emphasis on the ingenuity of artifice (and their personae as ingenious artificers) as the principal rationale for any performance. As I have shown elsewhere, illusionists exploring alternative paths often struggle to overcome these conventions, whether they are "new magicians" (Jones 2015a) seeking to provoke aesthetic interpretations or "gospel magicians" (Jones 2012) seeking to provoke religious, Christian interpretations. Ironically, for new magicians, gospel magicians, and others interested in shifting magic from a regime of explanation to a regime of interpretation, the most dangerous double isn't the charlatanic primitive magician. It is none other than the modern magician who magnifies the significance of technical secrets, wields them as an instrument of personal emphasis (Simmel 1950: 338), and asserts the serious nature of his endeavors against the foil of ridiculed non-modern Others who don't know how to explain tricks in technical terms.

Magical Illiteracy

I have already described how illusionists and anthropologists engaged in a process of what Bruno Latour calls *purification*. This involved "separating natural mechanisms from human passions, interests or ignorance," as Latour (1993b: 35) puts it, to leave modern magic on the former side, and primitive magic on the latter. Modern magicians self-consciously enact purification by separating mechanism from meaning, material causality from human fantasy.[10] As Keane (2007) demonstrates, Latour's account of modernity in terms of purification is also a story about changing "semiotic ideologies," ideas about how signs are understood to signify. If, in the conception of modern magicians, primitive magic effects signify by pointing to (non-existent) supernatural causes outside the magician, then modern magic effects signify by pointing to natural causes within the magician. By conventional expectation (if not always so in practice), a primitive magic effect is *never only* a trick; it is, at least, a depiction or, at most, a manifestation of powerful and hidden realities, imbued with fear and desire. A modern magic effect is *always just* a trick, a manifestation of the magicians' skill.

In modern magic, any audience response that does not prioritize the magician's technical prowess as the ultimate explanandum becomes a possible form of cognitive deviance. This may seem ironic since modern magicians are always promulgating hybrids onstage through tongue-in-cheek reference to the occult and paranormal, but the as-if register of suspended disbelief ultimately functions to reinforce, rather than destabilize, the separation of supernatural elements from magic (see Lamont 2013).

Beyond the realm of performance, I found that magicos enact purifying practices by circulating stories about deviantly credulous, non-modern attitudes toward magic. For instance, when I first met Georges Proust, the owner of the Parisian Académie de la Magie, a high-end boutique and manufacturer of stage illusions, he laughingly regaled me with stories about customers confusing entertainment magic and real magic: a Spiritualist medium who purchased a levitating table effect "in case his real powers ever failed him"; a wealthy client who ordered several expensive stage illusions but didn't want to learn how to use them. "I don't want to *use* them," the client explained. "I just want to acquire the powers of the Master."

Proust told me that one day a journalist came into the shop, took one picture, asked one or two questions, and left. Months later, the mailman delivered three giant crates of mail from West Africa. Apparently the journalist had published Proust's picture in front of all the little drawers of tricks along with his mailing address in a tabloid called *Banko*, with the caption "Georges Proust, Director of the French Academy of Magic." People wrote with all kinds of outlandish requests related to sorcery and witchcraft, Proust said. Months passed, and suddenly the same thing happened again. *Banko* had done a second run of the same issue.

While Proust didn't remember the specific requests so much as the sheer volume of mail, letters from people seeking occult intercession have often seemed to make their way to magic shops. In 1990, a magic magazine published a selection of the choicest letters received from the 1960s through the 1980s at France's oldest magic shop, whose owner had carefully archived them (Brahma 1990). Some of the requests were ethically dubious but ontologically sound—for example, the student seeking gimmicked objects for cheating on tests, or the rural politician hoping to order a custom-made double-bottomed ballot box. Other correspondents were clearly seeking supernatural succor, such as the COD order for "the mirror to read the past and future and . . . the magic ruby for heating and light," or the request for

"a product that, when placed in water, can relieve incurable illness: blind-
ness, gonorrhea, and abdominal worms that prevent women from giving
birth."

Other requests were from the lovelorn. One inquired about "increasing
the size of the male organ and rendering it very strong." Another had written,
"I want her to return to me through the power of your magic, and for her to
become as docile as a lamb, even a slave. Money is not an issue! Put the full
power of your magic to work so that she'll come back to me . . . Send her an
irresistible command." Many sought magical weapons, such as "the 'malicious wand' for striking down enemies" or the "electrifying fist for doubling
people over with negative current." One alarmingly wrote: "My academic life
is entangled, ensorcelled, enchanted by someone who's blocking my success . . .
I am not unaware that murder is wrong, but killing is a natural part of war.
I ask for your services: can you kill this sorcerer?" Another letter cautioned,
"Don't write 'magic' on the envelope—if the Post Office notices, you could
be arrested."

Modern magicians look mirthfully upon requests like these and the
category confusions they enact, and these letters—in spite of the spiritual
torment many of the authors seem to express—were published in an un-
ambiguous spirit of ridicule. What is important for my purposes is not that
so many people continue to conflate or confuse entertainment magic and
occult magic, but that the people who do should be singled out as targets
for derision among contemporary illusionists. From the perspective of these
entertainers, the benighted authors of letters like these are guilty of a kind
of magical illiteracy that would presumably render them incapable of being
good spectators who would competently credit the magician with skillful
ingenuity and manual dexterity rather than supernatural powers. Amaz-
ingly, these kinds of stories are common enough to constitute a stock literary trope among magic authors: Guillemin (1988: 86–87) reports receiving
comparable letters from Ivorian students at the junior high where he once
taught, and Vaisan (1981: 145–46) publishes a similar assortment of letters
that he received from throughout Francophone Africa.

Modern magicians also perpetuate projects of purification by actively
publicizing invidious comparisons with irrational non-modern Others. At
least since Robert-Houdin's *Confessions*, representations of indigenous and/
or primitive people who believe in supernatural magic—or of the ritual experts who exploit those beliefs—have been a commonplace in magicians'
travel narratives. In his television special "Fearless," the American magician
David Blaine (2002a) enacts this trope in segments featuring apparently
impromptu performances in Haiti and Venezuela. Haitians, he says in the

accompanying narration, "have a culture which is deeply rooted in magic"; for them, "magic and voodoo are considered the same thing." Scenes of Blaine performing card tricks and other illusionistic effects for people who don't always seem to understand what he is doing or why are intercut with images of a voodoo possession ritual and man-on-the-street interviews about the powers of witches and werewolves.

Blaine is next shown flying in a small plane over a dense rain forest, traveling to "a place where any other form of civilization was hours and hours away" to find out how Yanomamo Indians would react to his tricks. These are, he says, "the last discovered people on Earth," who have "no written language and virtually no contact with anybody in the outside world. Like the Haitians, they are a culture rooted in magic." As he is shown following a lone Yanomami man with a machete down a narrow jungle path, Blaine says in voiceover, "we were warned by everyone not to visit the Yanomami. The last group of outsiders had been chased away with poisonous spears." In a subsequent written account, Blaine invokes Robert-Houdin's trip to Algeria as an inspiration for trying to perform "magic in a different culture" (Blaine 2002b: 113).[11]

Thinking about the nature of magic through the lens of cross-cultural comparisons holds great intellectual appeal for Euro-American illusionists, and many approach the project with seriousness, sensitivity, and an eagerness to avoid ethnocentrism. Jacques Delord, for instance, published a long essay on a Congolese healer named Misère Apollinaire, whom he was able to observe while on tour in Brazzaville. "I long hesitated before committing my observations to paper," he writes (Delord 2005: 37), but "I feel the responsibility to break the wall of opacity and intolerance, both scientific and colonial, that proscribes . . . the recognition of the Other as a mirror of the Self." Delord describes a series of consultations in which Apollinaire extracted, by sucking, psychic projectiles—a serpent's tooth, small shells—shot by witches and lodged in victims' bodies. "I had complete freedom to observe the therapist's smallest gestures," writes Delord (39). "Since the early morning, our medicine man had been drinking liter upon liter of ordinary red wine . . . If there was trickery, it would only be there that a magician from the North could suspect it." The real trick, Delord concludes slyly, was how Apollinaire managed to absorb so much wine over the course of a single day's work.

More than any other illusionist I encountered, Breton magician Fanch Guillemin has made a life's work of traveling the globe to observe the performances of traditional, indigenous ritual experts, document their illusionary practices, and elicit local reactions to his own magic tricks. His exhaustive *Les sorciers du bout du monde* (Sorcerers at the Ends of the Earth) details his travels in sub-Saharan Africa, North Africa (where he sees 'Isawa in Ouargla, Algeria), South and East Asia, the Americas, and Oceania. Guillemin maintains a delicately balanced stance throughout, giving an illusionist's explanation of whatever effects he saw performed, but attempting to respect local beliefs about these performances. "I amply detail the kinds of local superstitions that particularly fascinate me," he writes (Guillemin 1988: 12). "But behind these intriguing stories I always look for the physical and visual effects, curious and observable things, in short all of the 'miracles' through which sorcerers make their powers concrete in the eyes of laymen . . . People, in essence, need a resemblance of proof to reinforce their faith" (12–13). When I asked Guillemin about the relationship of entertainment to instrumental magic, he told me simply, "shamanism is as much a form of entertainment as anything else."

In addition to probing the parameters of magic by circulating imagery of non-Western ritual magicians, modern magicians have played an active role in policing the boundaries between *mere* entertainment and more perfidious forms of charlatanism or illusionary deceit. Controversies can become particularly pitched when illusionists themselves or their close counterparts in the magic assemblage are thought to transgress such boundaries. For instance, in the early to mid-twentieth century, French illusionists engaged in heated attacks on fakirism, the exhibition of extreme feats of bodily mortification (see Lachapelle 2015). As magic historians Saltano and Joubert (1990: 51) put it:

> There are several types of stage fakirs: the real, the false, and the in-between— those who use fakery occasionally. Moved by a kind of professional ethics, illusionists have always considered real fakirs to be fellow artists, the occasional fakers to be acceptable as long as they performed as variety entertainers, and false fakirs to be traitors against the art of magic whom they were duty bound (because they know the tricks) to denounce before a mystified public.

Parapsychology has been another area of ongoing tension. During my time in the field, a number of magicos were particularly concerned about transgressions associated with the magical subgenre of mentalism, which mainly features psychic effects. Given the present-day vogue for astrology and channeling within the contemporary New Age movement, they worried about the potential for abusing tricks that simulate mind-reading, clairvoyance, thought-transmission, or fortune-telling. Many who performed mentalist effects felt it necessary to explain to audiences that they were only clever performers, not psychics. The Canadian mentalist Gary Kurtz, then touring Europe, provoked widespread criticism among my informants after refusing to acknowledge that he did not have supernatural powers on a French television program.

The association of modern magic with the normative values of Enlightenment reason is a constitutive feature of the genre (During 2002; Lachapelle 2015; Lamont 2013; Mangan 2007; Nadis 2005), which many of the magicians I worked with in France enact by aligning themselves with skeptical causes of debunking superstition and investigating claims of the paranormal. To get a sense of how powerful this vocational self-conception is for modern magicians, days after the horrific Paris terror attacks of November 2015, the director of the largest Francophone illusionism website wrote in an editorial: "Now more than ever . . . magicians must fight against obscurantism," likening radical Islam to other kinds of charlatanism illusionists have crusaded against.

During my time in the field, Gérard Majax was the French illusionist most actively involved in promoting these skeptical causes. Like his American counterpart the Amazing Randi, Majax began exposing the sham miracles of Uri Geller, the Israeli spoon-bender, in the 1960s. In addition to authoring a number of popular books on charlatanism (e.g., Majax 1996), he starred in the successful play *Zoltan* about a lapsed stage magician who founds a cult. He told me that, despite his earnest efforts, it could be frustratingly difficult to disabuse credulous people of superstitious beliefs. Laughing ruefully, he recalled a woman who told him that he had great mediumistic potential after attending a lecture in which he demonstrated the fraudulent tricks mediums employ to simulate supernatural powers.

Majax numbers among his collaborators in skeptical pursuits a team of paranormal investigators led by physicist Henri Broch at the University of Nice. Originally a professor of fluid dynamics, Broch created a Laboratory of Zeteticism (Laboratoire de Zététique) within the Physics Department—"zetetic" being another term for "skeptic," associated with the American sociologist and paranormal investigator Marcello Truzzi. Over the years, Broch has investigated everything from fire-walking to psychic surgery and UFOs, and has published extensive refutations of paranormal claims (e.g., Broch 2001).

As its only official member, Broch told me that the laboratory in fact functions principally as a club for people interested in "promoting scientific thought." When I visited a laboratory meeting several years ago, these included a Senegalese professor of materials science; a Canadian professor of biology; a Swiss graduate student writing the world's first doctoral dissertation in the field of Zeteticism; two high school science teachers (both named Denis); and Stéphane, an air-traffic controller form Monaco who was himself a highly adept semiprofessional magician.

Over dinner later that evening, Stéphane performed over an hour of enthralling close-up magic, much to everyone's delight. Common people's credulity and ignorance of science had been a recurring topic that evening, and Stéphane's tricks provided ample fodder for conversation. "It shows just how easy it is to fool people," one Zetetician said, "if he could manage to trick us from 50 centimeters away!" Stéphane was a seasoned performer, and had come equipped with a satchel full of material sufficient to entertain all evening. The younger of the two Denises was also an amateur magician, but much less experienced. When he tried to perform a simple card trick, he made the mistake of picking Broch as a volunteer. Broch was not a magician himself, but he had seen enough magic to know how to effectively trip one up. When Denis asked him to put the card he had selected back "anywhere" in the deck, Broch tried to stick it on the bottom, in the 52nd position, a location that would interfere with any attempt to manipulate it.

"Not there," Denis pleaded. Broch then tried to put it on top of the deck, which similarly would have made it impossible for Denis to gracefully complete the trick.

I don't want to delve into the social psychology of a situation like this— but the phenomenon of difficult spectators who aggressively try to confound the illusionist is well known among performers.[12] Whether because they feel threatened socially or intellectually, spectators themselves often frame entertainment magic in agonistic terms, as an interactional challenge. Certainly, some illusionists appear to relish the agonistic elements of magic performance, but for many of the magicos I worked with, like Denis in this example, modern magic's implicit agonism was a tremendous burden. Knowing how to anticipate, deter, and handle such conflicts constitutes a key professional skill (Stéphane, for instance, had no such problems).

That modern magicians should be so aware of the potential for conflict with spectators—magicos fervently believe that French spectators are the "worst" in the world in this regard[13]—reveals something important about the kinds of expectations associated with this genre of performance. They carefully strategize ways to avoid conflict and incorporate spectators into the co-constructedness of performance, using self-deprecatory humor, deliberately emitting "play signals," or engaging audiences in more imaginatively roundabout ways to shift the focus away from confrontational messages.[14]

This element of confrontation may be an inevitable consequence of a genre that emphasizes presenting *tricks as tricks*, "asymmetrical signs" elaborated to make a show of possessing hidden secrets (Kirshenblatt-Gimblett

1998: 254–55) that function to create social hierarchy. Jacques Delord was intensely aware of this dynamic, and his romantic critique of modern magic was closely connected to challenging what he viewed as a reductive focalization on skillful trickery as an end in itself. "The secret of being an artist is not the 'tricks' that you perform, nor your dexterity, nor your technical skill," he wrote (Delord 1987: 13). To be a true artist, he continued,

> the prestidigitator must have the courage to believe in Magic . . . Magic is at the origin of Mediterranean thought. Reasoning-reason, to advance human intelligence, has tried for more than two thousand years to forget its past. Now, to save humanity, it must . . . return to its origins . . . It is important that prestidigitators today stop tricking and finally start believing what their hands lead people to imagine . . . There are better things to do than condemn and persecute people whose "primitive" or "avant-garde" mentality inclines them to believe in a science whose psycho-intellectual foundations lie beyond our grasp.

Delord challenged illusionists to rethink magic without recourse to invidious contrasts with instrumental primitive magic, and without the modernist focus on self-referential technical skill. Essentially, he seemed to have in mind something like the illusionistic equivalent of symmetrical anthropology: a symmetrical magic that would banish distinctions between ritual and entertainment, belief and disbelief.[15]

Considered from the perspective of ethnohistorical reflexivity, Delord's critique of modern magic reveals precisely what I have been trying to show about the nature of its relationship with the anthropology of primitive magic. As they incorporated the imagery of illusionism in developing an intellectualist approach to instrumental magic, anthropologists worked within a paradigm that Stanley Tambiah (1990: 108) calls *causation*, "framed in terms of distancing, neutrality, experimentation, and the language of analytic reason." He contrasts this with a paradigm of *participation*, "framed in terms of sympathetic immediacy, performative speech acts, and ritual action. If participation emphasizes sensory and affective communication and the language of emotions, causality stresses the rationality of instrumental action and the language of cognition."

The claims of modern magic resonated with intellectualist currents in the anthropology of instrumental magic not only because both domains had a convergent interest in the figure of the primitive magician, but also because they similarly emphasized causality over participation. The normatively reflexive relationship between modern magicians who demonstrate effects and modern spectators who observe, assess, and analyze their performance stands as a conceptual antinomy to the way anthropologists theorized the sociality of deviant occult magic in which some people are unduly influential and others unduly influenced.

If modern magic succeeded in bringing anthropology under its spell by offering itself as such a generative analogue for intellectualist reasoning about ritual and religion, it is perhaps because the genre resonated so deeply with what Nancy Scheper-Hughes (1993: 21) describes as the long-standing "anthropological obsession with reason, rationality, and 'primitive' versus 'rational' thought" as "largely androcentric concerns." The practice of modern magic as Robert-Houdin defined it—closely associated with the cultural ideals of bourgeois, European masculinity—like anthropology, found in the primitive magician a figure of irrational alterity, a foundational Other, against which it can continue to define and refine itself, but which also, for that reason, imposes limits on what it can become.

Regimes of Enchantment

The model of analogical "mapping" seems to suggest a unidirectional process of thought passing through an already crystalline base to irradiate an otherwise hazy target. My analysis in *Magic's Reason*, however, confirms Strathern's (2008: 31) view that "analogistic reasoning offers insights into both terms being brought into relation with each other—illumination goes both ways." This dynamic of interillumination generates insight in two directions, as comparison subjects base and target domains alike to scrutiny and elaboration. Moreover, the starting point of an analogy, despite its seeming familiarity, is often anything but crystalline. Analogies also produce distortions that propagate bidirectionally; when patterns are misrecognized or misaligned, both domains under comparison become more, rather than less, obscure. Sometimes it seems most apt to say that what analogies produce is neither illumination nor distortion, but rather culture as a system that organizes and classifies patterns across domains according to its own priorities (Shore 1996).

There is no doubt that I have presented a kind of triumphalist account of increasing illumination and decreasing distortion along a ladder of conceptual development connecting successive ethnographies of instrumental magic. The gradual refinement and progressive disambiguation of the anthropological magic concept depended, at least in part, on purging traces of an originary analogy with entertainment magic and its cognitive—and cognitivist—traps. Indeed, the considerable work that previous generations of scholars had already put into disciplining the anthropological magic concept through a process suggesting that any connections with entertainment magic were "misanalogical" (Shelley 2002a) may partially explain why I initially had so much difficulty deploying it in an ethnography of entertainment magic.

In an important way, the disciplining of the concept of magic reflects Tylor's assertion that "analogy has always been the forerunner of scientific thought," relying on "experience" to "correct" and "restrict" it (1883: 207). However, science does not leave analogy behind in the backwaters of magic, but continues to rely on it as a basis for developing concepts and extending theories. The intellectualist view of magical thinking as analogy run rampant depended on a conviction that science could eventually eliminate analogy to arrive at a pure conception of things as they truly are. At least in anthropology, analogy will always remain a vital, indispensable—one might even argue foundational[1]—component of the scientific method.

A virtue of anthropological concepts—like any form of culture that must be adaptive—may be their ultimate imperfectability, the stubborn polysemy that makes them transportable and transposable from one case to the next through processes of endless analogy-making. They have comparative value because they are both mutable and immutable (Strathern 2007b). And magic, of course, is a prime example, combining fixity and fluidity as it ramifies through multiple, shifting, and often contradictory analogical combinations.

In part, what I have shown in *Magic's Reason* is the work that goes into sustaining foundational, charter analogies by keeping base and target domains distinct. If primitive and modern magic (or, say, occult and natural science, in Tylor's terms) turned out to be really the same thing, then any analogy between them would collapse, and with it an entire (cultural) conception of cultural difference. Analogy simply cannot exist without disanalogy. In this sense, the elaboration of primitive magic as a double for both modern magic and modern anthropology offers a powerful example of the role of disanalogy in cultural ontogenesis—particularly in the cultural production of Western modernity. Modern magic could, presumably, get along just fine without the foil of an irrational Other; I am less sure about anthropology's ability to forego a seemingly inbuilt need for figures of difference (see Kapferer 2013).

Anthropologists may have moved beyond the primitive/modern dichotomy that factored so centrally into the origination of the anthropological magic concept; it seems to be more difficult to disentangle that concept from its culturally inflected associations with other closely related dichotomies: enchantment/disenchantment, illusion/reality, participation/causality (Tambiah 1990), and ritual/sincerity (Seligman et al. 2008). I have emphasized the salience of one dichotomy—rationality/irrationality—but my account also raises deeper questions about the cultural nature of the category of belief, a construct as powerfully associated (in anthropology) with cultural identity as it is opposed to knowledge (in the scientific sense). Entertainment magic provided ethnographers and anthropologists with a cross-cultural counterpoint that facilitated mobilizing all of these dichotomies in accounts of not just non-Western magical beliefs, but also non-Western ritual practices, particularly—but not exclusively—those involving any kind of similitive artifice. These ritual practices, in a recursive movement, provided a foil for entertainment magicians and others to conceptualize illusionism—and showbiz more generally—as a domain of autonomous artifice for artifice's sake.

The structure of this book thus traces a circle from modern magic to the anthropology of primitive magic and back again. Beginning with Robert-Houdin, I demonstrated the close association of stage magic with enactments of Western modernity. Focusing on intercultural performances in nineteenth-century French colonial Algeria, the historiographical core of *Magic's Reason* shows how systematically and enduringly French ethnographic representations pit an indigenous Algerian ritual system, caricatured as pathologically enchanted, against a European genre of entertainment figured as normatively disenchanted. The 'Isawa's enthusiastic (but still unsympathetic) reception among Spiritualists and other members of French esoteric movements reflected a deeper ideological, epistemological, and metaphysical heterodoxy that modern magicians and Western anthropologists actively opposed.

Tracking tropes of trickery in French colonial culture established groundwork for the more general theoretical issue I took up in Chapter Five: how the analogue of modern magic informed intellectualist anthropological theories of primitive magic as false causal belief. Ethnographic representations of primitive charlatans (and anecdotal observations of supposedly atavistic Spiritualists) were part of the fabric from which Victorian anthropologists stitched comparative accounts of magical, religious, and scientific worldviews, setting an analytic agenda for future generations of cultural anthropologists. The correlative concepts of magical and scientific thinking—for Tylor and Frazer, both different ways of using analogies—were at the heart of intellectualist theory. The opposition between them shaped the course of anthropological conversations about comparative systems of belief, as I showed in Chapter Six, even as anthropologists have pushed themselves to transcend the conceptual limitations of this binary.

These historical processes highlight the significance of modern magic as a vital cultural component of Western modernity, as both an expressive practice and an interpretive apparatus. In the final chapter, I brought this analysis to bear on my own ethnography, showing how contemporary French illusionists theorize their performance practices through favorable and un-favorable comparisons with images of primitive Otherness. My primary purpose was not to critique primitivist ideologies so much as to show why representations of primitive magicians serve as such generative analogues for these entertainers thinking about both what they do so well and what they wish they could do differently. Using the technique of ethnohistorical reflexivity, I operationalized my admittedly limited intellectual history of anthropological magic theory within an ethnography of secular entertain-ment magic, ultimately revealing how professionals in both domains have asserted their modernity and expertise through claims of mastery over prim-itive magic.

Disclosing some of the hidden ways that anthropology had already incor-porated ideas about a topic—entertainment magic—which, on the surface, it largely appeared to eschew involved exploring analogical associations be-tween my ethnography and a body of anthropological literature often seeming to pull in a radically different direction. In a way, this was possible because my illusionist interlocutors pushed me to take this analogical leap, which to them was no leap at all. The result was to resituate anthropology and entertain-ment magic within a broader cultural context in which they had histori-cally already been made to connect by anthropologists and magicians alike, albeit in ways that the prevailing historiography of both fields had not yet made immediately apparent.

The shape of the anthropological magic concept anticipated the kind of meta-analogy I drew between illusionism and anthropology, formed as it was through (1) historical encounters between illusionists and ethnog-raphers or anthropologists; (2) the use of illusionism as an implicit and explicit comparative foil in anthropological theories of instrumental magic; and (3) a style of reasoning about "primitive" magic shared by both "mod-ern" anthropologists and "modern" magicians as Euro-American cultural producers working in the context of colonial and postcolonial ideologies of racial and civilizational hierarchy. These convergences point to an un-derlying cultural pattern in the way that Euro-Americans came to construe intellectual aptitudes for rationality and reflexivity as their own distinctive historical achievements.

Historians of anthropology have long known that the topic of primi-tive magic played such an important formative role in the development of the discipline precisely because it seemed, at least initially, to represent the utter absence of these supposedly modern mental attributes. Meanwhile, historians of modern magic have also established that illusionism resonated culturally in the nineteenth- and twentieth-century North Atlantic region (and, indeed, beyond) as a practice associated with these same qualities of mind and, by extension, with the normative ontology of Western modernity. What I have sought to add to both scholarly conversations is a focus on the way anthropology and modern magic worked in tandem to elaborate a shared figure of dangerous doubleness: the primitive magician, suspected of using legerdemain to exploit an irrational and unreflexive primitive public of which he is also, simultaneously, a part. My emphasis has been on showing that this figure, the primitive magician, is less a historical fact than a conceptual trope, a personification of alterity that anthropologists and illusionists collaboratively fleshed out and exploited as an analytic resource.

In staging this argument, I have probably overstated connections between modern magic and Western anthropology strictly in terms of disenchantment. In the eyes of many, modern magic is also a form of enchantment or reënchantment, positioned within a cultural complex—the magic assemblage—that incorporated many performers, from Western Spiritualists to Algerian 'Isawa, who blurred boundaries between entertainment and religion, spectacle and ritual. It remains important to think of not just entertainment magic but also anthropology as embedded within its own *regime of enchantment*, by which I mean something like a web of affect-laden agreements about how forms of human and non-human agency are distributed and interrelated within cosmological and/or sociopolitical systems.

For instance, Ehler Voss (2014) shows how commonly anthropologists have favorably likened themselves to shamans, liminal mediums capable of interacting with otherworldly agents to convey knowledge from distant realms. He then cleverly teases out some rather unfavorable implications of this analogy: if anthropologists have suspected shamans of "deceit or at least self-deceit," then they have also suspected each other of the same thing—using literary tricks to conjure worlds that they claim are empirically real (215–16).

Even the most famous shaman in the anthropological record, Quesalid, the skeptical initiate to Kwakwaka'wakw shamanism who discovers his own healing powers while denouncing others' tricks, turns out to be a literary construct conjured from the intercultural collaboration between Franz Boas and his key informant, George Hunt—himself the initiate—and later embellished by Lévi-Strauss (Whitehead 2000). Boas was not "a neutral observer and recording angel [who] somehow lucked out and found the one unique Enlightenment individual ready to challenge hocus-pocus and give the inside story," Taussig (2003: 293) writes. "The text itself, an artifact of the fledgling science of anthropology . . . is an utterly perfect instance of the confession of the secret, the very acme of the skilled revelation of skilled concealment" that is so central to what he calls the "profound magic" of anthropological representations.

Probably the best-known analogy between magical and anthropological enchantments comes from Malinowski himself, who says of his early experience doing fieldwork in the Trobriand Islands: "it was not until I was alone in the district that I began to make some headway; and, at any rate, I found out where lay the secret of effective field-work. What is then this *ethnographer's magic*, by which he is able to evoke the real spirit of the natives, the true picture of tribal life?" (1922: 6, emphasis mine). Malinowski responds that it is through "a patient and systematic application of a number of rules of common sense and well-known scientific principles, and not by the discovery of any marvelous short-cut." But this oft-quoted passage admits of multiple readings.

Many readers have concluded that, by deliberately invoking magic—one of his core analytic categories—in connection with his own scientific endeavors, Malinowski was doing something more than just being ironic. In terms of its mythopoetic qualities, this passage "announces the emergence of an authoritative persona: Bronislaw Malinowski, new-style anthropologist," who is "endowed with . . . a new kind of insight and experience" (Clifford 1988: 110). It also links fieldwork with ritual secrecy (de Jong 2004: 262), recalling Hubert and Mauss's assertion that "isolation, like the secret, is an almost perfect sign of the intimate nature of the magical rite" in which "the act and the actor are enveloped in mystery" (1902–1903: 18–19).[2] George Stocking (1995: 112) remarks on the parallel between the situations of insufficient skill that Malinowski says occasion Trobriand magic and "the gap between the specific methodological prescriptions of fieldwork and the vaguely defined goals of ethnographic knowledge" that this ethnographer fills with his own professional magic.

For my part, I note that what Malinowski is describing here doesn't seem to be, strictly speaking, the more-or-less-skillful techniques of data collection and analysis so much as the production of mimetic, similitive imagery—evoking a "true picture," as he puts it. To me, this sounds less like the instrumental magic of Trobriand gardening and seafaring and more like something much closer to the base domain of entertainment magic's captivating illusions—the magic of the magic assemblage. I would not go so far as to claim that it is in no uncertain terms. That this interpretation can suggest itself at all is sufficient to prove at least the basic point that, even in the rarefied realms of highly disciplined anthropological texts, the term *magic* retains an essential polysemy that allows connotations to jostle and referents to mingle.

Malinowski (1922: 7) links his "ethnographer's magic" to "being really in contact" with the natives, "[taking] part, *in a way*, in the village life" such that he woke "up every morning to a day, presenting itself to [him] *more or less* as it does to the native" (emphasis mine). Here, he provides a rationale for both conducting participant observation fieldwork and reading ethnographic texts in terms of the "willing suspension of disbelief" (Kapferer 2001): the ethnographer should come as close as possible to believing that he is a native, constituting himself as a dependable double, so that the reader can vicariously experience what it is like to see the world from "the native's point of view," in Malinowski's (1922: 25) words. It would seem that, along with Western stage magic, anthropology itself may be a "modern enchantment . . . that enchants and disenchants simultaneously" (Saler 2006: 702)—a mode of earnestly taking part in native life, but only "in a way" and "more or less," since everything irrational that natives do must eventually be accounted for according to analogies that render it acceptable to the rational norms of Western science.

The *as-if* protocols associated with spectatorship in the modern magic assemblage, in which "spectators agree to be entertained, manipulated, and tricked, but not to be conned" (Nardi 1984: 39), seem to resemble the anthropological conventions of suspending disbelief while conducting fieldwork on irrational beliefs or reading about them in ethnographic texts. Tanya Luhrmann (2012a: 372) argues that "late modern secular society values and cultivates an explicit as-if engagement in the spiritual domain . . . by explicitly inviting the suspension of disbelief as a response to the skepticism inherent to an open society."[3] Maybe this perspective should be extended to anthropology itself as not just a scientific activity, but also a "secularly humanistic" (Engelke 2014: 300) endeavor that reaches its fullest expression when confronted with secular reason's ultimate Other: magic.

It is problematic, however, to equate modern magic too narrowly with the willing suspension of disbelief. In fact, cultural historian Peter Lamont argues—admittedly, against other influential authors—that "it makes no sense" (2013: 44). "The essence of [modern] magic is that something impossible appears to happen in real time and space. To truly experience an impossible event, you must observe an event that you truly believe to be impossible. A willing suspension of disbelief can only diminish that experience" (45). Lamont continues, "the primary aim of magic as a performing art [is] the creation of a dilemma between the conviction that something cannot happen and the observation that it happens. It requires disbelief . . . If you suspend disbelief, willingly or otherwise, the magic disappears."

And so we are back again to disenchantment—or rather to disenchant-ment as its own regime of enchantment, bound up with the intellectual thrill of explanatory challenges—as the motif that most powerfully connects the domains of modern magic and anthropology. Magic performance and anthropological research unfold against a backdrop of conventionalized disbelief: an excess of belief and the entertainer risks becoming a charlatan or the ethnographer, "going native." But, as we have seen, when nineteenth-century anthropologists and modern magicians were at their most incredu-lous, aggressively debunking primitive magic and exposing the charlatan-ism of its exponents, they were also, in a paradoxical way, at their most credulous.

As Wittgenstein (1993: 116) writes, "the elimination of magic" in anthro-pological theory "has itself the character of magic." Confident in the accu-racy of their disanalogies, intellectualist anthropologists engaged in modes of reasoning that, in hindsight, seem difficult to distinguish from magical thinking as they themselves defined it: a misuse of analogy. Whatever illumi-nations and distortions their comparisons produced, they also, most power-fully, produced culture, working in tandem with the flourishing exoticism of the magic assemblage to reinforce conceptions of Western modernity as cognitively distinctive in its emphasis on rationality and reflexivity.

Do the messy interconnections—the underlying hybridities—between the categories of modern and primitive magic that I have detailed augur in favor of a radically enlarged or a radically reduced conception of magic? As we have seen, scholars and magicians alike, arriving at this intellectual fork, have taken diverging paths, some emphasizing analogy and continu-ity, others disanalogy and rupture. At the very least, an awareness of the deep history of analogical mappings and counter-mappings linking these domains should remind anthropologists of the dauntingly complex associa-tions embedded within one of their core comparative concepts, and make them more vigilant whenever they use it—or any other concept, for that matter—to analogize cases across cultures.

ACKNOWLEDGMENTS

A decade has elapsed since I began this fitful project. My process of researching and writing was not just lengthy, but also nonlinear, making it difficult
to reconstruct, and therefore adequately acknowledge, all the input and support I have received. Knowing in advance that I will not be able to recall
every conversation and encounter that has kept these ideas percolating over
the years, I thank everyone who has taken the time to discuss these topics
with me, even in passing.

Still, some influences stand out as decisive. The principal questions I
explore in *Magic's Reason* emerged from conversations with Bambi Schief-
felin and Fred Myers at NYU, and both have remained key interlocutors
and generous readers. Aaron Glass's insight into Franz Boas's depictions of
Kwakwaka'wakw ritual artifice provided additional early inspiration.

Others whom I wish to thank for contributions over the years include:
Lucia Allais, Jonathan Allen, Misty Bastian, Richard Bauman, Amahl Bishara,
James Boon, Dominic Boyer, Don Brenneis, Jon Daries, Omri Elisha, Mi-
chael Fischer, Julien Gavelle, Dedre Gentner, Michael Gilsenan, Emmanuel
Grimaud, Jennifer Hammer, Mary Harper, Jeff Himple, Michael Houseman,
James Howe, Jean Jackson, Erica James, Dave Kaiser, Clare Kim, Rena Leder-
man, Alaina Lemon, Tanya Luhrmann, Reed Malcolm, Emily Martin, Amy
Moran-Thomas, Ram Natarajan, Carol Rigolot, Joel Robbins, Lawrence Rosen,
Susan Silbey, Romain Simenel, Randall Styers, Michael Taussig, Karen Ver-
schooren, Chris Walley, Margaret Wiener, Martin Zillinger, and Angela Zito.

Among the opportunities I had to present portions of this project to
scholarly audiences, two were particularly pivotal. In 2008, members of the
Center for Historical Analysis at Rutgers University provided me with stimu-
lating and challenging comments on an early version of my research on
French colonial culture. In 2015, the honor of giving the Learner Lecture in

Religious Studies at NYU provided the perfect setting to work through some of the more mature arguments, particularly during the ensuing conversation with Adam Becker, Elayne Oliphant, and Geoffrey Pollick.

Parts of this book first appeared in *Comparative Studies in Society and History* (Jones 2010), where I am particularly grateful to Andrew Shryock, David Akin, and the five reviewers for the significant role they played in laying a firm early foundation. Versions of shorter passages also appear in *Cultural Anthropology* (Jones 2012), *Annual Review of Anthropology* (Jones 2014b), and the edited collection *Performing Magic on the Western Stage* (Jones 2008). I thank the editors and reviewers for their contributions, and the publishers for permission to use these materials here.

I thank all of the magicians who so generously contributed to the ethnographic components of this book, and to the agencies that funded that research: the Social Science Research Council and the Fulbright Foundation. Support for archival research in Paris and Aix-en-Provence came from the Gardner Magic Project at Princeton University.

My research assistants at various stages included Munir Kamal Fakher El-din, Violet Kozloff, Jia-Hui Lee, Saraswathi Shukla, and Mona Zaki. Phoebe Luckyn-Malone provided expert editorial assistance. My talented illustrator, Insil Choi, proved a key sounding board, pushing me to clarify my ideas about analogical reasoning as we tried various approaches to diagramming parallels between Korean *p'ansori* music and American blues. I thank Didier Morax and Céline Noulin for providing images, and Jérôme Cadéac for kind facilitation. Mike Healy was a tremendous help in preparing the final images for publication.

Several people generously read parts of this manuscript at various stages of completion, including Manduhai Buyandelger, Keith Murphy, and Heather Paxson. Stefan Helmreich earned my undying gratitude and boundless admiration for commenting on chapters almost as quickly as I could write them; his insight and wit infuse the marrow of this book. Jillian Cavanaugh, Shalini Shankar, and David Valentine gave transformative feedback on key sections of the manuscript at two crucial junctures.

After years of false starts, I might have abandoned this book project altogether were it not for a fortuitous meeting with a formidable editor. Without Priya Nelson's sagacious guidance and support, *Magic's Reason* simply would not exist. I also thank her colleagues at the University of Chicago Press, especially Dylan Montanari, as well as the Press's anonymous reviewers for their invaluable feedback. During the production process, this project profited from the involvement of many people, including Kristen Raddatz, Marianne Tatom, and Susan Karani.

I am deeply grateful for my family's moral support, especially during critical stages of the writing process. My parents, Richard and Carol, provided childcare at decisive moments; certain passages of this book will always remind me of the happy sounds of them playing with their grandchildren as I typed furiously in another room. I also thank the Wangs, Allan and Lisa, for their investment in this project.

My twins, August and Maurice, gave me a gift of their indulgence, even as they grew increasingly aware that this book was distracting me from building Duplos. Most of all, I am thankful to my wife, Val, who not only worked tirelessly to make space for me to write, but also coached me expertly though writing's turmoils. I thank all three of them for constantly reminding me how delightfully dangerous doubles can be.

NOTES

INTRODUCTION
1. For a discussion of Houdini's vexed, Oedipal relationship with Robert-Houdin, and its symbolic implications for French magicians today, see Jones (2008: 52–54).
2. Throughout, 'Isawiyya is used to refer to the Sufi order, 'Isawa to its members collectively, and 'Isawi to individual devotees. The term 'Isawi is also used adjectivally, to describe things relating to the order and its practices. The Arabic transliteration system followed in this book is a simplified version of that used in the *International Journal of Middle East Studies*. However, because much of the archival material presented here was either written in French or was based on French studies of North Africa, French-style spellings of Arabic words also appear in some of the quotations and citations; this is particularly true of proper names, which I generally leave as they are spelled in the original sources. In French transliterations, *Aïssaoua* is generally used for the name of this order.
3. Tylor revised and reissued *Primitive Culture* in 1873, the edition that I principally reference.
4. Scholars such as Eduardo Viveiros de Castro (2004, 2013) have subjected the premises of this dominant anthropological framework to radical epistemological critique.

CHAPTER ONE
1. For a more complete analysis of this work, see Jones (2008). I refer to this work as the *Confessions* throughout, and base my discussion on the 1859 mass-market French edition. That same year, Robert-Houdin's memoirs appeared in British and American editions, translated by Lascelles Wraxall. Over the years, English-language editions have employed a range of subtly tweaked titles (*Memoirs of Robert-Houdin: Ambassador, Author, and Conjurer; Life of Robert-Houdin, the King of the Conjurers*). For a recent, authoritative English edition, see Robert-Houdin (2006).
2. See Lamont (2013: 44–45) for the related argument that it is important to entertainment magicians that spectators *do not entirely* suspend their disbelief. Robert-Houdin is stressing a commonality with theater, while Lamont is emphasizing a generic difference.
3. See Tresch (2012: 171–76).
4. The value of "progress" is in many ways built into entertainment magic: to competently pull off deceptions, magicians must constantly update their material with

reference to the explanatory resources that particular audiences can access, given their background technical knowledge (Smith 2015).

5. Also see Lamont (2006, 2013), Landman (2013), and Nardi (1984). Moreover, these presentational skills of framing effects are something that illusionists learn and practice (Jones and Shweder 2003).

6. On the gun trick, see Steinmeyer (2005).

7. Centre des Archives d'Outre Mer, 80'Miom 475-1.

8. Although Robert-Houdin makes no mention of the intricately carved gold frame, describing the certificate as being presented to him "rolled up" (1859, vol. 2: 278), he almost certainly procured it in Algeria as well. The stylized text wreathing around the border reads "*illā Allāh*" (only God), as in "*Lā ilāha illā Allāh*" (there is no god but God).

9. Compare Becker (2005).

10. In the *Confessions*, he describes traveling with his wife to visit the encampments of individual chiefs in largely unpacified regions. Wherever he went, the conjuror demonstrated his talents, in one instance precipitating a magical duel of weapons and wits with a particularly jealous marabout. On this occasion, Robert-Houdin repeated an elaborate—and very risky—version of the bullet-catching feat, delivering a magical coup de grace that he claims reduced the marabout to "doubting everything, even the Prophet" (1859, vol. 2: 308). I hesitate to analyze this portion of the narrative in much detail because, in the absence of other corroborating historical evidence, I find it best to regard it as quite likely fictionalized. Although Robert-Houdin implies that his travels in the desert lasted only three or four days, Fechner (2002: 51), working with personal letters, has determined twelve days to be a more likely figure. Fechner attributes Robert-Houdin's relative silence about this probably dangerous, unpleasant mission to a sense of patriotic decorum.

CHAPTER TWO

1. For additional detail on this publication, see Triaud (1995: 15–18).

2. My discussion of North African Sufism draws on Andézian (1996, 2004), Cornell (1998), Crapanzano (1973: 15–21), Geertz (1968: 43–54), Gellner (1969), Hammoudi (1997), and Jenkins (1979) for general background. Several landmark ethnographies of Moroccan Sufi brotherhoods inform this account, primarily Eickelman (1976) on the *Sherqawi*; Kapchan (2007) on the *Gnawa*; and Crapanzano (1973) on the *Hamadsha*, whose self-mutilations some 'Isawiyya groups incorporate into their own ceremonies. On the place of Sufi orders in the contemporary Maghreb, see Scheele (2007) for Algeria, Spadola (2014, 2015) for Morocco, and Boissevain (2006) for Tunisia. Concerning the 'Isawiyya in particular, I discuss recent ethnographic work of Andézian (2001) and Zillinger (2014, 2015a) in Chapter Four; see also Jamous (1995, 2013) and Nabti (2010).

3. Writing about Egypt, Gilsenan (1973: 4) describes the *zawaya* as "schools, caravanserai, commercial and social focal points, law courts, banks, storehouses, poor houses, burial grounds, and the source and channel of divine grace."

4. Clancy-Smith (1994) offers an impressive historical study of the way relationships between maraboutic figures and Arab leaders shaped indigenous responses to colonialism in nineteenth-century Algeria. On chiliastic rebellions led by prophetic figures operating within the same cultural matrix of spiritual authority as the Sufis and saints, see von Sivers (1973).

5. Abi-Mershed (2010: 104) argues that de Neveu was correct "that the ideological stakes in the colonial war in Algeria had changed between 1841 and 1842," but that

the intensification of hostilities had less to do with a rise in religious extremism than with the expansion of France's political agenda.

6. Compare Silverstein (2004: 50).

7. For this reason, Catholicism also provided a basis for interpretations of Islam that diverged from the normative perspective of dominant French secularism. See, for instance, Daughton (2008) and Foster (2013).

8. De Neveu reports the miracle stories corresponding to the ritual consumption of dangerous substances. Other sources give the historical basis for additional ritual marvels in Ibn 'Isa's miraculous deeds. For instance, Bellemare (1858: 87) relates that Ibn 'Isa's unarmed disciples killed a band of marauding brigands by making slicing gestures with empty hands. Thus, in the hadra ceremony, "any 'Isawi who makes the gesture of striking his left arm with his right hand will draw blood, even if he is not armed."

9. Paradoxically, Stallybrass and White continue, "disgust always bears the imprint of desire. These low domains, apparently expelled as 'Other,' return as the object of nostalgia, longing and fascination" (1986: 191)—feelings that Robert-Houdin's portraits of other performers are clearly designed to arouse.

10. Compare de Neveu (1846: 15, 21).

11. *Le grand Robert de la langue française*, 2nd ed., s.v. "jongleur."

12. See also Butterworth (2005: 180 ff).

13. Compare Bailer-Jones (2002: 112).

14. Of course, I mean *knowledge* here in a sense broad enough to also accommodate more or less willful production of ignorance (High, Kelly, and Mair 2012) within the legitimating epistemological framework of colonial power-knowledge, since analogies often conceal much more than they reveal. My intention, however, is not to contribute to the growing field of ignorance studies (Proctor and Schiebinger 2008), but rather to point out the ways that analogy, via comparisons with the 'Isawa and other indigenous ritual experts, contributed to North Atlantic understandings of what entertainment magic was and how it signified.

CHAPTER THREE

1. For a wonderful profile of Rinn, see Trumbull (2009: 64–71).

2. Clancy-Smith (1990: 239) points out, "Rinn benefitted greatly from the not disinterested collaboration of several prominent sufi leaders."

3. It is also worth noting that anthropological interest in North African Sufi orders reflects a lasting preoccupation with secret societies. In American anthropology, Herdt (2003: 27) identifies Lewis Henry Morgan (who studied and imitated Iroquois secretive associations) as originating the image of the "anthropologist as cryptographer of secrecy." Mahmud (2012: 427) argues that there is an "elective affinity between anthropology and secret societies," which often figure into ethnographic accounts as metonyms for society in general.

4. These paintings are now held, respectively, at the Minneapolis Museum of Art and the Musée des Beaux Arts Hyacinthe Rigaud in Perpignan, France.

5. This was a pattern with clear parallels in other imperial settings, such as British Nigeria, where "the colonial perspective on native rituals and traditions transformed them into spectacles through categorical reframing, altering the context and projecting the object into wider spheres of circulation" (Apter 2002: 589).

6. According to a satirical Algerian ballad (Ben Omar 1899), it was the radical ethnomusicologist Francisco Salvador-Daniel who arranged for the 'Isawa's first trip to Paris.

7. Fauser (2005: 238–41) discusses reactions to 'Isawi music in 1889.
8. Presumably, some of the musicians depicted in this series may have also been 'Isawa, although they are not identified as such.
9. See Pougin (1890: 118).
10. Brower (2010: 135) describes how Dicksonn was enlisted by skeptic Paul Heuzé to help debunk spirit mediums. "The magician's conviction that all mediums . . . were cheats" was so widely known that one Spiritist researcher worried he might use his prestidigitatory skill to not only expose but also frame mediums as frauds: "'I wouldn't want Dicksonn at my experiments . . . because I have no confidence in his good faith. He could easily simulate the discovery of some trick'" (135). See also Lachapelle (2015).
11. During the same period, the European magic assemblage also featured other Maghrebian performers, including renowned acrobats from Morocco (Escher 1999; Simour 2013). Like the 'Isawa, these acrobats were typically Sufis, members of the *tariqa* founded by Sidi Ahmad U-musa (Rhani 2012).
12. For further anthropological analysis of the contemporary culture of French secularism, also see Oliphant (2015).
13. On the place of embodiment in North African Sufism, see Amster (2013).
14. A rough sense of how much the 'Isawa might have been paid for these engagements can be gleaned from reports of a suit the troupe filed against the impresario in 1900 for non-payment of salary. According to that case, the 'Isawa performing at the Paris World's Fair contracted to receive 3,550 francs fortnightly, roughly 18,000 $US (in 2015 terms), plus 33 percent of the box-office take (*Le Temps* 1900).
15. Kapchan (2007: 141–46) describes the place of money in Moroccan Gnawa trance rituals performed traditionally as healing ceremonies and, more recently, as aestheticized commodities in the global cultural marketplace.

CHAPTER FOUR

1. A number of other French spectators described the hypnotic power of the hadra as so strong that it threatened to utterly entrance them; for example, Beaucé (1850) and Bellemare (1858).
2. A comprehensive engagement with the flourishing historiographical literatures on modern, North Atlantic esotericism transcends the scope of the present study. I engage selectively with recent research pertaining most directly to my case study and its specific interpretive context. Readers interested in a more general historical overview can begin with surveys by Bell (2007), Geoghegan (2015), Harvey (2015), Monroe (2007), and Saler (2006).
3. Lamont (2005: 49) similarly describes "a link between Victorian spiritualism and Indian juggling."
4. Théophile Gautier was also deeply influenced by Mesmerism, which, in the 1840s, "became a facet of *la vie de bohème*" that attracted "journalists, Romantic Socialists, literary writers, and visionary working-class autodidacts" (Monroe 2008: 70). When "the 'Isawa had reached the degree of orgasm necessary for the celebration of their rites," he describes their condition as "magnetic ecstasy" (Gautier 1881: 99–100). Also see Bordeau (2007).
5. Lachapelle (2015: 83) also notes that fakirs engaged in activities of cultural critique.
6. Even within critical sources, some polyvocality emerges. For instance, in 1856, Émile Carrey published a scathing article on the 'Isawa that nevertheless included a long interview with an 'Isawi who patiently explains that the order performs "to be agreeable

to God, and because our ceremonies are prescribed by the Saint that I serve. It costs us money [to stage them] rather than earning us income" (quoted in Morin 1857: 258).

7. Andézian (2001: 113) suggests that the duplex structure of the hadra lent itself to the detachment of the ritual's religious and performative components, with the latter coming to circulate as "desacralized" folkloric performance—increasingly as an element of Maghrebian cultural patrimony (see also Goodman 1998; Kapchan 2007).

8. Fitting into this general pattern of liminal transgression, in which the immanence of divine grace is enacted through the demonstrations of imperviousness to normally dangerous objects and acts, the impersonation of wild animals is a carefully scripted commemoration of the legend that Ibn 'Isa once traveled accompanied by wild beasts he called his "disciples" (Jamous 1995: 69).

9. Nabti (2010: 309) writes: "According to muqaddams, the desire to participate in a hadra comes from a willingness to detach oneself from the terrestrial realm to elevate oneself towards God and to let oneself be invaded by the divine presence. The trance that they call 'ecstasy' . . . is seen as a method for accessing divinity." See also Jamous (2013).

10. Andézian (1996: 397) insists that "there is absolutely no trace of political involvement from the 'Isawiyya" under either Ottoman or French rule.

11. See also Zillinger (2017).

CHAPTER FIVE

1. For more on the Davenports' innovations, see Steinmeyer (2003: 63).

2. In the circumpolar shamanic traditions, where the medium's own spirit leaves his body, the angakok ends the séance with his restraints still in place. By contrast, in the Shaking Tent tradition, where the spirits come to assist the medium who himself remains present, the unfastening of the restraints is part of the spirit manifestation. In the case of Spiritualist performances "designed to eliminate the possibility that [mediums] were responsible" for manufacturing spirit manifestations, "the Davenports were tied up with rope explicitly to rule out the notion that they might be responsible for events" (Lamont 2006: 26).

3. Colombo (2004) provides extensive documentation for this ethnographic tradition.

4. It is interesting to compare Le Jeune's reports on the Shaking Tent ceremony from 1634 and 1637. At first, he seems quite convinced that the performance is, at worst, a ruse perpetrated by clever charlatans on credulous spectators. He even seems enraptured himself by the ceremony as a form of entertainment (see Thwaites 1897: 165–67). After three years in Quebec, however, he was much less sure if the jugglers' Shaking Tent performance could be accomplished without the assistance of demonic agency (see Thwaites 1898: 17).

5. See Petit (2007).

6. Compare Collins and Pinch (1979); Pinch and Collins (1984).

7. For a discussion of *Cock Lane and Common-Sense* in the context of Lang's life and work, and in respect to his evolving relationship with Tylor, see Stocking (1995: 56–57).

8. Kellar, along with other contemporary illusionists, indeed assisted the American psychologist Joseph Jastrow in his research on the psychology of conjuring (see Petit 2007: 169–70). Similarly, Lachapelle (2015: 107) describes collaboration with psychologist Alfred Binet's research on the psychology of perception as a way for nineteenth-century Parisian conjurors to "display their allegiance to the world of science."

9. See Parris et al. (2009) for a cognitive and neurobiological perspective on the type of fascination magic tricks induce.

10. For a further discussion of the survival/revival motif in the historiography of modern magic, see Mangan (2007: 9–15).

11. Lewis (2002) shows how shifting and uncertain the meaning such performances of sucking shamanism can be.

12. See also Kapchan (2007: 24–25).

13. On Hallowell's research and attitude of suspended disbelief toward these performances, see Stocking (2004: 209–11).

14. Interestingly, Granzberg, Steinbring, and Hamer (1977: 155) report that Cree-speaking communities in Northern Manitoba gave "TV as well as radio the same Cree name by which the shaking tent is known—*koosabachigan*," co-classifying all three as forms of spiritual communication at a distance.

15. Steinmeyer (2003) argues that these symbolic triumphs in many ways compensated for Houdini's mediocre technical abilities as a magician.

16. Motifs of sexuality were omnipresent in Victorian Spiritualism. See for instance Beckman (2003).

CHAPTER SIX

1. See Darnell (1988: 110–14).

2. On this effect in the context of Houdini's career, see Kalush and Sloman (2006: 32); Mangan (2007: 150); Solomon (2010: 85); Silverman (1996: 8–13); Steinmeyer (2003: 148).

3. See Lamont and Wiseman (1999: 11–13).

4. As Silverman (1996: 13) writes, "the impact . . . depends on speed. To stun and baffle as it can, the exchange must occur in a blink."

5. Although I draw primarily on cognitive psychology here, analogy is a topic that has engaged a wide variety of different fields: rhetoric, philosophy, linguistics, and psychology, to name but a few (for an overview, see Itkonen 2005). In anthropology, cultural patterns of analogy-making (e.g., Brenneis 2008, 2013; Helmreich 2016; Strathern 2011) and cultural penchants for analogism (Descola 2013; cf. Helmreich 2014) have been popular topics, all the more so if we consider, following Gentner and Jeziorski (1993) and Genter et al. (2001), metaphor to be a subspecies of analogy (e.g., Lakoff 1993; Obeyesekere 1992; Sahlins 1981).

6. Compare to Markman and Wisniewski (1997).

7. Max Weber similarly argues in *Economy and Society* that "the syllogistic constructions of concepts through rational subsumption only gradually replaced analogical thinking, which originated in symbolistically rationalized magic, whose structure is wholly analogical" (1968, vol. 2: 407).

8. Compare to Goertz (2006) and Sartori (1970) on the inverse relationship between a concept's "intension" and "extension."

9. See also Evans-Pritchard (1969: 266) on the comparison of "relations between relations," as also discussed by Kockelman (2011).

10. Invoking a concept is a way of fitting the case into a "category" or "class" (Becker 1998: 123–25), characterizing it as an "example of" something. This makes it possible to anchor qualitative research in previous literature, contribute to social theory, and generalize from a case. As Becker puts it, "concepts are empirical generalizations, which need to be tested and refined on the basis of empirical research results" (128). If previous conceptual models can't account for features of our case, they must be revised or outright discarded (211–12).

11. Considered in the broadest terms (Hofstadter 2001), analogistic reasoning is the

linchpin of any form of qualitative fieldwork that involves identifying any kind of recurring behavioral patterns. Some of the deepest kinds of anthropological insights come from drawing analogies between spheres of activity endogenous to a particular sociocultural system, thereby revealing deeper levels of underlying organization. Whether they are just methodologically muddling through or following the prescriptive protocols of grounded theory (Charmaz 2006), analytic ethnography (Snow, Morrill, and Anderson 2003), or abductive analysis (Tavory and Timmermans 2014), all good ethnographers hope to achieve the kind of holistic synthesis that comes with recognizing repeated patterns across divergent institutions within the society they study.

12. Compare to Boyer and Howe's (2015) notion of "portable analytics."

13. Becker (1998: 141) calls this "enlarging a concept's reach."

14. Analogy has a storied role in the history of scientific thought (see Bailer-Jones 2002). Kepler used the base domain of light to reason about gravitational force (Gentner et al. 1997); Maxwell used a mechanical analogy of ball bearings and vortices as a heuristic for theorizing electromagnetic fields (Nersessian 1987); and Rutherford speculated that electrons orbit the nucleus of an atom the way planets orbit the sun (Gentner and Landers 1985). In addition to the work of scientific analogy as "a high-level reasoning process" constituting a "deliberate, conscious activity" (Gentner and Smith 2012: 136), unconscious analogies can also creep into scientific reasoning in the form of tacit, paradigmatic assumptions, for instance: the mapping of industrial production onto reproductive biology (Martin 1991) or biological reproduction onto nuclear weapons (Cohn 1987; Gusterson 1996).

15. Just consider the range of antecedent analogues that have factored into the development of anthropology's main conceptual construct, culture itself—everything from living organisms, machines, languages, and literary texts (Boon 1972; Keesing 1974; Manganaro 2002) to seawater (Helmreich 2011). In formulating theories of culture, anthropologists themselves "have been misled by the analogies they draw—to texts, organisms, or works of art. They have mistakenly read the presuppositions of their methods of approach into what they study" (Tanner 1997: 38).

16. One might view such ideological overdeterminations in terms of "analogical priming" (Spellman, Holyoak, and Morrison 2001).

17. Compare Hoffman, Eskridge, and Shelley (2009: 139).

18. For an extended discussion, see Jones (2013).

19. Di Leonardo (1998) calls this the "anthropological gambit."

20. For one account of the difference between magical and scientific analogy, see Greenwood and Goodwyn (2016).

21. A collection from Landy and Saler (2009) offers a complementary interdisciplinary perspective from the humanities.

CHAPTER SEVEN

1. Delord wrote a number of often moving essays for the magazine *Magicus* reflecting on his experiences touring throughout Africa and Asia.

2. In my case, that meant following Charles Briggs's (1986) advice to take on the role of an apprentice magician (Jones 2011: 46–47).

3. Compare to Helmreich's (2007) and Maurer's (2005) calls for "lateral" approaches to studying knowledge practices that converge with anthropological theories.

4. See also Asad (1997) and Herzfeld (1997).

5. Compare Pels (1998).

6. For other expressions of this view from magician-authors whom I frequented during my fieldwork, see, for instance, Alzaris (1999: 14–15); Hladik (2004: 7); Saltano and Joubert (1990: 7–8).

7. On the broader resonance of primitivist motifs in French popular culture, see Sally Price (2007).

8. Burger and Neale themselves have been associated with a movement called "bizarre magic," which has sought to renew the depth and meaning in magical performances through the use of paranormal stories and motifs (see Taylor and Nolan 2015).

9. Mangan (2007: 9) argues against Burger and Neale for a more "symmetrical" (Latour 1993b) reading of the relationship between shaman and showman, suggesting that "the relationship between belief and disbelief need not be that of mutually exclusive binary opposition"; drawing on performance theory, he goes on to question the implicit dichotomization of ritual and theater (16–18).

10. Antimodern magicians like Burger and Neale (and also romantics like Jacques Delord) arguably aim to revalorize Latourian hybrids of meanings and mechanism, materiality and fantasy.

11. Also on Blaine, see Mangan (2007: 190–91).

12. See Jones (2011: 149–50).

13. See Jones (2011: 39).

14. See Jones (2011: 151–56).

15. Elsewhere, he wrote that "if the concept of magic was evacuated of content by rational and objective thought, it was through a deliberate will and force" but "other modes of thought still exist, equally valid and perhaps more profound, such as symbolic thought" (Delord 1992: 12).

CONCLUSION

1. For Dilthey, sciences of the spirit "arise because we are obliged to endow animal and human organisms with mental activity. We transfer to them, on the basis of their life-expressions, an analogue of what is given to us in our own inner experience" (quoted in Outhwaite 1976: 28). In other words, the scientific practice of ethnography is only possible in the first place because interpersonal knowledge—and intrapersonal knowledge, Dilthey would add—comes through analogy: "we understand ourselves and others only when we transfer our own lived experience into every kind of expression of our own and other people's life" (quoted in Hodges 2010: 142).

2. Secrecy (see Jones 2014b) is perhaps another reason that makes the meta-analogy between modern magic and anthropology particularly fitting. As archetypes, the modern magician and the modern anthropologist both enjoy a privileged relationship with secrecy. The illusionist is an embodiment of what Johnson (2002) terms "secretism," a cultivation of the reputation for possessing secrets. The anthropologist engages in projects of "revelatory publicity" (Boyer 2013: 3), seeking to "uncover society's secrets" (Mahmud 2012: 427). If illusionists performatively reveal the concealment of their own secret skills not only to enchant but also to disenchant, then anthropologists penetrate and reveal others' secrets not only to disenchant, but also to enchant.

3. In studies ranging from contemporary British witchcraft and neo-paganism (Luhrmann 1989b, 2012b) to Evangelical Christianity in the contemporary United States (Luhrmann 2012c: 320–21), she has shown that suspending disbelief is a cultural practice that can be cultivated as a skillful activity by contemporary religious practitioners along with the ethnographers who study them (Luhrmann 1989a).

REFERENCES

Abi-Mershed, Osama W. 2010. *Apostles of Modernity: Saint-Simonians and the Civilizing Mission in Algeria.* Stanford, CA: Stanford University Press.

Alzaris, Stefan. 1999. *Illusionnisme et magie.* Paris: Flammarion.

Amster, Ellen J. 2013. *Medicine and the Saints: Science, Islam, and the Colonial Encounter in Morocco, 1887–1956.* Austin: University of Texas Press.

Andézian, Sossie. 1996. "L'Algérie, le Maroc, la Tunisie." In *Les voies d'Allah: Les ordre mystiques dans l'Islam des origines à aujourd'hui,* edited by Alexandre Popovic and Gilles Veinstein, 389–408. Paris: Fayard.

———. 2001. *Expériences du divin dans l'Algérie contemporaine: Adeptes des saints dans la région de Tlemcen.* Paris: CNRS éditions.

———. 2004. "Old Practices and New Meanings: Saint Veneration in Western Algeria." In *On Archaeology of Sainthood and Local Spirituality in Islam: Past and Present Crossroads of Events and Ideas,* edited by Georg Stauth, 107–25. Piscataway, NJ: Transaction Publishers.

Apter, Andrew. 2002. "On Imperial Spectacle: The Dialectics of Seeing in Colonial Nigeria." *Comparative Studies in Society and History* 44 (3): 564–96.

Arnould, Eric J., and Julien Cayla. 2015. "Consumer Fetish: Commercial Ethnography and the Sovereign Consumer." *Organization Studies* 36 (10): 1361–86.

Artaud, Antonin. 1964. *Le theatre et son double: Le theatre de seraphin.* Paris: Gallimard.

Asad, Talal. 1983. "Anthropological Conceptions of Religion: Reflections on Geertz." *Man* 18 (2): 237–59.

———. 1997. "Brief Note on the Idea of 'An Anthropology of Europe.'" *American Anthropologist* 99 (4): 719–21.

———. 2011. "Thinking about Religion, Belief and Politics." In *The Cambridge Companion to Religious Studies,* edited by Robert A. Orsi, 36–57. Cambridge: Cambridge University Press.

Ashforth, Adam. 2005. *Witchcraft, Violence, and Democracy in South Africa.* Chicago: University of Chicago Press.

Bailer-Jones, Daniela M. 2002. "Models, Metaphors and Analogies." In *The Blackwell Guide to the Philosophy of Science,* edited by Peter K. Machamer and Michael Silberstein, 108–27. Malden, MA: Blackwell.

Bakhtin, M. M. 1981. *The Dialogic Imagination: Four Essays.* Edited by Michael Holquist. Translated by Caryl Emerson and Michael Holquist. Austin: University of Texas Press.

Barthes, Roland. 1957. *Mythologies*. Paris: Éditions du Seuil.

Bateson, Gregory. 1972. *Steps to an Ecology of Mind*. New York: Ballantine Books.

Baudelaire, Charles. 1887. *Oeuvres posthumes et correspondances inédites, précédées d'une étude biographique*. Edited by Eugène Crépet. Paris: Maison Quantin.

Bauman, Richard, and Charles L. Briggs. 1990. "Poetics and Performance as Critical Perspectives on Language and Social Life." *Annual Review of Anthropology* 19: 59–88.

Bazerman, Charles. 2012. "Writing with Concepts: Communal, Internalized, and Externalized." *Mind, Culture, and Activity* 19 (3): 259–72.

Beaucé, Vivant. 1850. "Journal d'un colon." *L'Illustration*, April 27, 263–66.

Becker, Adam H. 2005. "Doctoring the Past in the Present: E. A. Wallis Budge, the Discourse on Magic, and the Colonization of Iraq." *History of Religions* 44 (3): 175–215.

Becker, Howard Saul. 1982. *Art Worlds*. Berkeley: University of California Press.

———. 1991. *Outsiders: Studies in the Sociology of Deviance*. New York: Free Press.

———. 1998. *Tricks of the Trade: How to Think about Your Research While You're Doing It*. Chicago: University of Chicago Press.

Beckman, Karen Redrobe. 2003. *Vanishing Women: Magic, Film, and Feminism*. Durham, NC: Duke University Press.

Beidelman, T. O. 1990. "*Persuasions of the Witch's Craft: Ritual Magic in Contemporary England* by T. M. Luhrmann (Review)." *Anthropos* 85 (4–6): 621–23.

Bellemare, Alexandre. 1858. "Les sociétés secrètes musulmanes de l'Algérie." *Revue contemporaine* 6: 76–94.

Bell, Karl. 2007. "Breaking Modernity's Spell: Magic and Modern History." *Cultural and Social History* 4 (1): 115–22.

———. 2012. *The Magical Imagination: Magic and Modernity in Urban England, 1780–1914*. Cambridge: Cambridge University Press.

Bennett, Drake. 2008. "How Magicians Control Your Mind." *Boston Globe*, August 3, C1.

Ben Omar, Qaddour. 1899. "Les Aïssaoua à Paris." *Journal Asiatique* 14: 121–56.

Bialecki, Jon, Naomi Haynes, and Joel Robbins. 2008. "The Anthropology of Christianity." *Religion Compass* 2 (6): 1139–58.

Bishara, Amahl. 2013. *Back Stories: U.S. News Production and Palestinian Politics*. Stanford, CA: Stanford University Press.

Blaine, David. 2002a. *David Blaine: Fearless*. DVD. Buena Vista Home Entertainment.

———. 2002b. *Mysterious Stranger*. New York: Villard.

Boas, Franz. 1896. "The Limitations of the Comparative Method of Anthropology." *Science* 4 (103): 901–8.

Boëtsch, Gilles. 2014. "Science, Scientists, and the Colonies (1870–1914)." In *Colonial Culture in France Since the Revolution*, edited by Pascal Blanchard, Sandrine Lemaire, Nicolas Bancel, and Dominic Thomas, translated by Alexis Pernsteiner, 98–105. Bloomington: Indiana University Press.

Boissevain, Katia. 2006. *Sainte parmi les saints: Sayyda Mannûbiya ou les recompositions culturelles dans la Tunisie contemporaine*. Paris: Maisonneuve & Larose.

Boon, James A. 1972. "Further Operations of 'Culture' in Anthropology: A Synthesis of and for Debate." *Social Science Quarterly* 53 (2): 221–52.

———. 2000. "Showbiz as a Cross-Cultural System: Circus and Song, Garland and Geertz, Rushdie, Mordden, . . . and More." *Cultural Anthropology* 15 (3): 424–56.

Bordeau, Catherine. 2007. "Gender and Universal Fluid in Théophile Gautier." *French Forum* 32 (1–2): 89–102.

Bowen, John Richard. 2010. *Can Islam Be French? Pluralism and Pragmatism in a Secularist State*. Princeton, NJ: Princeton University Press.

Boyer, Dominic. 2007. "Of Dialectical Germans and Dialectical Ethnographers: Notes from an Engagement with Philosophy." In *Ways of Knowing: Anthropological Approaches to Crafting Experience and Knowledge*, edited by Mark Harris, 27–41. New York: Berghahn Books.

———. 2013. *The Life Informatic: Newsmaking in the Digital Era.* Ithaca, NY: Cornell University Press.

Boyer, Dominic, and Cymene Howe. 2015. "Portable Analytics and Lateral Theory." In *Theory Can Be More Than It Used to Be: Learning Anthropology's Method in a Time of Transition*, edited by Dominic Boyer, James D. Faubion, and George E. Marcus, 15–38. Ithaca, NY: Cornell University Press.

Brahma, Pierre. 1990. "Drôles de clients (suite)." *Magicus*, July–September: 7–13.

Brenneis, Donald. 2008. "Telling Theories." *Ethos* 36 (1): 155–69.

———. 2013. "Trading Fours: Creativity, Analogy, and Exchange." *American Ethnologist* 40 (4): 619–23.

Briggs, Charles L. 1986. *Learning How to Ask: A Sociolinguistic Appraisal of the Role of the Interview in Social Science Research.* Cambridge: Cambridge University Press.

Brinton, Daniel G. 1894. "Nagualism: A Study in Native American Folk-Lore and History." *Proceedings of the American Philosophical Society* 33 (144): 11–73.

Broch, Henri. 2001. *Le paranormal: Ses documents, ses hommes, ses méthodes.* Paris: Seuil.

Brower, M. Brady. 2010. *Unruly Spirits: The Science of Psychic Phenomena in Modern France.* Urbana: University of Illinois Press.

Brown, Michael F. 1997. "Thinking about Magic." In *Anthropology of Religion: A Handbook*, edited by Stephen D. Glazier, 121–36. Westport, CT: Greenwood Press.

Brunel, René. 1926. *Essai sur la confrérie religieuse des 'Aïssâoûa au Maroc.* Paris: P. Geuthner.

Burger, Eugene. 2009a. "The Shaman's Magic." In *Magic and Meaning Expanded*, edited by Eugene Burger and Robert E. Neale, 25–37. Seattle, WA: Hermetic Press.

———. 2009b. "Stories of the Origin of Magic." In *Magic and Meaning Expanded*, edited by Eugene Burger and Robert E. Neale, 57–82. Seattle, WA: Hermetic Press.

Burke, Edmund. 2014. *The Ethnographic State: France and the Invention of Moroccan Islam.* Berkeley: University of California Press.

Butterworth, Philip. 2005. *Magic on the Early English Stage.* Cambridge: Cambridge University Press.

Buyandelger, Manduhai. 2013. *Tragic Spirits: Shamanism, Memory, and Gender in Contemporary Mongolia.* Chicago: University of Chicago Press.

Carr, E. Summerson. 2010. "Enactments of Expertise." *Annual Review of Anthropology* 39: 17–32.

Çelik, Zeynep. 1992. *Displaying the Orient: Architecture of Islam at Nineteenth-Century World's Fairs.* Berkeley: University of California Press.

Çelik, Zeynep, and Leila Kinney. 2008. "Ethnography and Exhibitionism at the Expositions Universelles." In *Genealogies of Orientalism: History, Theory, Politics*, edited by Edmund Burke and David Prochaska, 154–73. Lincoln: University of Nebraska Press.

Chakrabarty, Dipesh. 2000. *Provincializing Europe: Postcolonial Thought and Historical Difference.* Princeton, NJ: Princeton University Press.

Chamedes, Giuliana, and Elizabeth A. Foster. 2015. "Introduction: Decolonization and Religion in the French Empire." *French Politics, Culture & Society* 33 (2): 1–10.

Charmaz, Kathy. 2006. *Constructing Grounded Theory: A Practical Guide through Qualitative Analysis.* Thousand Oaks, CA: Sage Publications.

Chau, Adam Y. 2005. *Miraculous Response: Doing Popular Religion in Contemporary China.* Stanford, CA: Stanford University Press.

Chavigny, Jean. 1970. *Le roman d'un artiste: Robert-Houdin, rénovateur de la magie blanche.* 2nd ed. Orléans: Imprimerie industrielle.

Cheak, Aaron. 2004. "Magic through the Linguistic Lenses of Greek mágos, Indo-European *mag(h)-, Sanskrit mâyâ and Pharaonic Egyptian heka." *Journal for the Academic Study of Magic* 1 (2): 260–86.

Christopher, Milbourne. 2006. *The Illustrated History of Magic.* Updated ed. New York: Carroll & Graf Publishers.

Clancy-Smith, Julia. 1990. "In the Eye of the Beholder: Sufi and Saint in North Africa and the Colonial Production of Knowledge, 1830–1900." *Africana Journal* 15: 220–57.

———. 1994. *Rebel and Saint: Muslim Notables, Populist Protest, Colonial Encounters: Algeria and Tunisia, 1800–1904.* Berkeley: University of California Press.

———. 2006. "Le regard colonial: Islam, genre et identités dans la fabrication de l'Algérie française, 1830–1962." *Nouvelles Questions Féministes* 25 (1): 25–40.

Clifford, James. 1988. *The Predicament of Culture: Twentieth-Century Ethnography, Literature, and Art.* Cambridge, MA: Harvard University Press.

Cohn, Carol. 1987. "Sex and Death in the Rational World of Defense Intellectuals." *Signs* 12 (4): 687–718.

Collins, Harry M., and Trevor J. Pinch. 1979. "The Construction of the Paranormal: Nothing Unscientific Is Happening." *Sociological Review* 27 (May): 237–70.

Collins, Samuel Gerald. 2015. "Networked Spirits and Smart Séances: Aura and the Anthropological Gaze in the Era of the Internet of Things." *Anthropology and History* 26(4): 419–36.

Colombo, John Robert, ed. 2004. *The Mystery of the Shaking Tent.* Shelburne, ON: The Battered Silicon Dispatch Box.

Comaroff, Jean, and John L. Comaroff. 1999. "Occult Economies and the Violence of Abstraction: Notes from the South African Postcolony." *American Ethnologist* 26 (2): 279–303.

———. 2012. *Theory from the South: Or, How Euro-America Is Evolving toward Africa.* Boulder, CO: Paradigm Publishers.

Conklin, Alice L. 2013. *In the Museum of Man: Race, Anthropology, and Empire in France, 1850–1950.* Ithaca, NY: Cornell University Press.

Cook, James W. 2001. *The Arts of Deception: Playing with Fraud in the Age of Barnum.* Cambridge, MA: Harvard University Press.

Cooper, John M. 1944. "The Shaking Tent Rite among Plains and Forest Algonquians." *Primitive Man* 17 (3–4): 60–84.

Cornell, Vincent J. 1998. *Realm of the Saint: Power and Authority in Moroccan Sufism.* Austin: University of Texas Press.

Crapanzano, Vincent. 1973. *The Hamadsha: A Study in Moroccan Ethnopsychiatry.* Berkeley: University of California Press.

———. 1995. "The Moment of Prestidigitation: Magic, Illusion, and Mana in the Thought of Emile Durkheim and Marcel Mauss." In *Prehistories of the Future: The Primitivist Project and the Culture of Modernism,* edited by Elazar Barkan and Ronald Bush, 95–113. Stanford, CA: Stanford University Press.

Dadswell, Sarah. 2007. "Jugglers, Fakirs, and *Jaduwallahs*: Indian Magicians and the British Stage." *New Theatre Quarterly* 23 (1): 3–24.

Darnell, Regna. 1988. *Daniel Garrison Brinton: The "Fearless Critic" of Philadelphia.* Philadelphia: Department of Anthropology, University of Pennsylvania.

Daughton, J. P. 2008. *An Empire Divided: Religion, Republicanism, and the Making of French Colonialism, 1880–1914.* Oxford: Oxford University Press.

Davasse, Jules. 1862. *Les Aïssaoua, ou, Les charmeurs de serpents.* Paris: E. Dentu.

Davidson, Naomi. 2012. *Only Muslim: Embodying Islam in Twentieth-Century France.* Ithaca, NY: Cornell University Press.

Davies, Charlotte Aull. 2008. *Reflexive Ethnography: A Guide to Researching Selves and Others.* New York: Routledge.

De Jong, Ferdinand. 2004. "The Social Life of Secrets." In *Situating Globality: African Agency in the Appropriation of Global Culture,* edited by Wim M. J. van Binsbergen and Rijk van Dijk, 257–76. Leiden: Brill Publishers.

Delord, Jacques. 1987. "La nostalgie du mérveilleux." *Magicus,* May: 13.

———. 1990. "J'aime l'Afrique." *Magicus,* March: 19–20.

———. 1992. "C'est toujours à la magie qu'il faut en revenir." *Magicus,* May: 12–13.

———. 2005. "Un guérisseur à Brazzaville." *Magicus,* May–June: 37–39.

Dermenghem, Émile. 1954. *Le culte des saints dans l'Islam maghrébin.* Paris: Gallimard.

Descola, Philippe. 2013. *Beyond Nature and Culture.* Translated by Janet Lloyd. Chicago: University of Chicago Press.

Desprez, Charles. 1880. *L'hiver à Alger.* 4th ed. Algiers: Adolphe Jourdan.

Dicksonn. 1927. *Médiums, fakirs et prestidigitateurs.* Paris: Albin Michel.

Dif, Max. 1986. *Histoire illustrée de la prestidigitation.* Paris: Maloine.

di Leonardo, Micaela. 1998. *Exotics at Home: Anthropologies, Others, American Modernity.* Chicago: University of Chicago Press.

Douglas, Mary. 2002. *Purity and Danger.* New York: Routledge.

Doutté, Edmond. 1900. *Les Aïssaoua à Tlemcen.* Châlons-sur-Marne: Martin Frères.

Downey, Greg. 2005. *Learning Capoeira: Lessons in Cunning from an Afro-Brazilian Art.* Oxford: Oxford University Press.

Du Bois, John W. 2007. "The Stance Triangle." In *Stancetaking in Discourse: Subjectivity, Evaluation, Interaction,* edited by Robert Englebretson, 139–82. Amsterdam: John Benjamins Publishers.

Dunbar, Kevin. 1995. "How Scientists Really Reason: Scientific Reasoning in Real-World Laboratories." In *The Nature of Insight,* edited by Robert J. Sternberg and Janet E. Davidson, 365–95. Cambridge, MA: MIT Press.

du Potet, Jules. 1854. "Danse des Aïssaoua." *Journal du Magnétisme* 13: 352–55.

During, Simon. 2002. *Modern Enchantments: The Cultural Power of Secular Magic.* Cambridge, MA: Harvard University Press.

Durkheim, Émile. 1912. *Les formes élémentaires de la vie religieuse: Le système totémique en Australie.* Paris: Félix Alcan.

Eamon, William. 1994. *Science and the Secrets of Nature: Books of Secrets in Medieval and Early Modern Culture.* Princeton, NJ: Princeton University Press.

L'Echo de l'au-delà et d'ici-bas. 1901. *Les Aïssaouas à l'Exposition de 1900.* La Roche-sur-Yon: Petite Imprimerie Vendéenne.

Eggan, Fred. 1954. "Social Anthropology and the Method of Controlled Comparison." *American Anthropologist* 56 (5): 743–63.

Eickelman, Dale F. 1976. *Moroccan Islam: Tradition and Society in a Pilgrimage Center.* Austin: University of Texas Press.

———. 1998. *The Middle East and Central Asia: An Anthropological Approach.* Upper Saddle River, NJ: Prentice Hall.

Emerson, Robert M., Rachel I. Fretz, and Linda L. Shaw. 2011. *Writing Ethnographic Fieldnotes.* 2nd ed. Chicago: University of Chicago Press.

Engelke, Matthew. 2012. "Material Religion." In *The Cambridge Companion to Religious Studies,* edited by Robert A. Orsi, 209–29. New York: Cambridge University Press.

———. 2014. "Christianity and the Anthropology of Secular Humanism." *Current Anthropology* 55 (S10): 292–301.

Era. 1889. "The Aissaouas in London." September 7.

Escher, Anton. 1999. "Les acrobates marocains dans les cirques allemands." In *Migrations internationales entre le Maghreb et l'Europe—les effects sur les pays de destination et d'origine. Actes du 4ème colloque Maroco-Allemand Munich 1997*, edited by M. Berriane and H. Popp, S249–58. Passau: Faculté des Lettres et des Sciences Humaine de Rabat.

Evans-Pritchard, E. E. 1937. *Witchcraft, Oracles, and Magic among the Azande*. Oxford: Clarendon Press.

———. 1965. *Theories of Primitive Religion*. Oxford: Clarendon Press.

———. 1969. *The Nuer: A Description of the Modes of Livelihood and Political Institutions of a Nilotic People*. Oxford: Oxford University Press.

———. 1976. *Witchcraft, Oracles, and Magic among the Azande*. Abridged ed. Oxford: Clarendon Press.

Fabian, Johannes. 2000. *Out of Our Minds: Reason and Madness in the Exploration of Central Africa*. Berkeley: University of California Press.

———. 2002. *Time and the Other: How Anthropology Makes Its Object*. New York: Columbia University Press.

Falcone, Jessica Marie. 2013. "The Hau of Theory: The Kept-Gift of Theory Itself in American Anthropology." *Anthropology and Humanism* 38 (2): 122–45.

Fassin, Didier. 2015. "In the Name of the Republic: Untimely Meditations on the Aftermath of the Charlie Hebdo Attack." *Anthropology Today* 31 (2): 3–7.

Faucon, Narcisse. 1889. *Le livre d'or de l'Algérie: Historie politique, militaire, administrative, événements et faits principaux, biographie des hommes ayant marqué dans l'armée, les sciences, les lettres, etc., de 1830 à 1889*. Paris: Challamel.

Fauser, Annegret. 2005. *Musical Encounters at the 1889 Paris World's Fair*. Rochester, NY: University of Rochester Press.

Favret-Saada, Jeanne. 1980. *Deadly Words: Witchcraft in the Bocage*. Cambridge: Cambridge University Press.

———. 2015. *The Anti-Witch*. Translated by Matthew Carey. Chicago: HAU Books.

Fechner, Christian. 2002. *The Magic of Robert-Houdin: An Artist's Life*. Edited by Todd Karr. Translated by Stacey Dagron. Vol. 2. Boulogne: Editions FCF.

Fernando, Mayanthi L. 2014. *The Republic Unsettled: Muslim French and the Contradictions of Secularism*. Durham, NC: Duke University Press.

Flaherty, Gloria. 1992. *Shamanism and the Eighteenth Century*. Princeton, NJ: Princeton University Press.

Foster, Elizabeth Ann. 2013. *Faith in Empire: Religion, Politics, and Colonial Rule in French Senegal, 1880–1940*. Stanford, CA: Stanford University Press.

Frankenberg, Ruth. 1993. *White Women, Race Matters: The Social Construction of Whiteness*. Minneapolis: University of Minnesota Press.

Frazer, James George. 1900. *The Golden Bough: A Study in Magic and Religion*. 2nd ed. Vol. 1. London: Macmillan.

Fun. 1867. "From Our Stall." November 23.

Gautier, Théophile. 1851. "Les Aïssaoua, ou les khouan de Sidi Mhammet-Ben-Aïssa." *Revue de Paris*, November: 175–85.

———. 1867. "Revue des théâtres." *Le moniteur universel*, July 29.

Geertz, Clifford. 1968. *Islam Observed: Religious Development in Morocco and Indonesia*. New Haven, CT: Yale University Press.

———. 1973. *The Interpretation of Cultures: Selected Essays*. New York: Basic Books.

Gell, Alfred. 1988. "Technology and Magic." *Anthropology Today* 4 (2): 6–9.

———. 1996. "Vogel's Net Traps as Artworks and Artworks as Traps." *Journal of Material Culture* 1 (1): 15–38.

———. 1998. *Art and Agency: An Anthropological Theory*. Oxford: Clarendon Press.

Gellner, Ernest. 1969. *Saints of the Atlas*. Chicago: University of Chicago Press.

———. 1981. *Muslim Society*. Cambridge: Cambridge University Press.

Gentner, Dedre. 1983. "Structure-Mapping: A Theoretical Framework for Analogy." *Cognitive Science* 7 (2): 155–70.

Gentner, Dedre, Brian Bowdle, Phillip Wolff, and Conseulo Boronat. 2001. "Metaphor Is Like Analogy." In *The Analogical Mind: Perspectives from Cognitive Science*, edited by Dedre Gentner, Keith James Holyoak, and Boicho N. Kokinov, 199–253. Cambridge, MA: MIT Press.

Gentner, Dedre, Sarah Brem, Ronald W. Ferguson, Arthur B. Markman, Bjorn B. Levidow, Phillip Wolff, and Kenneth D. Forbus. 1997. "Analogical Reasoning and Conceptual Change: A Case Study of Johannes Kepler." *Journal of the Learning Sciences* 6 (1): 3–40.

Gentner, Dedre, and Michael Jeziorski. 1993. "The Shift from Metaphor to Analogy in Western Science." In *Metaphor and Thought*, edited by Andrew Ortony, 2nd ed., 447–80. Cambridge: Cambridge University Press.

Gentner, Dedre, and Russell Landers. 1985. "Analogical Reminding: A Good Match Is Hard to Find." In *Proceedings of the International Conference on Systems, Man, and Cybernetics*. Tucson, AZ.

Gentner, Dedre, and Arthur B. Markman. 1997. "Structure Mapping in Analogy and Similarity." *American Psychologist* 52 (1): 45–56.

Gentner, Dedre, and Laura L. Namy. 1999. "Comparison in the Development of Categories." *Cognitive Development* 14 (4): 487–513.

Gentner, Dedre, and Linsey A. Smith. 2012. "Analogical Reasoning." In *Encyclopedia of Human Behavior*, edited by Vilayanur Ramachandran, 130–36. Oxford: Academic Press.

Geoghegan, Bernard Dionysius. 2015. "Occult Communications: On Instrumentation, Esotericism, and Epistemology." *Communication+1* 4 (Article 1).

Geshiere, Peter. 2013. *Witchcraft, Intimacy and Trust: Africa in Comparison*. Chicago: University of Chicago Press.

———. 2016. "Witchcraft, Shamanism, and Nostalgia." *Comparative Studies in Society and History* 58 (1): 242–65.

Gilsenan, Michael. 1973. *Saint and Sufi in Modern Egypt: An Essay in the Sociology of Religion*. Oxford: Clarendon Press.

Goertz, Gary. 2006. *Social Science Concepts: A User's Guide*. Princeton, NJ: Princeton University Press.

Goldenweiser, Alexander. 1937. *Anthropology: An Introduction to Primitive Culture*. New York: F. S. Crofts & Co.

Good, Byron. 1994. *Medicine, Rationality, and Experience: An Anthropological Perspective*. Cambridge: Cambridge University Press.

Goodman, Jane E. 1998. "Singers, Saints, and the Construction of Postcolonial Subjectivities in Algeria." *Ethos* 26 (2): 204–28.

Goodwin, Charles. 1994. "Professional Vision." *American Anthropologist* 96 (3): 606–33.

Goto-Jones, Christopher. 2014. "Magic, Modernity, and Orientalism: Conjuring Representations of Asia." *Modern Asian Studies* 48 (6): 1451–76.

Graeber, David. 2015. *The Utopia of Rules: On Technology, Stupidity, and the Secret Joys of Bureaucracy.* Brooklyn, NY: Melville House.

Granzberg, Gary, Jack Steinbring, and John Hamer. 1977. "New Magic for Old: TV in Cree Culture." *Journal of Communication* 27 (4): 154–58.

Green, Nile. 2015. "The Global Occult: An Introduction." *History of Religions* 54 (4): 383–93.

Greenwood, Susan. 2009. *The Anthropology of Magic.* Oxford: Berg.

Greenwood, Susan, and Erik D. Goodwyn. 2016. *Magical Consciousness: An Anthropological and Neurobiological Approach.* New York: Routledge.

Grison, Georges. 1889. "Courrier de l'Exposition." *Le Figaro,* August 3.

Guillemin, Fanch. 1988. *Les sorciers du bout du monde.* Paris: Pensée universelle.

Gusterson, Hugh. 1996. *Nuclear Rites: A Weapons Laboratory at the End of the Cold War.* Berkeley: University of California Press.

———. 2004. "How Far Have We Traveled? Magic, Science, and Religion Revisited." *Anthropology News* 45 (8): 7–11.

Hadibi, Mohand Akli. 2004. "From 'Total Fullness' to 'Emptiness': Past Realities, Reform Movements and the Future of the Zawiyas in Kabylia." In *On Archaeology of Sainthood and Local Spirituality in Islam: Past and Present Crossroads of Events and Ideas,* edited by Georg Stauth, 73–90. Piscataway, NJ: Transaction Publishers.

Hagen, Aina Landsverk. 2015. " 'Calling It a Crisis': Modes of Creative Labour and Magic in an Elite Architect Company." *Journal of Business Anthropology* 4 (2): 201–18.

Hale, Dana S. 2008. *Races on Display: French Representations of Colonized Peoples, 1886–1940.* Bloomington: Indiana University Press.

Hallowell, A. Irving. 1942. *The Role of Conjuring in Salteaux Society.* Philadelphia: University of Pennsylvania Press.

Hammoudi, Abdellah. 1997. *Master and Disciple: The Cultural Foundations of Moroccan Authoritarianism.* Chicago: University of Chicago Press.

Hannoum, Abdelmajid. 2010. *Violent Modernity: France in Algeria.* Cambridge, MA: Harvard University Press.

———. 2015. "Cartoons, Secularism, and Inequality." *Anthropology Today* 31 (5): 21–24.

Harrison, Carol E. 1999. *The Bourgeois Citizen in Nineteenth-Century France: Gender, Sociability, and the Uses of Emulation.* Oxford: Oxford University Press.

Harrison, Faye V. 1997. *Decolonizing Anthropology: Moving Further Toward an Anthropology for Liberation.* Arlington, VA: Association of Black Anthropologists, American Anthropological Association.

Harvey, David Allen. 2015. "Elite Magic in the Nineteenth Century." In *The Cambridge History of Magic and Witchcraft in the West: From Antiquity to the Present,* edited by David J. Collins, 547–75. Cambridge: University of Cambridge Press.

Hees, Syrinx von. 2005. "The Astonishing: A Critique and Re-Reading of ʿAǧāʾib Literature." *Middle Eastern Literatures* 8 (2): 101–20.

Helmreich, Stefan. 2001. "After Culture: Reflection on the Apparition of Anthropology in Artificial Life, a Science of Simulation." *Cultural Anthropology* 16 (4): 612–27.

———. 2007. "An Anthropologist Underwater: Immersive Soundscapes, Submarine Cyborgs, and Transductive Ethnography." *American Ethnologist* 34 (4): 621–41.

———. 2011. "Nature/Culture/Seawater." *American Anthropologist* 113 (1): 132–44.

———. 2014. "The Left Hand of Nature and Culture." *HAU: Journal of Ethnographic Theory* 4 (3): 373–81.

———. 2016. "Gravity's Reverb: Listening to Space-Time, or Articulating the Sounds of Gravitational-Wave Detection." *Cultural Anthropology* 31 (4): 464–92.

Herdt, Gilbert H. 2003. *Secrecy and Cultural Reality: Utopian Ideologies of the New Guinea Men's House*. Ann Arbor: University of Michigan Press.

Herzfeld, Michael. 1989. *Anthropology through the Looking-Glass: Critical Ethnography in the Margins of Europe*. Cambridge: Cambridge University Press.

———. 1992. *The Social Production of Indifference: Exploring the Symbolic Roots of Western Bureaucracy*. Chicago: University of Chicago Press.

———. 1997. "Theorizing Europe: Persuasive Paradoxes." *American Anthropologist* 99 (4): 713–15.

———. 2001. *Anthropology: Theoretical Practice in Culture and Society*. Malden, MA: Blackwell.

Hess, David. 1993. *Science in the New Age: The Paranormal, Its Defenders and Debunkers, and American Culture*. Madison: University of Wisconsin Press.

Hesse, Mary. 1967. "Models and Analogies in Science." In *The Encyclopedia of Philosophy*, edited by Paul Edwards, vols. 5 and 6: 354–59. New York: Macmillan.

High, Casey, Ann Kelly, and Jonathan Mair, eds. 2012. *The Anthropology of Ignorance: An Ethnographic Approach*. New York: Palgrave Macmillan.

Hinsley, Curtis M. 2016. "Ambiguous Legacy." In *Coming of Age in Chicago: The 1893 World's Fair and the Coalescence of American Anthropology*, edited by Curtis M. Hinsley and David R. Wilcox, 99–109. Lincoln: University of Nebraska Press.

Hladik, Jean. 2004. *La prestidigitation*. Paris: Presses universitaires de France.

Hodges, H. A. 2010. *Wilhelm Dilthey: An Introduction*. New York: Routledge.

Hoffman, Robert R., Tom Eskridge, and Cameron Shelley. 2009. "A Naturalistic Exploration of Forms and Functions of Analogizing." *Metaphor and Symbol* 24 (3): 125–54.

Hofstadter, Douglas R. 2001. "Epilogue: Analogy as the Core of Cognition." In *The Analogical Mind: Perspectives from Cognitive Science*, edited by Dedre Gentner, Keith J. Holyoak, and Boicho N. Kokinov, 499–538. Cambridge, MA: MIT Press.

Holm, Gustav. 1914. "Ethnological Sketch of the Angmagsalik Eskimo." In *The Ammassalik Eskimo Contributions to the Ethnology of the East Greenland Natives*, edited by William Thalbitzer, translated by Grenville Grove and H. M. Kyle. Vol. 1. Copenhagen: Reitzels.

Houdini, Harry. 1920. *Miracle Mongers and Their Methods: A Complete Exposé of the Modus Operandi of Fire Eaters, Heat Resisters, Poison Eaters, Venomous Reptile Defiers, Sword Swallowers, Human Ostriches, Strong Men, etc.* New York: E. P. Dutton & Co.

———. 1924. *A Magician among the Spirits*. New York: Harper & Brothers.

Hubert, Henri, and Marcel Mauss. 1902–3. "Esquisse d'une théorie générale de la magie." *L'Année sociologique* 7: 1–146.

Hugonnet, F. 1858. "Les Aïssaoua." *L'Illustration*, October 9, 231–32.

Hultkrantz, Ake. 1967. "Spirit Lodge, a North American Shamanic Séance." In *Studies in Shamanism*, edited by Carl-Martin Edsman, 32–68. Stockholm: Almqvist & Wiksell.

Hutchins, Edwin. 2012. "Concepts in Practice as Sources of Order." *Mind, Culture, and Activity* 19 (3): 314–23.

Idoux. 1898. "La secte des Aïssaoua." *Mémoires de la Société bourguignonne de géographie et d'histoire* 14: 163–92.

L'Illustration. 1881. "Les Aïssaouas." August 13, 116.

Itkonen, Esa. 2005. *Analogy as Structure and Process: Approaches in Linguistic, Cognitive Psychology, and Philosophy of Science*. Amsterdam: John Benjamins.

James, Erica Caple. 2010. *Democratic Insecurities: Violence, Trauma, and Intervention in Haiti*. Berkeley: University of California Press.

Jamous, Raymond. 1995. "Le saint et le possédé." *Gradhiva* 17: 63–84.

———. 2013. "De la tombe au sang: La question des substituts dans les confréries religieuses marocaines." *Archives de sciences sociales des religions* 161: 189–99.

Jastrow, Joseph. 1900. *Fact and Fable in Psychology*. Boston: Houghton, Mifflin and Co.

Jaucourt, Louis de. 1765. "Tours de cartes et de mains (*art d'Escamotage*)." *Encyclopédie; ou, Dictionnaire raisonné des sciences, des arts et des métiers*, edited by Denis Diderot. Neufchâtel: Samuel Faulche.

Jenkins, R. G. 1979. "The Evolution of Religious Brotherhoods in North and Northwest Africa 1523–1900." In *The Cultivators of Islam*, edited by John Ralph Willis, 40–77. London: F. Cass.

Johnson, Paul C. 2002. *Secrets, Gossip, and Gods: The Transformation of Brazilian Candomblé*. Oxford: Oxford University Press.

Jones, Graham M. 2008. "The Family Romance of Modern Magic: Contesting Robert-Houdin's Cultural Legacy in Contemporary France." In *Performing Magic on the Western Stage: From the Eighteenth Century to the Present*, edited by Francesca Coppa, Lawrence Hass, and James Peck, 33–60. New York: Palgrave Macmillan.

———. 2010. "Modern Magic and the War on Miracles in French Colonial Culture." *Comparative Studies in Society and History* 52 (1): 66–99.

———. 2011. *Trade of the Tricks Inside the Magician's Craft*. Berkeley: University of California Press.

———. 2012. "Magic with a Message: The Poetics of Christian Conjuring." *Cultural Anthropology* 27 (2): 193–214.

———. 2013. "Slower than the Eye: Time, Artifice, and Concealment's Revelations." In *Jamie Isenstein: Will Return*, edited by Stephanie Snyder, 57–79. Portland, OR: Reed Institute.

———. 2014a. "Reported Speech as an Authentication Tactic in Computer-Mediated Communication." In *Indexing Authenticity: Sociolinguistic Perspectives*, edited by Véronique Lacoste, Jakob Leimgruber, and Thiemo Breyer, 188–208. Berlin: De Gruyter.

———. 2014b. "Secrecy." *Annual Review of Anthropology* 43 (1): 53–69.

———. 2015a. "New Magic as an Artification Movement: From Speech Event to Change Process." *Cultural Sociology*. Advance online publication. doi: 10.1177/1749975515584082.

———. 2015b. "Politics and the 'Magic Negro.'" *The Enemy* (blog). January 9. http://theenemy reader.org/tricks-politics-magic-negro/.

Jones, Graham M., and Lauren Shweder. 2003. "The Performance of Illusion and Illusionary Performatives: Learning the Language of Theatrical Magic." *Journal of Linguistic Anthropology* 13 (1): 51–70.

Kafka, Franz. 1976. *The Diaries, 1910–1923*, edited by Max Brod, p. 393. New York: Schocken.

Kaiser, David. 2011. *How the Hippies Saved Physics: Science, Counterculture, and the Quantum Revival*. New York: W. W. Norton.

Kalush, William, and Larry Sloman. 2006. *The Secret Life of Houdini: The Making of America's First Superhero*. New York: Atria Books.

Kapchan, Deborah A. 2007. *Traveling Spirit Masters: Moroccan Gnawa Trance and Music in the Global Marketplace*. Middletown, CT: Wesleyan University Press.

Kapferer, Bruce. 2001. "Anthropology. The Paradox of the Secular." *Social Anthropology* 9 (3): 341–44.

———. 2013. "How Anthropologists Think: Configurations of the Exotic." *Journal of the Royal Anthropological Institute* 19 (4): 813–36.

Keane, Webb. 2007. *Christian Moderns: Freedom and Fetish in the Mission Encounter*. Berkeley: University of California Press.

Keaton, Trica Danielle. 2006. *Muslim Girls and the Other France: Race, Identity Politics, & Social Exclusion*. Bloomington: Indiana University Press.

Keesing, Roger M. 1974. "Theories of Culture." *Annual Review of Anthropology* 3 (1): 73–97.

Keller, Richard C. 2007. *Colonial Madness: Psychiatry in French North Africa.* Chicago: University of Chicago Press.

Kelly, John D. 2014. "Introduction: The Ontological Turn in French Philosophical Anthropology." *Hau* 4 (1): 259–69.

Kieckhefer, Richard. 1994. "The Specific Rationality of Medieval Magic." *American Historical Review* 99 (3): 813–36.

———. 1998. *Forbidden Rites: A Necromancer's Manual of the Fifteenth Century.* University Park: Pennsylvania State University Press.

———. 2000. *Magic in the Middle Ages.* Canto ed. Cambridge: Cambridge University Press.

Kirby, E. T. 1974. "The Shamanistic Origins of Popular Entertainments." *The Drama Review: TDR* 18 (1): 5–15.

Kirshenblatt-Gimblett, Barbara. 1998. *Destination Culture: Tourism, Museums, and Heritage.* Berkeley: University of California Press.

Kockelman, Paul. 2011. "Biosemiosis, Technocognition, and Sociogenesis: Selection and Significance in a Multiverse of Sieving and Serendipity." *Current Anthropology* 52 (5): 711–39.

Kreiser, B. Robert. 1978. *Miracles, Convulsions, and Ecclesiastical Politics in Early Eighteenth-Century Paris.* Princeton, NJ: Princeton University Press.

Kris, Ernst, and Otto Kurz. 1979. *Legend, Myth, and Magic in the Image of the Artist: A Historical Experiment.* New Haven, CT: Yale University Press.

Lachapelle, Sofie. 2011. *Investigating the Supernatural: From Spiritism and Occultism to Psychical Research and Metapsychics in France, 1853–1931.* Baltimore: Johns Hopkins University Press.

———. 2015. *Conjuring Science: A History of Scientific Entertainment and Stage Magic in Modern France.* New York: Palgrave Macmillan.

Lakoff, George. 1993. "The Contemporary Theory of Metaphor." In *Metaphor and Thought,* edited by Andrew Ortony, 2nd ed., 202–51. Cambridge: Cambridge University Press.

Lamond, Grant. 2014. "Analogical Reasoning in the Common Law." *Oxford Journal of Legal Studies* 34 (3): 567–88.

Lamont, Peter. 2004. "Spiritualism and a Mid-Victorian Crisis of Evidence." *Historical Journal* 47 (4): 897–920.

———. 2005. *The Rise of the Indian Rope Trick: How a Spectacular Hoax Became History.* New York: Thunder's Mouth Press.

———. 2006. "Magician as Conjuror: A Frame Analysis of Victorian Mediums." *Early Popular Visual Culture* 4 (1): 21–33.

———. 2013. *Extraordinary Beliefs: A Historical Approach to a Psychological Problem.* Cambridge: Cambridge University Press.

Lamont, Peter, and Richard Wiseman. 1999. *Magic in Theory: An Introduction to the Theoretical and Psychological Elements of Conjuring.* Hatfield: University of Hertfordshire Press.

Landman, Todd. 2013. "Framing Performance Magic: The Role of Contract, Discourse and Effect." *Journal of Performance Magic* 1 (1): 47–68.

Landy, Joshua, and Michael T. Saler, eds. 2009. *The Re-Enchantment of the World: Secular Magic in a Rational Age.* Stanford, CA: Stanford University Press.

Lang, Andrew. 1896. *Cock Lane and Common-Sense.* 2nd ed. London: Longmans Green & Co.

Latour, Bruno. 1993a. *The Pasteurization of France.* Cambridge, MA: Harvard University Press.

———. 1993b. *We Have Never Been Modern.* Cambridge, MA: Harvard University Press.

———. 2007. "The Recall of Modernity: Anthropological Approaches." *Cultural Studies Review* 13 (1): 11–30.

Lave, Jean, and Etienne Wenger. 1991. *Situated Learning: Legitimate Peripheral Participation*. Cambridge: Cambridge University Press.

Le Chatelier, Alfred. 1887. *Les confréries musulmanes du Hedjaz*. Paris: Ernest Leroux.

Le grand Robert de la langue française. 1986. 2nd ed. 9 vols. Paris: Le Robert.

Lemaire, Sandrine, and Pascal Blanchard. 2014. "Exhibitions, Expositions, Media Coverage, and the Colonies (1870–1914)." In *Colonial Culture in France Since the Revolution*, edited by Pascal Blanchard, Sandrine Lemaire, Nicolas Bancel, and Dominic Thomas, translated by Alexis Pernsteiner, 90–97. Bloomington: Indiana University Press.

Lemaire, Sandrine, Pascal Blanchard, and Nicolas Bancel. 2014. "Milestones in Colonial Culture under the Second Empire (1851–1870)." In *Colonial Culture in France Since the Revolution*, edited by Pascal Blanchard, Sandrine Lemaire, Nicolas Bancel, and Dominic Thomas, translated by Alexis Pernsteiner, 75–89. Bloomington: Indiana University Press.

Lemon, Alaina. 2013. "Touching the Gap: Social Qualia and Cold War Contact." *Anthropological Theory* 13 (1–2): 67–88.

Lenôtre, G. 1890. "Les Aïssaouas." In *L'Exposition de Paris de 1889*, vols. 3–4: 275–77. Paris: Librarie illustrée.

Lépinay, Vincent A. 2011. *Codes of Finance: Engineering Derivatives in a Global Bank*. Princeton, NJ: Princeton University Press.

Levallois, Michel. 2012. "François Édouard de Neveu." In *Dictionnaire des orientalistes de langue française*, edited by François Pouillon. Paris: IISMM-Karthala.

Lévi-Strauss, Claude. 1963. "The Sorcerer and His Magic." In *Structural Anthropology*. Translated by Claire Jacobson and Brooke Grundfest Schoepf, 167–85. New York: Basic Books.

Lewis, Gilbert. 2002. "Between Public Assertion and Private Doubts: A Sepik Ritual of Healing and Reflexivity." *Social Anthropology* 10 (1): 11–21.

Lewis, I. M. 1989. *Ecstatic Religion: A Study of Shamanism and Spirit Possession*. New York: Routledge.

Lorcin, Patricia. 1995. *Imperial Identities: Stereotyping, Prejudice and Race in Colonial Algeria*. New York: St. Martin's Press.

Luhrmann, Tanya M. 1989a. "The Magic of Secrecy." *Ethos* 17 (2): 131–65.

———. 1989b. *Persuasions of the Witch's Craft: Ritual Magic in Contemporary England*. Cambridge, MA: Harvard University Press.

———. 1997. "Magic." In *The Dictionary of Anthropology*, edited by Thomas Barfield, 298–99. Malden, MA: Blackwell.

———. 2012a. "A Hyperreal God and Modern Belief: Toward an Anthropological Theory of Mind." *Current Anthropology* 53 (4): 371–95.

———. 2012b. "Touching the Divine: Recent Research on Neo-Paganism and Neo-Shamanism." *Reviews in Anthropology* 41 (2): 136–50.

———. 2012c. *When God Talks Back: Understanding the American Evangelical Relationship with God*. New York: Alfred A. Knopf.

Maarouf, Mohammed. 2012. "The Cultural Foundations of the Islamist Practice of Charity in Morocco." *Journal of Religion and Popular Culture* 24 (1): 29–66.

Mahmud, Lilith. 2012. "'The World Is a Forest of Symbols': Italian Freemasonry and the Practice of Discretion." *American Ethnologist* 39 (2): 425–38.

———. 2014. *The Brotherhood of Freemason Sisters: Gender, Secrecy, and Fraternity in Italian Masonic Lodges*. Chicago: University of Chicago Press.

Maire, Catherine-Laurence. 1985. *Les convulsionnaires de Saint-Médard: Miracles, convulsions et prophéties à Paris au XVIIIe siècle*. Paris: Gallimard.

Maire, Joseph. 1883. "Souvenirs d'Alger." *La Revue lyonnaise* 6: 534–40.

Majax, Gérard. 1996. *Gare aux gourous: Les trucs des sectes*. Paris: Arléa.

Malinowski, Bronislaw. 1922. *Argonauts of the Western Pacific: An Account of Native Enterprise and Adventure in the Archipelagoes of Melanesian New Guinea*. New York: E. P. Dutton.

———. 1935. *Coral Gardens and Their Magic: A Study of the Methods of Tilling the Soil and of Agricultural Rites in the Trobriand Islands*. 2 vols. London: G. Allen & Unwin.

———. 1948. *Magic, Science and Religion and Other Essays*. Boston: Beacon Press.

Mangan, Michael. 2007. *Performing Dark Arts: A Cultural History of Conjuring*. Chicago: Intellect.

Manganaro, Marc. 2002. *Culture, 1922: The Emergence of a Concept*. Princeton, NJ: Princeton University Press.

Markman, Arthur B., and Dedre Gentner. 1997. "The Effects of Alignability on Memory." *Psychological Science* 8 (5): 363–67.

———. 2001. "Thinking." *Annual Review of Psychology* 52 (1): 223–47.

Markman, Arthur B., and Edward J. Wisniewski. 1997. "Similar and Different: The Differentiation of Basic Level Categories." *Journal of Experimental Psychology: Learning, Memory, and Cognition* 23 (1): 54–70.

Marett, R. R. 1936. *Tylor*. New York: John Wiley.

Martin, Emily. 1991. "The Egg and the Sperm: How Science Has Constructed a Romance Based on Stereotypical Male-Female Roles." *Signs: Journal of Women in Culture and Society* 16 (3): 485–501.

Martin, Michèle. 2006. *Images at War: Illustrated Periodicals and Constructed Nations*. Toronto: University of Toronto Press.

Masuzawa, Tomoko. 2000. "Troubles with Materiality: The Ghost of Fetishism in the Nineteenth Century." *Comparative Studies in Society and History* 42 (2): 242–67.

Maurer, Bill. 2005. *Mutual Life, Limited: Islamic Banking, Alternative Currencies, Lateral Reason*. Princeton, NJ: Princeton University Press.

Maxwell, Joseph. 1992. "Understanding and Validity in Qualitative Research." *Harvard Educational Review* 62 (3): 279–301.

McDougall, James. 2006. *History and the Culture of Nationalism in Algeria*. Cambridge: Cambridge University Press.

McGarry, Molly. 2008. *Ghosts of Futures Past: Spiritualism and the Cultural Politics of Nineteenth-Century America*. Berkeley: University of California Press.

Merad, Ali. 1967. *Le réformisme musulman en Algérie de 1925 à 1940: Essai d'histoire religieuse et sociale*. Paris: Mouton & Co.

Merton, Robert K. 1949. *Social Theory and Social Structure*. Glencoe, IL: Free Press.

Metzner, Paul. 1998. *Crescendo of the Virtuoso: Spectacle, Skill, and Self-Promotion in Paris during the Age of Revolution*. Berkeley: University of California Press.

Meyer, Birgit, and Peter Pels, eds. 2003. *Magic and Modernity: Interfaces of Revelation and Concealment*. Stanford, CA: Stanford University Press.

Mitchell, Timothy. 1989. "The World as Exhibition." *Comparative Studies in Society and History* 31 (2): 217–36.

Moeran, Brian. 2015. *The Magic of Fashion: Ritual, Commodity, Glamour*. New York: Routledge.

Monroe, John Warne. 2007. "The Way We Believe Now: Modernity and the Occult." *Magic, Ritual, and Witchcraft* 2 (1): 68–78.

———. 2008. *Laboratories of Faith: Mesmerism, Spiritism, and Occultism in Modern France*. Ithaca, NY: Cornell University Press.

Moore, Henrietta L. 2004. "Global Anxieties: Concept-Metaphors and Pre-Theoretical Commitments in Anthropology." *Anthropological Theory* 4 (1): 71–88.

Morin, André-Saturnin. 1857. "Les Aïssaouas." *Journal du magnétisme* 16: 253–62.

———. 1859. "Robert Houdin." *Journal du magnétisme* 18: 213–22.

Mullings, Leith. 2005. "Interrogating Racism: Toward an Antiracist Anthropology." *Annual Review of Anthropology* 34 (1): 667–93.

Nabti, Mehdi. 2010. *Les Aïssawa: Soufisme, musique et rituels de transe au Maroc*. Paris: L'Harmattan.

Nader, Laura. 1996. "The Three-Cornered Constellation: Magic, Science, and Religion Revisited." In *Naked Science: Anthropological Inquiry into Boundaries, Power, and Knowledge*, edited by Laura Nader, 259–75. New York: Routledge.

Nadis, Fred. 2005. *Wonder Shows: Performing Science, Magic, and Religion in America*. New Brunswick: Rutgers University Press.

Nardi, Peter M. 1984. "Toward a Social Psychology of Entertainment Magic (conjuring)." *Symbolic Interaction* 7 (1): 25–42.

Natale, Simone. 2011. "The Medium on the Stage: Trance and Performance in Nineteenth-Century Spiritualism." *Early Popular Visual Culture* 9 (3): 239–55.

———. 2013. "Spiritual Stars: Religion and Celebrity in the Careers of Spiritualist Mediums." *Celebrity Studies* 4 (1): 94–96.

Neale, Robert E. 2009. "Early Conjuring Performances." In *Magic and Meaning Expanded*, edited by Eugene Burger and Robert E. Neale, 39–56. Seattle, WA: Hermetic Press.

Nersessian, Nancy J. 1987. "A Cognitive-Historical Approach to Meaning in Scientific Theories." In *The Process of Science: Contemporary Philosophical Approaches to Understanding Scientific Practice*, edited by Nancy J. Nersessian, 161–78. Dordrecht: Martinus Nijhoff Publishers.

Neveu, François-Édouard de. 1846. *Les Khouan: Ordres religieux chez les Musulmans de l'Algérie*. 2nd ed. Paris: A. Guyot.

Ney, N. 1881a. "Les sociétés secrètes en Algérie." *L'Illustration*, July 30, 77–78.

———. 1881b. "Les sociétés secrètes en Algérie." *L'Illustration*, August 6, 87–90.

Nouvellet, Joseph. 1887. "Une soirée dans l'autre monde." *Revue du Lyonnais* 3 (6): 433–43.

Obeyesekere, Gananath. 1992. *The Apotheosis of Captain Cook: European Mythmaking in the Pacific*. Princeton, NJ: Princeton University Press.

Oliphant, Elayne. 2015. "Beyond Blasphemy or Devotion: Art, the Secular, and Catholicism in Paris." *Journal of the Royal Anthropological Institute* 21 (2): 352–73.

Outhwaite, William. 1976. *Understanding Social Life: The Method Called Verstehen*. New York: Holmes & Meier.

Owen, Alex. 2004. *The Darkened Room: Women, Power, and Spiritualism in Late Victorian England*. Chicago: University of Chicago Press.

Pang, Laikwan. 2004. "Magic and Modernity in China." *Positions: East Asia Cultures Critique* 12 (2): 299–327.

Parris, Ben A., Gustav Kuhn, Guy A. Mizon, Abdelmalek Benattayallah, and Tim L. Hodgson. 2009. "Imaging the Impossible: An fMRI Study of Impossible Causal Relationships in Magic Tricks." *NeuroImage* 45 (3): 1033–39.

Peirce, Charles S. 1991. *Peirce on Signs: Writings on Semiotic*. Edited by James Hoopes. Chapel Hill: University of North Carolina Press.

Pels, Peter. 1998. "The Magic of Africa: Reflections on a Western Commonplace." *African Studies Review* 41 (3): 193–209.

———. 2003a. "Introduction: Magic and Modernity." In *Magic and Modernity: Interfaces of Revelation and Concealment*, edited by Birgit Meyer and Peter Pels, 1–38. Stanford, CA: Stanford University Press.

———. 2003b. "Spirits of Modernity: Alfred Wallace, Edward Tylor, and The Visual Politics of Fact." In *Magic and Modernity: Interfaces of Revelation and Concealment*, edited by Birgit Meyer and Peter Pels, 241–71. Stanford, CA: Stanford University Press.

———. 2008. "The Modern Fear of Matter: Reflections on the Protestantism of Victorian Science." *Material Religion* 4 (3): 264–83.

———. 2013. "Amazing Stories: How Science Fiction Sacralizes the Secular." In *Deus in Machina: Religion, Technology, and the Things in Between,* edited by Jeremy Stolow, 213–38. New York: Fordham University Press.

———. 2014. "Magic." In *Encyclopedia of Aesthetics,* edited by Michael Kelly, 233–36. Oxford: Oxford University Press.

Petit, Michael. 2007. "Joseph Jastrow, the Psychology of Deception, and the Racial Economy of Observation." *Journal of the History of the Behavioral Sciences* 43 (2): 159–75.

Pigg, Stacy Leigh. 1996. "The Credible and the Credulous: The Question of 'Villagers' Beliefs' in Nepal." *Cultural Anthropology* 11 (2): 160–201.

Pilbeam, Pamela M. 2014. *Saint-Simonians in Nineteenth-Century France: From Free Love to Algeria.* Basingstoke: Palgrave Macmillan.

Pinch, Trevor J., and Harry M. Collins. 1984. "Private Science and Public Knowledge: The Committee for the Scientific Investigation of the Claims of the Paranormal and Its Use of the Literature." *Social Studies of Science* 14 (4): 521–46.

Poole, Fitz John Porter. 1986. "Metaphors and Maps: Towards Comparison in the Anthropology of Religion." *Journal of the American Academy of Religion* 54 (3): 411–57.

Pougin, Arthur. 1890. *Le théâtre à l'Exposition universelle de 1889: Notes et descriptions, histoire et souvenirs.* Paris: Librairie Fischbacher.

Prévost, Jean. 1584. *La première partie des subtiles et plaisantes inventions, comprenant plusieurs jeux de récréation et traicts de souplesse, par le discours desquels les impostures des bateleurs sont descouvertes.* Lyon: Antoine Bastide.

Price, Sally. 2007. *Paris Primitive: Jacques Chirac's Museum on the Quai Branly.* Chicago: University of Chicago Press.

Prochaska, David. 1990a. *Making Algeria French: Colonialism in Bône, 1870–1920.* Cambridge: Cambridge University Press.

———. 1990b. "The Archive of Algérie Imaginaire." *History and Anthropology* 4 (2): 373–420.

Proctor, Robert, and Londa L. Schiebinger, eds. 2008. *Agnotology: The Making and Unmaking of Ignorance.* Stanford, CA: Stanford University Press.

Rabourdin, Lucien. 1881. "Les âges de pierre du Sahara central." *Bulletins de la Société d'Anthropologie de Paris* 4: 113–62.

Rasmussen, Knud. 1938. "Shamans." In *Knud Rasmussen's Posthumous Notes on the Life and Doings of the East Greenlanders in Olden Times,* edited by H. Ostermann, 94–129. Copenhagen: Reitzels.

Ravet, Alfred. 1888. "Une soirée chez les Aïssaoua." In *Bulletin de l'année 1888,* vol. 10, 389–97. Rouen: Société normande de Géographie.

Raynaly, Édouard. 1894. *Les propos d'un escamoteur: Étude critique et humoristique.* Paris: Imprimerie de Charles Noblet.

Revue spirite: Journal d'études psychologique. 1868. "Les Aïssaoua, Ou les convulsionnaires de la rue Le Peletier." *Revue spirite: Journal d'études psychologique* 11 (1): 18–23.

Rhani, Zakaria. 2012. "Sidi Ahmed Ou Moussa: Une tradition mystique d'art acrobatique." In *Taoub le groupe acrobatique de Tanger,* edited by Ileana Marchesani and Karine Joseph, 190–203. Casablanca: Éditions du Sirocco.

Rhani, Zakaria, and Hlaoua Aziz. 2014. "Soufisme et cultes des saints au Maroc." In *Hamadcha Du Maroc: Rituels musicaux, mystiques et de possession,* edited by Brigitte Maréchal and Felice Dassetto, 17–30. Louvain: Presses universitaires de Louvain.

Rinn, Louis. 1884. *Marabouts et Khouan: Étude sur l'Islam en Algérie.* Algiers: Adolphe Jourdan.

Robert-Houdin, Jean-Eugène. 1859. *Confidences d'un prestidigitateur: Une vie d'artiste*. 2 vols. Paris: Librairie nouvelle.

——. 1861. *Les tricheries des Grecs dévoilées: L'art de gagner à tous les jeux*. Paris: A. Bourdilliat.

——. 1868. *Les secrets de la prestidigitation et de la magie: Comment on devient sorcier*. Paris: Michel Lévy frères.

——. 1877. *Magie et physique amusante*. Paris: Calmann Lévy.

——. 2006. *Essential Robert-Houdin*. Edited by Todd Karr. Los Angeles: Miracle Factory.

Romberg, Raquel. 2009. *Healing Dramas: Divination and Magic in Modern Puerto Rico*. Austin: University of Texas Press.

Saaïdia, Oissila. 2013. "Islam et ordre colonial dans les empires britannique et français: Entre collaboration et contestation." *Histoire, monde et cultures religieuses* 25 (1): 75–105.

Sahlins, Marshall. 1981. *Historical Metaphors and Mythical Realities: Structure in the Early History of the Sandwich Islands Kingdom*. Ann Arbor: University of Michigan Press.

Said, Edward W. 1979. *Orientalism*. New York: Vintage Books.

Saler, Michael. 2006. "Modernity and Enchantment: A Historiographic Review." *American Historical Review* 111 (3): 692–716.

Saltano, Maurice, and Bernard Joubert. 1990. *Les magiciens: Le monde fantastique de l'illusionnisme*. Paris: Syros-Alternatives.

Sapir, Edward. 1924. "Culture, Genuine and Spurious." *American Journal of Sociology* 29 (4): 401–29.

Sartori, Giovanni. 1970. "Concept Misformation in Comparative Politics." *American Political Science Review* 64 (4): 1033–53.

Scheele, Judith. 2007. "Recycling 'Baraka': Knowledge, Politics, and Religion in Contemporary Algeria." *Comparative Studies in Society and History* 49 (2): 304–28.

Scheper-Hughes, Nancy. 1993. *Death without Weeping: The Violence of Everyday Life in Brazil*. Berkeley: University of California Press.

Schmidt, Leigh Eric. 1998. "From Demon Possession to Magic Show: Ventriloquism, Religion, and the Enlightenment." *Church History* 67 (2): 274–304.

Schwartz, Vanessa R. 1998. *Spectacular Realities: Early Mass Culture in Fin-de-Siècle Paris*. Berkeley: University of California Press.

Scott, Joan Wallach. 2007. *The Politics of the Veil*. Princeton, NJ: Princeton University Press.

Seldow, Michel. 1971. *Vie et secrets de Robert-Houdin*. Paris: Fayard.

Seligman, Adam B., Robert P. Weller, Michael J. Puett, and Bennett Simon. 2008. *Ritual and Its Consequences: An Essay on the Limits of Sincerity*. Oxford: Oxford University Press.

Sessions, Jennifer E. 2011. *By Sword and Plow: France and the Conquest of Algeria*. Ithaca, NY: Cornell University Press.

Shapin, Steven, and Simon Schaffer. 2011. *Leviathan and the Air-Pump: Hobbes, Boyle, and the Experimental Life*. Princeton, NJ: Princeton University Press.

Shelley, Cameron. 2002a. "Analogy Counterarguments and the Acceptability of Analogical Hypotheses." *British Journal for the Philosophy of Science* 53 (4): 477–96.

——. 2002b. "The Analogy Theory of Disanalogy: When Conclusions Collide." *Metaphor and Symbol* 17 (2): 81–97.

Shore, Bradd. 1996. *Culture in Mind: Cognition, Culture, and the Problem of Meaning*. New York: Oxford University Press.

Siari-Tengour, Ouanassa. 2009. "Pratiques culturelles, transferts de saviors et réseaux: L'apport des Saint-Simoniens en Algérie." In *Réforme de l'État et réformismes au Maghreb (XIXe–XXe siècles)*, edited by Odile Moreau, 223–33. Paris: L'Harmattan.

Siegel, Lee. 1991. *Net of Magic: Wonders and Deceptions in India*. Chicago: University of Chicago Press.

Silverman, Kenneth. 1996. *Houdini!!! The Career of Ehrich Weiss: American Self-Liberator, Europe's Eclipsing Sensation, World's Handcuff King & Prison Breaker*. New York: HarperCollins Publishers.

Silverstein, Michael. 2005. "Axes of Evals: Token versus Type Interdiscursivity." *Journal of Linguistic Anthropology* 15 (1): 6–22.

———. 2013. "Discourse and the No-Thing-Ness of Culture." *Signs and Society* 1 (2): 327–66.

Silverstein, Paul A. 2004. *Algeria in France: Transpolitics, Race, and Nation*. Bloomington: Indiana University Press.

Simmel, Georg. 1950. *The Sociology of Georg Simmel*, translated by Kurt H. Wolff. Glencoe, IL: Free Press.

Simour, Lhoussain. 2013. "American Fair Expositions Revisited: Morocco's Acrobatic Performers between the Industry of Entertainment and the Violence of Racial Display." *Journal for Cultural Research* 17 (3): 295–322.

Small, Mario Luis. 2009. " 'How Many Cases Do I Need?' On Science and the Logic of Case Selection in Field-Based Research." *Ethnography* 10 (1): 5–38.

Smith, Wally. 2015. "Technologies of Stage Magic: Simulation and Dissimulation." *Social Studies of Science* 45 (3): 319–43.

Snow, David A., Calvin Morrill, and Leon Anderson. 2003. "Elaborating Analytic Ethnography Linking Fieldwork and Theory." *Ethnography* 4 (2): 181–200.

Solomon, Matthew. 2010. *Disappearing Tricks: Silent Film, Houdini, and the New Magic of the Twentieth Century*. Urbana: University of Illinois Press.

Spadola, Emilio. 2008. "The Scandal of Ecstasy: Communication, Sufi Rites, and Social Reform in 1930s Morocco." *Contemporary Islam* 2 (2): 119–38.

———. 2014. *The Calls of Islam: Sufis, Islamists, and Mass Mediation in Urban Morocco*. Bloomington: Indiana University Press.

———. 2015. "Rites of Reception: Trance, Technology, and National Belonging in Morocco." In *Trance Mediums and New Media: Spirit Possession in the Age of Technical Reproduction*, edited by Heike Behrend, Anja Dreschke, and Martin Zillinger, 137–55. New York: Fordham University Press.

Spellman, Barbara A., Keith James Holyoak, and Robert G. Morrison. 2001. "Analogical Priming via Semantic Relations." *Memory & Cognition* 29 (3): 383–93.

Srinivas, Tulasi. 2015. "Doubtful Illusions: Magic, Wonder and the Politics of Virtue in the Sathya Sai Movement." *Journal of Asian and African Studies*. Advance online publication. doi: 10.1177/0021909615595987.

Stafford, Barbara Maria. 1994. *Artful Science: Enlightenment, Entertainment, and the Eclipse of Visual Education*. Cambridge, MA: MIT Press.

Stahl, Christopher. 2008. "Outdoing Ching Ling Foo." In *Performing Magic on the Western Stage: From the Eighteenth Century to the Present*, edited by Francesca Coppa, Lawrence Hass, and James Peck, 151–76. New York: Palgrave Macmillan.

Stallybrass, Peter, and Allon White. 1986. *The Politics and Poetics of Transgression*. Ithaca, NY: Cornell University Press.

Steinmeyer, Jim. 2003. *Hiding the Elephant: How Magicians Invented the Impossible and Learned to Disappear*. New York: Carroll & Graf Publishers.

———. 2005. *The Glorious Deception: The Double Life of William Robinson, aka Chung Ling Soo, the "Marvelous Chinese Conjurer."* New York: Carroll & Graf Publishers.

Stocking, George W. 1971. "Animism in Theory and Practice: E. B. Tylor's Unpublished 'Notes on Spiritualism.' " *Man* 6 (1): 88–104.

———. 1982. *Race, Culture, and Evolution: Essays in the History of Anthropology*. Reprinted. Chicago: University of Chicago Press.

------. 1987. *Victorian Anthropology*. New York: Free Press.

------. 1995. *After Tylor: British Social Anthropology, 1888–1951*. Madison: University of Wisconsin Press.

------. 2004. "A. I. Hallowell's Boasian Evolutionism: Human Ir/rationality in Cross-Cultural, Evolutionary, and Personal Context." In *Significant Others: Interpersonal and Professional Commitments in Anthropology*, edited by Richard Handler, 196–260. Madison: University of Wisconsin Press.

Stone, David. 2006. *Close-up: Les vrais secrets de la magie: Petites recettes et grande cuisine du close-up professionnel*. Paris: Pamadana éditions.

Strathern, Marilyn. 1992a. *After Nature: English Kinship in the Late Twentieth Century*. Cambridge: Cambridge University Press.

------. 1992b. *Reproducing the Future: Essays on Anthropology, Kinship, and the New Reproductive Technologies*. New York: Routledge.

------. 2007a. "Interdisciplinarity: Some Models from the Human Sciences." *Interdisciplinary Science Reviews* 32 (2): 123–34.

------. 2007b. "Useful Knowledge." In *Proceedings of the British Academy, Volume 139, 2005 Lectures*, edited by Peter James Marshall, 73–110. Oxford: Oxford University Press.

------. 2008. "Old and New Reflections." In *How Do We Know? Evidence, Ethnography, and the Making of Anthropological Knowledge*, edited by Liana Chua, Casey High, and Timm Lau, 20–35. Newcastle: Cambridge Scholars Publishing.

------. 2011. "What Is a Parent?" *HAU: Journal of Ethnographic Theory* 1 (1): 245–78.

Styers, Randall. 2004. *Making Magic: Religion, Magic, and Science in the Modern World*. New York: Oxford University Press.

Tambiah, Stanley Jeyaraja. 1990. *Magic, Science, Religion, and the Scope of Rationality*. Cambridge: Cambridge University Press.

Tanner, Kathryn. 1997. *Theories of Culture: A New Agenda for Theology*. Minneapolis: Fortress Press.

Taussig, Michael. 1991. *Shamanism, Colonialism and the Wild Man: A Study in Terror and Healing*. Chicago: University of Chicago Press.

------. 1993. *Mimesis and Alterity: A Particular History of the Senses*. New York: Routledge.

------. 1997. *The Magic of the State*. New York: Routledge.

------. 1999. *Defacement: Public Secrecy and the Labor of the Negative*. Stanford, CA: Stanford University Press.

------. 2003. "Viscerality, Faith, and Skepticism: Another Theory of Magic." In *Magic and Modernity: Interfaces of Revelation and Concealment*, edited by Birgit Meyer and Peter Pels, 272–306. Stanford, CA: Stanford University Press.

Tavory, Iddo, and Stefan Timmermans. 2014. *Abductive Analysis: Theorizing Qualitative Research*. Chicago: University of Chicago Press.

Taylor, Nik, and Stuart Nolan. 2015. "Performing Fabulous Monsters: Re-Inventing the Gothic Personae in Bizarre Magic." In *Monstrous Media/Spectral Subjects: Imaging Gothic from the Nineteenth Century to the Present*, edited by Fred Botting and Catherine Spooner, 128–42. Manchester: Manchester University Press.

Taylor, Rogan P. 1985. *The Death and Resurrection Show: From Shaman to Superstar*. London: Anthony Blond.

Teller. 1999. "Witchcraft as Statecraft: A Tale of a Trick and Entreaty." *New York Times Magazine*, April 18, 84.

Le Temps. 1900. "Tribunaux." *Le Temps*, July 19, 3E.

Terrio, Susan J. 2000. *Crafting the Culture and History of French Chocolate*. Berkeley: University of California Press.

———. 2009. *Judging Mohammed: Juvenile Delinquency, Immigration, and Exclusion at the Paris Palace of Justice*. Stanford, CA: Stanford University Press.

Thwaites, Reuben Gold, ed. 1897. *The Jesuit Relations and Allied Documents*. Vol. 6. Cleveland: Burrows Brothers.

———. 1898. *The Jesuit Relations and Allied Documents*. Vol. 12. Cleveland: Burrows Brothers.

Timmermans, Stefan, and Iddo Tavory. 2012. "Theory Construction in Qualitative Research from Grounded Theory to Abductive Analysis." *Sociological Theory* 30 (3): 167–86.

Tresch, John. 2012. *The Romantic Machine: Utopian Science and Technology after Napoleon*. Chicago: University of Chicago Press.

Triaud, Jean-Louis. 1995. *La légende noire de la Sanûsiyya: Une confrérie musulmane saharienne sous le regard français (1840–1930)*. 2 vols. Paris: Éditions de la Maison des sciences de l'homme.

Triplett, Norman. 1900. "The Psychology of Conjuring Deceptions." *American Journal of Psychology* 11 (4): 439–510.

Trumbull, George R. 2007. " 'Au Coin Des Rues Diderot et Moïse': Religious Politics and the Ethnography of Sufism in Colonial Algeria, 1871–1906." *French Historical Studies* 30 (3): 451–83.

———. 2009. *An Empire of Facts: Colonial Power, Cultural Knowledge, and Islam in Algeria, 1870–1914*. Cambridge: Cambridge University Press.

Turner, Victor. 1982. *From Ritual to Theatre: The Human Seriousness of Play*. New York: PAJ.

Tylor, Edward Burnett. 1873. *Primitive Culture: Researches into the Development of Mythology, Philosophy, Religion, Language, Art and Custom*. 2nd ed. Vol. 1. London: Murray.

———. 1881. *Anthropology: An Introduction to the Study of Man and Civilization*. London: Macmillan.

———. 1883. "Magic." In *Encyclopaedia Britannica*, 200–207. 9th ed. New York: Charles Scribner's Sons.

Vaisan, Roger. 1981. *Pied de nez au destin malicieux: Mémoires*. Langres: Dominique Guéniot.

Vapereau, Gustave. 1859. *L'année littéraire et dramatique (1858)*. Paris: Librarie de L. Hachette & Cie.

Viveiros de Castro, Eduardo. 2004. "Perspectival Anthropology and the Method of Controlled Equivocation." *Tipití: Journal of the Society for the Anthropology of Lowland South America* 2 (1): 3–22.

———. 2013. "The Relative Native." *HAU* 3 (3): 473–502.

von Sivers, Peter. 1973. "The Realm of Justice: Apocalyptic Revolts in Algeria (1849–1879)." *Humaniora Islamica* 1: 47–60.

Voss, Ehler. 2014. "A Sprout of Doubt: The Debate on the Medium's Agency in Mediumism, Media Studies, and Anthropology." In *Religion, Tradition and the Popular: Transcultural Views from Asia and Europe*, edited by Judith Schlehe and Evamaria Sandkühler, 205–24. Bielefeld: Transcript.

Wagner, Roy. 1981. *The Invention of Culture*. Chicago: University of Chicago Press.

Wallace, Alfred Russel. 1875. *On Miracles and Modern Spiritualism*. London: James Burns.

Warnier, A. 1867. "Les Arabes, ou Les Aïssaoua au Théâtre international." In *L'Exposition universelle de 1867 illustrée*, edited by François Ducuing, vol. 2, 37–40. Paris: J. Claye.

Weber, Max. 1958. *From Max Weber: Essays in Sociology*. Edited and translated by H. H. Gerth and C. Wright Mills. New York: Oxford University Press.

———. 1968. *Economy and Society: An Outline of Interpretive Sociology*. Edited by Guenther Roth and Claus Wittich. Translated by Ephraim Fischoff. 3 vols. New York: Bedminster Press.

Weller, Robert P. 1994. *Resistance, Chaos and Control in China: Taiping Rebels, Taiwanese Ghosts, and Tiananmen*. Seattle: University of Washington Press.

Whitehead, Harry. 2000. "The Hunt for Quesalid: Tracking Lévi-Strauss' Shaman." *Anthropology & Medicine* 7 (2): 149–68.

Wiener, Margaret J. 2003. "Hidden Forces: Colonialism and the Politics of Magic in the Netherlands Indies." In *Magic and Modernity: Interfaces of Revelation and Concealment*, edited by Birgit Meyer and Peter Pels, 129–58. Stanford, CA: Stanford University Press.

———. 2013. "Magic, (colonial) Science and Science Studies." *Social Anthropology* 21 (4): 492–509.

———. 2015. "Colonial Magic: The Dutch East Indies." In *The Cambridge History of Magic and Witchcraft in the West: From Antiquity to the Present*, edited by David J. Collins, 482–517. Cambridge: Cambridge University Press.

Williams, Raymond. 1960. "The Magic System." *New Left Review* 1 (4): 27–32.

Wittgenstein, Ludwig. 1993. *Philosophical Occasions, 1912–1951*, edited by James Carl Klagge and Alfred Nordmann. Indianapolis: Hacket.

Wolf, Eric. 1995. *Europe and the People Without History*. Berkeley: University of California Press.

Young, Jeremy C. 2014. "Empowering Passivity: Women Spiritualists, Houdini, and the 1926 Fortune Telling Hearing." *Journal of Social History* 48 (2): 341–62.

Zarcone, Thierry. 2009. "Confrérisme, maraboutisme et culte des saints face au réformisme. Le cas de la Turquie d'Atatürk et de la Tunisie de Bourguiba." In *Réforme de l'État et réformismes au Maghreb (XIXe–XXe siècles)*, edited by Odile Moreau, 323–36. Paris: L'Harmattan.

Zarobell, John. 2010. *Empire of Landscape: Space and Ideology in French Colonial Algeria*. University Park: Pennsylvania State University Press.

Zetterberg, J. Peter. 1980. "The Mistaking of 'the Mathematicks' for Magic in Tudor and Stuart England." *Sixteenth Century Journal* 11 (1): 83–97.

Zhan, Mei. 2009. *Other-Worldly: Making Chinese Medicine through Transnational Frames*. Durham, NC: Duke University Press.

Zillinger, Martin. 2014. "Media and the Scaling of Ritual Spaces in Morocco." *Social Compass* 61 (1): 39–47.

———. 2015a. "Absence and the Mediation of the Audio-Visual Unconscious." In *Trance Mediums and New Media: Spirit Possession in the Age of Technical Reproduction*, edited by Heike Behrend, Anja Dreschke, and Martin Zillinger, 77–99. New York: Fordham University Press.

———. 2015b. "Screening Trance, Mediating Absence." Presentation at the Visibility, Embodiment, and Empathy: Explorations of Human Intersubjectivity Symposium, Harvard University, Cambridge, MA, March 27.

———. 2017. "Graduated Publics: Mediating Trance in the Age of Technical Reproduction." *Current Anthropology* 58 (S15): 41–55.

INDEX